School Law for Public, Private, and Parochial Educators

Leo H. Bradley

Rowman & Littlefield Education
Lanham, Maryland • Toronto • Oxford
2005

Published in the United States of America
by Rowman & Littlefield Education
A Division of Rowman & Littlefield Publishers, Inc.
A wholly owned subsidary of The Rowman & Littlefield Publishing Group, Inc.
4501 Forbes Boulevard, Suite 200, Lanham, Maryland 20706
www.rowmaneducation.com

PO Box 317
Oxford
OX2 9RU, UK

British Library Cataloguing in Publication Information Available

Library of Congress Cataloging-in-Publication Data
Bradley, Leo H., Ed. D.
  School law for public, private, and parochial educators / Leo H. Bradley.
     p. cm.
  Includes index.
  ISBN 978-1-57886-263-4 — ISBN 1-57886-263-9
(pbk. : alk. paper)
  1. Educational law and legislation—United States. 2. Educators—
United States—Handbooks, manuals, etc. I. Title.
  KF4119.8.E3B73 2005
  344.73'07—dc22

                                                    2005004412

∞™ The paper used in this publication meets the minimum requirements of
American National Standard for Information Sciences—Permanence of Paper
for Printed Library Materials, ANSI/NISO Z39.48-1992. Manufactured in the
United States of America.

To Leo Herman II, Michael Jacob, and Vincent Charles.
My legacy is yours, to have and to grow.
Dad

Contents

Preface

In the day-to-day operation of public, private, and parochial schools, a constant question asked by administrators and teachers alike is, "Am I acting legally in this situation?" The failure to know the answer to this question can be catastrophic. Educators must be confident that they possess the basic knowledge of school law at a level sufficient to administer their schools and classrooms legally. They must also have the knowledge and wisdom to know when they need legal council. The purpose of this book is to assist educators—public, private, and parochial—in gaining the knowledge they need to administer their schools with confidence that what they are doing is legal as well as proper.

There are aspects of school law that apply only to public schools. There are aspects of school law that apply to all kinds of schools, but may impact one type of school more than another. There are extrapolations of public school law that private and parochial schools can make to more efficiently operate their schools. Therefore, when appropriate, differentiated curriculum to accommodate all types of schools is present in this book, thus making it appropriate for educators regardless of where they practice their profession. Students of school law should also keep in mind that over the course of a career, they may teach or administer in many different types of schools. Therefore, a study of school law that incorporates all the different entities is theoretically sound. Even if an educator never intends to enter the public arena, he or she will have to interact with public schools in relation to federal and state programs that aid parochial and private schools. Current trends toward parental choice in relation to attendance law point to more and more relationships among all the various types of school systems now in existence: public, private, parochial, charter, and homeschooling. Therefore, knowledge of school law that incorporates all possible governance structures will best serve the graduate students of today.

The study of school law is often viewed by students as one of the more difficult courses in graduate schools of education. This is especially true of students with little or no academic experience in the law or political science. School law books traditionally contain much text and vocabulary written by lawyers. These authors use legal language, which is foreign to many educators. The landmark case opinions—majority, concurring, and dissenting—are authored mostly by U.S. Supreme Court justices, state supreme court justices, and federal appeals (circuit) court justices. Thus, these decisions contain references to many aspects of the law that educators do not deal with in their professional lives. This text will attempt to bridge the language gap between education and law so that the educator, for whom this text is written, can better comprehend the legal meaning of constitutional law, statutes, and case law. It is imperative that this translation does not change the meaning of the law. It is also imperative that the student of school law not expect to master knowledge of school law without learning vocabulary and principles of law. However, it is a purpose of this book to help the student understand school law without having to spend an inordinate amount of time trying to decipher terms and language that are required only for attorneys. This will allow the education student to spend more time on understanding the principles of law upon which school statutes and case law are based.

Since the United States has a decentralized educational structure, it is sometimes hard to identify single rules of law that apply to all fifty states. Therefore, it is sometimes difficult to summarize or characterize some aspects of school law. Needless to say, for most points of law, many case law decisions have been handed down. It would be impractical to attempt to include them all. Therefore, landmark cases, generally recognized as the most powerful precedents currently in existence, are included at the conclusion of each chapter.

Chapter 1 deals with the legal system, specifically the nature of the state and federal court systems. Also, the powers and functions of the courts are explained.

Chapter 2 examines the federal role in education. It discusses the constitutional sources from which federal controls emanate. This role is ever expanding and has become more prevalent in recent years. Since the concept of federalism is in continual debate and flux, the role of the federal government in education will undoubtedly continue to evolve.

The Tenth Amendment to the federal Constitution is the basis for state control of education. Chapter 3 looks at how the states have, through statutory enactment, established the governance structure for public education.

Chapter 4 looks at church-state relationships. Since the U.S. Supreme Court issued the *Cochran* decision in 1932, the bricks in the so-called wall of separation, as described by Jefferson in the founding days of the republic, have been slowly crumbling. This chapter explains the Court's rationale for deciding when there is proper separation of church and state and when the separation is not legally necessary.

Chapter 5 presents the evolving concept of school attendance. The emergence of vouchers and other parental choice plans are remaking the legal concept of bona fide residence as the basis for legal school attendance.

Chapter 6 studies the legal correlation between curriculum and instruction, and examines the many aspects of teaching and learning that gather legal issues. It is within the instructional aspect of school law that much litigation involving teacher and community roles occurs. Educational malpractice, a natural by-product of the national accountability movements, is discussed.

The courts have stated, "A child's constitutional rights are not shed at the schoolhouse door." It is no longer possible for schools to have student regulation policies that could be summarized under the following heading: Do it because I said you had to do it. Societal norms and mores continue to play havoc with school's attempts to balance students' rights with their own right and obligation to provide a safe and orderly environment for learning. Chapter 7 weighs the legal principles upon which this legal balance rests.

Teacher contracts, rights, freedoms, tenure, and licensure are extremely important legal areas for administrators. The educational leader must know how to supervise, monitor, evaluate, and recommend employment issues relative to performance. In addition, administrators must be able to balance the legal control of school personnel to maintain an orderly and effective learning environment with the First Amendment right to free expression that all Americans enjoy, including teachers. This is the purpose of chapter 8.

There is significant litigation in torts. Although chapter 9 will define all types of torts, negligence will receive special emphasis. School personnel supervise the most precious possession of most people: their children. Therefore, school personnel, both teachers and administrators, must be knowledgeable in how to give a standard of care to students under their supervision and purview.

Since the inception of Public Law 94-142 (IDEIA), the question of handicapped education has evolved through federal statute, state accommodation, and voluminous case law. Informal assessments of a principal's time on task indicate that administrators are spending a significant portion of most school days on issues revolving around handicapped children. Therefore, chapter 10 presents the school law principles that govern handicapped education, from identification through assessment.

Chapter 11 discusses the never-ending saga of school desegregation. Since the Supreme Court issued the *Brown v. Topeka* ruling in 1954, the country has wrestled with the implementation of this historic decision. Changing demographics and housing patterns in recent decades have not tended to create a nation integrated racially. Although most school systems have been released from court orders to desegregate in order to eliminate de jure segregation, de facto segregation still exists.

Cases

Cases by Topic

1

The Legal System

Public schools are state schools. Therefore, in legal matters, schools are often referred to as the state. They are an arm of the state's police power, which is exercised to provide for the health, safety, and welfare of its citizens. The purpose of the state is to use the concerted action of the body politic for the benefit of human beings, and to provide the greatest good to the greatest number. State schools have been determined by all the states to be one of the mechanisms to accomplish these societal goals.

SOURCES OF SCHOOL LAW IN THE UNITED STATES

There are three sources of school law in the United States:

1. Constitutions (federal and state)
2. State Statutes
3. Case Law (often referred to as common law or judge-made law)

Characteristics of Constitutions

Both the federal and state constitutions in the United States are written to make provisions for securing the fundamental personal, property, and political rights of individuals. All the constitutions that provide the foundation

1

for school law contain provisions for authorized modifications. For example, the federal Constitution has been amended twenty-seven times.

The federal Constitution of the United States provided for the separation of powers into the executive, legislative, and judicial branches of government. The federal Constitution did not dictate that the states adopt the separation of powers. However, all fifty states have done so. Proof that the federal model did not have to be adopted at the state level can be seen in Nebraska. This state adopted a unicameral legislature as opposed to the two-house structure of the federal government and the other forty-nine states.

All fifty state constitutions make provision for a system of free, public education. The state constitutions vary greatly as to the specificity of the educational provision. Some are vague and only indicate that education will forever be pursued within the state. Other state constitutions are more specific about the state responsibility in the educational domain.

Characteristics of State Statutes

State statutes are acts of the state legislatures expressing its will and constitute the laws of the state. Statutes are an effective means of making new laws that meet the needs of society, and changing old laws that are no longer serving the interests of the people. Public schools are governed by statutes enacted by the state legislatures. Rules and regulations of boards of education, most often called board policies, fall within the category of the statutory source of school law. Boards of education must, in devising policies for the administration of the public schools, do so within the limits defined by the state statutes. However, legislatures may, through statute, confer administrative duties upon a state agency, such as a public school, or upon school officials such as the board of education, the clerk-treasurer, and in rare instances, superintendents or principals.

Case Law

Case law is sometimes referred to as common law or judge-made law. The word *common* in this context means being derived from custom, or reliance on precedent. American jurisprudence is premised on the principle of "stare decisis," which means "let the decision stand." Although why you are following the law. To continue to administer unconstitutional policies will be indefensible if and when the policy is challenged. Remember, it only takes one person to challenge and bring down an illegal policy. The law is not based solely on will of the majority but on the constitution and statutes of the state. We are a nation of laws. School board and administrative behavior should reflect this basic principle of civilization.

THE AMERICAN COURT SYSTEM

Since the United States has a federal system of government, it is necessary to have a dual judicial system, state and federal. Cases involving public schools may be heard at either level, depending upon the question to be decided. Most cases are state controversies, but in recent years there has been a substantial increase in federal litigation involving public and private schools. The following table is presented as an illustration of how public and private schools may be involved with both court systems.

State Courts

State constitutions generally prescribe the powers and the jurisdiction of the state courts. The legislature, through power granted in the constitution, provides for the specific operation of the courts, and creates additional courts as needed, so long as such power is found in the constitution.

Table 1.1.

Legal Issue	Jurisdiction	Source of Jurisdiction
1. Teacher contract	State	State Statute
2. Discrimination	Federal	504 Federal Civil Rights Act based on disability
3. Teacher strike	State	State Statute
4. Race discrimination	Federal	Equal Protection Clause of 14th amendment
5. IEP for handicapped student	Federal	IDEIA
6. Corporal punishment	State	State Statute

State courts consist of four categories (see figure 1.1):

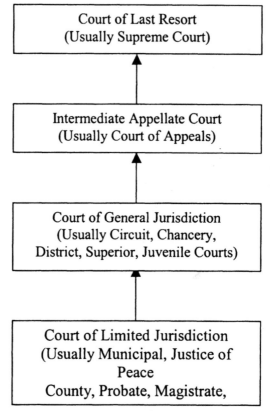

Figure 1.1.   **General Structure of State Court Systems**

1. Courts of last resort, usually called state supreme courts
2. Intermediate appellate courts, often called courts of appeal
3. Courts of general jurisdiction
4. Courts of limited jurisdiction

Courts of Last Resort

This court is the highest state jurisdiction, and is established by the state constitution. This court hears two types of appeals: mandatory and discretionary. State statutes sometimes dictate that certain issues must be heard by the court of last resort. These types of appeals are called mandatory. Other appeals are only heard at the discretion of the court of last resort. Mandatory appeals are automatically heard by the court. In discretionary jurisprudence, a party must file a petition to seek redress of the court. The court then decides whether to accept or reject the case.

Intermediate Appellate Courts

These courts hear appeals from lower courts as specified by state statute. The role of these appellate courts is to review specific trial court proceedings to correct errors in the application of the law, and to serve to extend and expand the law for the good of the community. Incidentally, these two roles are also the purview of the court of last resort. Like the court of last resort, intermediate appellate courts hear both mandatory and discretionary appeals as prescribed in the state constitution.

Courts of General Jurisdiction

With few exceptions, most court cases involving schools will originate at this jurisdiction level. These courts hold a variety of names, including common pleas and juvenile. If the case involves personnel, the case will originate in the court of common pleas or some other similar name. If the case involves children under eighteen, the juvenile court will be the court of original jurisdiction.

Courts of Limited Jurisdiction

These courts are lower trial courts with specific jurisdiction such as traffic violations and small claims. Schools are seldom involved with these courts.

Federal Courts

Article III of the Constitution of the United States states that "The judicial power of the United States shall be vested in one supreme court, and in such inferior courts as the Congress shall from time to time ordain and establish." Pursuant to that provision, Congress has created a court system consisting of district courts, courts of appeals, special federal courts, and the Supreme Court. (See figure 1.2.)

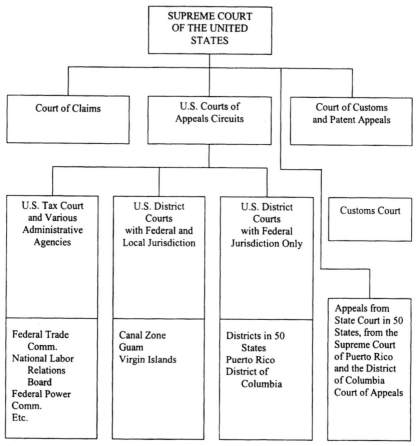

Figure 1.2.   The U.S. Court System

All states have a least one federal district court, with most having two
or more. California, New York, and Texas have four. Cases that are liti-
gated in the federal courts are classified under two groups:

1. Cases involving citizens of different states
2. Cases involving litigation of federal statutes of the federal Constitution

Decisions of the federal district courts can be appealed to the courts of
appeal. These courts often referred to as the federal circuits, consist of
thirteen different jurisdictions. (See figure 1.3.) The most significant aspect of circuit rulings for school administrators is that the ruling of the

highest court in one jurisdiction (e.g., Tenth Circuit) does not take precedence over a conflicting ruling from the highest court of another jurisdiction (e.g., Sixth Circuit). Therefore, unless the U.S. Supreme Court renders a decision on appeal, there could be conflicting rulings in effect in different parts of the country.

Let's look at an example to clarify this point. In the Tenth Circuit, located in Denver, Colorado, the court rules for the parent in an inclusion case and declares that the least restrictive environment is the regular classroom. This ruling will apply to the states of Wyoming, Utah, Colorado, Kansas, Oklahoma, and New Mexico since they are the states that constitute the Tenth Circuit. Any situations involving facts identical to the ones upon which the case was decided would indicate that the least restrictive environment would be the regular classroom.

In Cincinnati, Ohio, the seat of the Sixth Circuit, a very similar case is heard. The court rules for the school and denies inclusion as the least restrictive environment. This ruling, which is diametrically opposite to the ruling in the Tenth Circuit, applies to the states of Michigan, Ohio, Kentucky, and Tennessee, since they are the states that make up the Sixth Circuit. Any situations involving facts identical to the ones upon which this case was decided would indicate that the least restrictive environment would not be the regular classroom.

Therefore, the country would be under two different judicial rulings until the U. S. Supreme Court decided the matter for the entire country. Perhaps they would accept the Sixth Circuit ruling or the Tenth Circuit ruling. Or perhaps they would issue a ruling that did not fully accept either circuits' reasoning. Whatever they decide would become the law in the Sixth and Tenth Circuits, as well as the rest of the country.

The U.S. Supreme Court decides what cases it will hear on appeal by granting a writ of certiorari. A writ of certiorari is granted to an inferior court by the Supreme Court whereby a case is removed from an inferior court to a superior court for trial. The Supreme Court may grant or deny a writ of certiorari at their discretion. Cases may be accepted by the U.S. Supreme Court from lower federal courts or from state supreme courts when a state statute or federal statute is questioned as to its validity under the federal Constitution or where title, right, privilege, or immunity is claimed under the Constitution. All cases reach the U.S. Supreme Court through a writ of certiorari.

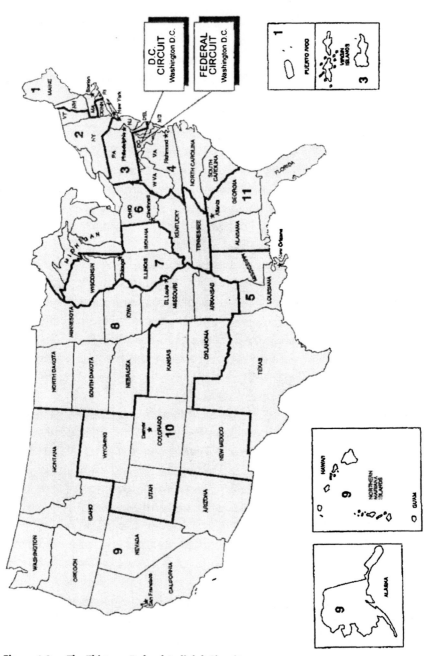

Figure 1.3.   The Thirteen Federal Judicial Circuits

SIGNIFICANT IMPLICATIONS FOR
SCHOOL ADMINISTRATION/LEADERSHIP

This chapter should help the school administrator to know how to administer her school on a day-to-day basis with confidence that her actions are legal and proper from a constitutional and statutory perspective. Secondly, this chapter points out a legal principle that every school administrator should know—that is, that any state statute, board of education policy, or administrative policy or procedure is considered to be constitutional unless it is challenged. Therefore, the school administrator should not assume that all policies and procedures are legal just because they have been in force for any period of time. The school administrator should not wait for questionable policies to be challenged, but should constantly scrutinize policies to ensure their constitutionality and be proactive in assuring that her school is one that recognizes and follows the law.

2

Federal Role In Education

The Tenth Amendment to the federal Constitution states that "powers not delegated to the United States by the Constitution, nor prohibited by it to the States, are reserved to the States respectfully, or to the people." Since public education is not mentioned in the federal Constitution, it is presumably reserved to the states or to the people.

Therefore, federal involvement in public education is an indirect role, and emanates from three sources:

1. The general welfare clause of the Constitution
2. The commerce clause of the Constitution
3. Actions by federal courts enforcing federal constitutional provisions protecting individual rights and freedoms.

EDUCATION AND GENERAL WELFARE

Article I, section 8 of the Constitution states, "The Congress shall have the power to lay and collect taxes, duties, imports and excises, to pay the debts and provide for the common defense and general welfare of the United States." In subsequent cases, the Supreme Court has ruled conclusively that Congress can tax and spend under the general welfare clause. The courts have said that the general welfare concept is not static but flexible, and Congress may tax and expend money for general welfare so long as it does not demonstrate a display of arbitrary power. With this elastic definition of general welfare, Congress is free to define education as general welfare and to tax and appropriate funds for educational purposes.

The federal government influences education under the general welfare clause by providing grant money to states for educational purposes. The states are not obligated to accept the grants. However, if the states acquiesce and accept the grant money, they also accept the rules and regulations put forth in the grant. Therefore, federal influence is inserted into schools, both public and private, since most federal grants offer the opportunity for involvement by both types of schools.

In recent decades, the federal government has increased its involvement in education by including extensive accountability measures within its grant proposals. These accountability measures are so strong that they have begun to dictate specific conditions in highly technical areas of education such as curriculum, instruction, and student assessment. In fact, state acquiescence to general welfare grants is drawing the nation closer and closer to a national curriculum and assessment model. In many instances, the states are acquiescing because the amount of money being provided by the federal government is so extensive that to refuse it would create severe fiscal problems. The federal government applies pressure to the states to accept their general welfare grants by tying the acquiescence to other federal monies not related to educational funds, such as highway allocations and assistance. In fact, state refusal of major federal funds is almost nonexistent.

In recent decades, public education has become a major issue in presidential elections. This seems to indicate that the federal government intends to continue to play a major role in education. Currently, states seem to be willing to accept federal regulations as a prerequisite to receiving the federal dollars. It will be interesting to see if this state attitude of acquiescence continues.

EDUCATION AND COMMERCE

Under the commerce clause, Congress has the power to regulate commerce with foreign nations, among the several states, and with the Indian tribes. Education has been most affected by the commerce clause through regulations and standards in safety, transportation, and labor. Because of the commerce clause, education must meet the standards and regulations of such agencies as OSHA, meet the minimum wage laws, and follow other federal standards and regulations with regard to the safety of buildings and school busses.

One naturally assumes that the term *commerce* refers to the buying, selling, and trading of goods among states in the pursuit of commercial activity. However, the Supreme Court has given the term *commerce* a broader meaning. In *Gibbons v. Ogden*, Chief Justice John Marshall maintained that commerce was intercourse, not merely an exchange of goods but also a means for the advancement of society, labor, transportation, intelligence, care, and various other mediums of exchange. The inclusion of intelligence in this interpretation of commerce opens the door to the inclusion of educational matters within the commerce clause.

That education is a foundation of commerce is not a new idea nor is it hard to defend. The significance of literacy to a civilization, and indeed the right of every human being to pursue it, began with printing. By the eighteenth century, knowledge became the subject of a brisk and universal trade among the peoples of the world. In this broad context, education could be brought within the scope of the commerce clause in that the movement of an intelligent citizenry among the states is vital to the growth and prosperity of the nation.

It is interesting to speculate how far the courts might go with regard to the commerce clause and a national curriculum. Due to the wide discrepancy among the states with regard to student achievement and taxable wealth, a broad interpretation of the commerce clause could infer that the lack of consistency from state to state with regard to quality indicators is hindering the intellectual growth of the nation. Therefore, through the power of the commerce clause, the federal government could pass standards and regulations that, in effect, would create a national curriculum. This would theoretically ensure that all students, regardless of their state of residency, would receive the same curriculum, thus increasing the quality of intelligence flowing from state to state.

The courts are constantly asked to balance the educational powers granted to the states by the Tenth Amendment against the apparent boundless scope of the commerce clause. Although schools have come increasingly under additional standards and regulations of the commerce clause, recent Supreme Court decisions have indicated that there are limits to the expansion of the commerce clause powers. For example, in *United States v. Lopez*, 1995, the Court held that the Gun Free School Zones Act was unconstitutional because there was no regulation of any commercial activity and it was not connected in any way to interstate commerce. This and other similar decisions by a conservative Court indicate a trend away from an expanded intrusion into educational commerce by the federal government.

Every day that a school is in session, that school is full of people—students and adults—who have constitutional rights. These rights are largely based on constitutional constraints that enforce individual rights and freedoms. When there are controversies involving these rights and freedoms, the federal court system has jurisdiction. The First and Fourteenth Amendment rights seem to permeate the caseload. However, if any aspect of the federal constitutional rights or constraints is in controversy, the federal courts will hear the case. Thus, in case law, the federal government exercises extensive control and influence.

SUPREMACY CLAUSE

There are occurrences when a state law is passed that comes into direct conflict with a federal law. When this happens, the state law must give way and accede primacy to the federal law. The supremacy clause elevates the authority of congressional legislation above that of state legislation in areas where Congress possesses constitutional delegation of authority. However, it should be noted that a state is not obligated to expend federal funds for purposes that violate its state constitution (see *Wheeler v. Barrera*).

In essence, the supremacy clause clarifies that, although the United States is made up of fifty sovereign states, we are one nation under one set of enumerated, federal laws that are the supreme law of the land. When the supremacy clause is called into question, the issue is not whether or not federal law takes precedent over state law. It is clear that the federal law prevails. However, there is always the issue of whether the federal law in question is a valid exercise of national power. The supremacy clause applies when the federal law is a power enumerated in the Constitution and therefore a legal exercise of federal authority.

SIGNIFICANT IMPLICATIONS FOR
SCHOOL ADMINISTRATION/LEADERSHIP

School administrators, both private and public, are going to be dealing more and more with grants authorized under the general welfare clause. The philosophical argument about education being solely a state function is purely rhetorical. Current legislation, such as the No Child Left Behind Act, is forcing both public and private schools to react to federal mandates. This act, often referred to by the initials NCLB, imposes annual testing of all public school students in reading and math, grades 3 through 8, and high school, by the 2005–2006 school year. The act also requires annual report cards on school performance, contains a third-grade reading assurance, and calls for a highly qualified teacher in every public school classroom by 2005. All of these requirements are laden with mandates that will project the federal government into the curriculum, instruction, and staff development programs of public schools. Of course, the states could refuse to accept the mandates but in doing so they run the danger of losing federal funding for other school programs. Political ramifications would also surface. Since NCLB is still in its infancy, it will probably undergo change. However, the role of the federal government in public education seems to be an ever-increasing trend. Despite the Tenth Amendment, the school administrator is going to have to deal with federal law on a more increasing basis.

Needless to say, administrators need to know the constitutional protection afforded the students, licensed personnel, and classified personnel. To not be informed concerning these rights and freedoms is to invite federal litigation, which costs the school both monetary and human resources. Each of these federal legal considerations will be discussed in the appropriate chapters.

3

State Role in Education

States have broad power to govern education. This power is guaranteed by the Tenth Amendment, which states, "The powers not delegated to the United States by the Constitution, nor prohibited by it to the states, are reserved to the states respectfully, or to the people." Since education is not mentioned in the federal constitution, education is a reserved power. Therefore, the states base their governance on their respective constitutions. State constitutions give general powers to the legislatures who then establish school systems as they see fit. In some states the constitutions are very specific in spelling out the powers and authority given to the various levels of boards of education, and prescribing organizational structure. Other states only refer to education in general terms such as "the state will forever encourage education," and leave the specifics of how to implement education totally in the hands of the legislatures.

LIMITATIONS OF POWER

Boards of education created by the state are limited to powers granted to them by the state constitution or by legislative statute. In most instances, these powers concentrate on educating all children within the state between the ages of five and eighteen. As schools have become more complex in their function, it often appears that the school is involved in many other kinds of activities that would not meet this definition of limitations

17

of powers. Keep in mind that the limitations basically refer to the use of public tax money that supports public education. There are many federal and state programs that contain funds designated for a specific purpose that are implemented within the state's public school districts. An example is adult basic education. These programs are financially self-sufficient and therefore not a violation of the boards' limitation of powers. In the spirit of community relations, many school districts open their buildings up to community use. However, it would not be legal for these programs to be supported by public tax money that is constitutionally or legislatively earmarked for the education of children ages five to eighteen.

The definition of education has increased in liberal interpretation as the needs of states and communities have grown. Beginning with the famous *Kalamazoo* case in Michigan, where the courts approved state tax support for high schools as well as grades 1 through 8, and with subsequent cases such as *Hartzell v. Connell*, which incorporated extracurricular activities as an integral part of education, the courts have upheld the expanding role of education in the society.

EDUCATION PROVISIONS OF STATE CONSTITUTIONS

In recent decades the courts have been more assertive in invoking the state constitutions with regard to state educational policymaking. The courts have been especially interested in how the states are meeting their constitutional definitions of a state school system that is "efficient," "uniform," or "thorough." At the center of this controversy is how states fund public schools to adequately and equitably provide for education of all its citizens. Of particular interest is the Kentucky case of *Rose v. The Council for Better Education, Inc.*, in which the Kentucky Supreme Court found the entire system of public education in Kentucky to be unconstitutional. From this decision, and others like it, such as the *DeRolph* case in Ohio, certain principles about the state role and obligation in providing for an efficient, unitary state school system have emerged. They can be summarized as follows:

1. The "sole responsibility" for providing a system of free and common schools lies with the state legislatures. This responsibility cannot be delegated to local boards.

2. State legislatures must provide a cohesive and unitary system.
3. Equity and equality are required.
4. Public schools are controlled and governed by the body politic. It is neither private nor quasi private.

In the *Rose* case, the Kentucky Supreme Court raised the following points:

1. Court held that education was a "fundamental right" in Kentucky. Previous to this ruling, it was not clear in many states that education was a right. It was considered more of an opportunity.
2. The current school system did not satisfy the constitutional requirement of an "efficient" system.
3. The school system was not uniform or adequate.
4. The system of schools must be adequately funded to achieve its goals and be substantially uniform throughout the state.
5. The court found that Kentucky schools were overall inadequate when compared to the schools of the rest of the nation.
6. Great disparity in fiscal capacity, revenues per pupil, curriculum, and educational services existed throughout the state.
7. "Efficient" was defined as: First, the system should impose no financial hardship or advantage on any group of citizens. Further, local school districts must make comparable tax efforts. Second, resources provided by the system must be adequate and uniform throughout the state. Third, the system must not waste resources. Efficient has also been defined as a system that is unitary, thus one in which there is uniformity throughout the state. It implies a system that gives all students equal opportunities regardless of economic status, or place of residence. Summarizing, an efficient state school system is one that is unitary, uniform, adequate, and properly managed.
8. The "sole responsibility" for providing a system of common schools lay with the General Assembly and could not be delegated to local boards.

These rulings underscore and emphasize the fact that providing for free and common public schools is a state responsibility. Despite the long-held tradition of "local control of schools," the fact remains that the state holds the constitutional responsibility to provide and maintain efficient and equitable schools for all its citizens. If local control exists, it is because the state legislatures have granted discretionary powers to local boards. This means that they could also take them away through legislative action.

The conflict between the courts and the state legislatures over this matter is due to questions of financial obligation. It is one thing for the courts to mandate a state school system that is uniform and equitable. It is another matter to fund such a mandate. Great disparity in local wealth among school districts exists. To bring the poor districts up to the standards of the wealthy requires a redistribution of the wealth. How much redistribution is fair? What can the state do if wealthy districts are willing to tax themselves locally to the point that disparity between themselves and poor areas will surface? What form of tax should be used?

The issue, based on financial disparity within the state, has brought state constitutions to the forefront of the legal debate. State legislatures are trying to figure out how to meet the constitutional mandate of providing common schools within the reality of economic diversity. Although it is a philosophical debate, it becomes political because the redistribution of wealth and the determination of how to tax the public are controversial and give rise to special interest advocacy.

FUNCTIONS OF BOARDS OF EDUCATION/ADMINISTRATIONS

School authorities exercise three kinds of powers: legislative, executive, and quasi judicial. Because this broad and comprehensive power base cuts across the traditional separation of powers, the courts closely scrutinize school implementation of authority to ensure impartiality and to prevent abuse of power.

1. Legislative Function

The legislative function is carried out by the board of education, through the passage of policies that form the governance structure for operation of the school, and by administrators who create administrative policy necessary for the day-to-day operation of the school. Administrative policy is quasi and must not be in conflict with board policy. Since education is a state function, and the powers of the various boards of education are created by the state, local school board members are considered to be state officers.

It should be noted that the legislative function could only be exercised by school officers. School officers are those persons or entities that are given specific legislative authority by the state statutes.

In most states, boards of education and clerk-treasurers are usually the only full-time school officers. Superintendents, principals, other administrators, teachers, and classified personnel are considered to be employees and thus not school officers. However, if the statutes specifically authorize a school employee, such as the superintendent, to perform a discretionary power, in that instance, she is a school officer. For example, in the state of Ohio, the statutes authorize the superintendent to approve and monitor homeschooling. The board of education has no authority in this matter. Therefore, in this instance, the superintendent is a school officer.

In order to understand the role of school officers, you must be able to differentiate between discretionary and ministerial authority. School officers exercise discretionary powers, while school employees exercise ministerial authority.

The legislative function is accomplished through discretionary decision making. Discretionary functions are judgmental and represent substantial prerogative. They could be considered general as opposed to specific. These powers have a direct link to the origin of the authority. In the case of education, the statutes empower specific bodies with decision-making responsibility. Although it is a general rule of law that discretionary powers cannot be delegated or subdelegated, there is a tendency in the courts to allow more and more discretion in this matter due to the increasingly complex nature of schools. Discretionary power is usually derived from the policies that are created by the board of education.

2. Executive Function

The executive function is carried out by the school employees, administrators, teachers, and classified personnel. The authority to perform the executive functions connected to the day-to-day operation of the school is delegated to school employees by the board of education. Discretionary powers are not specific enough to serve the diverse needs and happenings that occur daily in any school. Administrators and teachers must have some latitude in organizing and controlling the learning environment. They exercise those powers, which are referred to as ministerial.

Ministerial duties consist of all the authority exercised by the school employees that are not purely discretionary. School officers cannot delegate discretionary powers but can delegate ministerial ones.

3. Quasi-Judicial Function

A school board has quasi-judicial authority. A school board exercises this authority by exercising due process hearings in expelling students, dismissing a teacher or classified employee under contract, and other instances where a judicial judgment is called for. Although it is clear that school boards have this quasi-judicial authority, their judgments can be challenged in the courts. In such cases, the fundamental question is whether or not the school board has acted in fairness and neutrality. For example, if the board dismisses a teacher under contract, the reasons for such dismissal would have to be for reasons clearly pertaining to performance and not based on personal grievance or other reasons beyond the scope of the board's powers. *Ultra vires* is a legal term for a public agency, such as a board of education, that acts beyond the scope of its constitutional or legislative authority in either good or bad faith. If such evidence is found, the courts may void the board's actions.

SCHOOL OFFICERS

In order to understand the legality of decision-making delegation, the difference between a school officer and a school employee is vital. School officers possess discretionary or judgmental powers derived from either the state constitution or state statute. Other characteristics of school officers are: 1) a required oath of office, 2) the existence of a statutory provision for removal, 3) a position that is elected instead of appointed, and 4) a term of office specified by law. School board members are school officers. In most states, clerk-treasurers are officers, although they are appointed by the board of education. However, they are directly responsible to the board of education, and not subject to the authority of the superintendent.

In the performance of their duties, school administrators occasionally act as officers. This occurs when the statutes specifically give them discretionary authority. For example, in most states, the assignment of pupils is a discretionary power of the superintendent, not subject to review by the board of education. In many states, the issue of approving homeschooling is a discretionary power of the superintendent, also not subject to review by the board of education. As a general rule, school administrators are employees, not officers, and thus exercise ministerial functions only.

In summary, school officers are enumerated in the state constitution and statutes. As such, they are considered state officers and possess a portion of the state sovereignty, and can therefore exercise discretionary authority. Included in this discretionary authority is the power to delegate ministerial powers to employees, such as administrators and teachers.

SCHOOL BOARD MEETINGS

Regular Board Meetings

At an annual organizational meeting, the board elects its officers and establishes its meeting times and dates for the year. This meeting is usually held in early January. If the board does not deviate from the time and dates established, no further public notification is legally required. At regularly scheduled board meetings, the board's agenda can be any business that comes before the board that is within its legal purview. School systems prepare agendas for regular meetings, which are prepared by the superintendent and clerk-treasurer. This agenda will list the bills to be approved for payment, superintendent items for discussion, public participation requests, and other agenda items. In most cases, the prepared agenda will constitute the business of the meeting. However, if matters not mentioned on the agenda arise, the board can legally act upon them.

If the board chooses to move its meetings from place to place each month, the public must be notified of the address changes. Oftentimes boards of education represent a number of small communities that make up the school district. In those instances they sometimes choose to move the board meetings among the communities that make up the school district. The public must be notified of any change in time or place that varies from the established meeting schedule.

Special Board Meetings

From time to time, boards of education call special board meetings. Business may become so extensive that the board cannot get its responsibilities carried out within the time constraints of the regularly scheduled meetings. Crises also arise that require a special meeting. When a board of education calls a special meeting, it must give the public twenty-four hours notice in the local media. Local media is defined as newspapers, television, radio, and community bulletin boards. The most common media used is the newspapers. This public notification must include the following:

- Date
- Time
- Place (complete address)
- Agenda

At special board meetings, the board may only act upon the preestablished agenda. For example, if the special meeting was called to award a contract for blacktopping the parking lots, the board could not award the superintendent a new contract at that meeting. The only official business the board could conduct is to award the contract for the blacktopping. Other discussions may arise, but the board could take no official actions beyond the published notice of the reason for the special board meeting. This legal procedure prevents boards of education from acting without the opportunity for public knowledge. In controversial actions, the law wants to make sure that the board cannot avoid public scrutiny by delaying or avoiding controversial discussions and votes in regular meetings and "slipping them through" in special meetings that are not as well attended.

Executive Sessions

There are instances when boards of education can go into executive session to discuss matters deemed by the law as too sensitive for public consumption. A board of education cannot vote in executive session, only deliberate. A board of education could take a straw vote in executive session to determine where the various board members stood on an issue. However, such a straw vote is unofficial and must be repeated in public session to be legal. In addition, a board member could change his vote from the executive session straw vote to the legal motion presented in public session. Therefore, a straw vote in executive session is nothing more that a part of the deliberation. Items deemed legal subject matter for executive session are as follows:

- Appointments, employment, dismissal, promotion, demotion, or compensation for employees.
- Investigations of charges or complaints against employees.
- Purchase or sale of school property.
- Attorney conferences.
- Preparations for or conducting of professional negotiations or collective bargaining.
- Specialized details of security arrangements.
- Matters required to be kept confidential by federal law/rules or state statute.

Sunshine Laws

Many states have passed sunshine laws in an attempt to strengthen and clarify the limitations on executive sessions. As the workings of boards of education became more complex, legal issues arose that were not specifically covered by executive session statutes. For example, many boards of education operate from a committee structure instead of always meeting as a committee of the whole. Many legal issues involving the personal relationship of board members outside of official meetings influencing board decisions have arisen. These and other issues have motivated states to pass sunshine laws. Following is a discussion of the most commonly asked questions about sunshine laws as they apply to boards of education.

- To what entities does the sunshine law apply?

  The sunshine law has always applied to boards of education. The law also applies to any committee or subcommittee of a board of education.

- What is a committee or a subcommittee to which the Sunshine Law applies?

    A committee or subcommittee created by board action would seem to clearly be covered by the law. If the committee is named by the superintendent, arguably it is not a committee or subcommittee of the board to which the law applies (1994 Opinions of the Ohio Attorney General 94-096). The law does not cover entities such as booster clubs, PTA's and PTO's, which are not created by the board.

- Does the membership of the committee or subcommittee make a difference? Is it important that the committee or subcommittee has board members among its membership? Presume the law applies to a board committee or subcommittee, whether its membership includes any board members or not.

    One court has held that "public body" includes a building leadership team established by the negotiated agreement, making team meetings subject to the requirements of Ohio Revised Code (ORC) 121.22 (*Weissfield v. Akron Public School Dist.*, 94 Oapp3d 455, 640 NE2d 1201[1994]).

- Must a board adopt rules?

    Yes. Each board, committee, and subcommittee must adopt rules by which any person may learn the time and place of all regular meetings and the time, place, and purpose of all special meetings. The rules must provide for giving notice of meetings to any person and any news media who so request. The board, committee, or subcommittee may charge a reasonable fee for giving such notice.

- What constitutes a meeting?

    A meeting constitutes any prearranged discussion of public business of a board of education, committee, or subcommittee by a majority of its members. "Discussion" suggests exchange of words, comments, or ideas between members of the public body (*Springfield Board of Education v. OAPSE Local 530*, et al. [1990], 106 Oapp3d 855). Regardless of what name is given a gathering (work session, study group, retreat, etc.) if it meets this definition, it is a meeting. The Ohio Supreme Court has held that a series of meetings, each with a minority of members of a public body, without giving proper notice, can constitute a Sunshine Law violation (*State ex rel. Cincinnati Dist. v. Cincinnati* [1996] 76 Ohio St. 3d 540).

- Can a majority of the members of a board, a committee, or a subcommittee get together without violating the Sunshine Law?

  Yes. If there was not a prearranged discussion of the business of the board, committee, or subcommittee, it would not be a meeting as defined by statute. A majority of board members could, for example, get together on social occasions, ride together to an event, or attend a seminar without violating the law, so long as discussions of board business do not take place. The same is true of the members of a committee or subcommittee. Common examples include holiday parties, graduation ceremonies, and candidate forums, where there is no prearranged discussion of board business by a majority of its members.

- Can a board, a committee, or a subcommittee lawfully hold meetings outside the school district?

  Yes, there is no prohibition on holding meetings out of the district. However, provisions of the Sunshine Law are applicable and the public would be entitled to be present. If "out of district" meetings were conducted in order to curtail public accessibility, the practice would be in contravention of the spirit of the Sunshine Law and could be enjoined.

- When can a board hold an executive session?

  Only in conjunction with a regular or special meeting of the board, a committee, or subcommittee.

- What can a board do in executive session?

  Deliberate only. No action of any kind can be taken during an executive session.

- What topics may a board discuss in executive session?

  a) The appointment, employment, dismissal, discipline, promotion, demotion, or compensation of an employee or official or the investigation of charges or complaints against an employee, official, licensee or student, unless the employee, official, licensee or student requests a public hearing.

  b) The purchase of property for public purposes or the sale of property at competitive bidding.

  c) Conferences with the board's attorney to discuss matters that are the subject of pending or imminent court action.

  d) Preparing for, conducting, or reviewing negotiations or bargaining sessions with employees.

e) Matters required to be kept confidential by federal law or rules or state statutes.

f) Specialized details of security arrangements.

Each executive session discussion must be limited to the purposes stated. It is unlawful to state only one purpose for an executive session, and then to discuss a second topic, although an executive session may be called for the purpose of discussing several topics (*Vermillion Teachers' Assn. v. Vermillion Local School Dist. Board of Education* [1994] 98 Oapp3d 524). Board members, as a matter of ethics, should not divulge executive session discussions. Furthermore, it should be noted that some matters discussed in executive session can also be legally confidential. In fact, most sunshine laws provide that confidentiality of information shared in executive sessions is legally required when (1) notice of a subject's confidentiality is given, and (2) when confidentiality is necessary for the proper conduct of government business.

If this process is violated, it is a misdemeanor of the first degree.

- Must a board follow a particular procedure to go into executive session?

Yes. There must be a motion to go into executive session followed by a roll call vote. The motion must state which of the purposes listed of the law is the purpose for the executive session. If the executive session is to discuss a personnel matter, the motion must state exactly which type of personnel action is to be discussed, but need not include the name of any person to be considered (*Caldwell v. Westlake Bd. of Educ.* [1991] Cuyahoga Ct. App. No. 210345). A session to discuss a personnel matter must be about an individual or individuals, rather than about a subject in general (e.g., a board may discuss the nonrenewal of one or more specific people, but not nonrenewable procedures in general). See *Gannett Satellite Information Network v. Chillicothe City School District, 4th Dist. Ct. App., Ross Co.,* Case No. 1427 (April 4, 1988).

The resolution to adjourn into executive session should choose words from the statutory list. While it is fine to use general topics to help remember the reason(s) the board can properly go into executive session, the actual wording of the resolution must incorporate the works found in the statute. Mistakes may be able to be "cured" by subsequent action taken in public; see *Biesel v. Monroe Co. Bd. of Educ.*, Case No. 6A-678 (Monroe Co. AP, 8-29-90) unreported, *Kuhlman v. Village of Leipsic*, (Putnam Co. Court of Appeals No. 12-94-9), unreported, (3-27-95).

- Who is entitled to attend executive sessions?

All of the members of the board, committee, or subcommittee. The board, committee, or subcommittee may invite any other person that it wishes into an executive session. This means the board can hold an executive session without the superintendent or treasurer if it so chooses.

- Must minutes be kept of executive sessions?

No, minutes should not be kept of executive sessions. However, the minutes of the meeting at which the executive session occurs must reflect the general subject matter discussed in the executive session.

- What notice must be given of special board meetings?

The board, committee, or subcommittee must comply with its own rules to provide notice to any person who has requested it. The board, committee, or subcommittee must also provide at least twenty-four hours advance notice to the news media that have previously requested notice of the time, place, and purpose of any special meetings.

Thus, failure to notify local media of an emergency or special meeting as required by law could make action taken invalid.

- Can a board, a committee, or a subcommittee hold an emergency meeting?

Yes. An emergency meeting can be called upon immediate notification to all news media who have previously requested notice. The two-day notice provision to board members remains in effect, but is satisfied if all members attend the meeting.

- Must an employee be notified if the employee is to be the subject of an executive session discussion?

The Sunshine Law states that investigations of charges or complaints against an employee, official, or student can be heard in executive session unless the individual requests a public hearing. This option may trigger a need to notify the individual. In addition, laws

regarding employee nonrenewals and terminations have specific requirements.

- Does the Sunshine Law grant the public the right to participate in
  meetings of a board, a committee, or a subcommittee?

  No. The Sunshine Law contains no such provision. However, most
  boards of education provide an opportunity for public participation.
  The board may adopt reasonable rules to control public comments.

- Can a member of a board, a committee, or a subcommittee participate
  in meetings when he or she is not physically present?

  A member of a board, committee, or subcommittee can participate
  but cannot vote. Members can participate in discussions even though
  they are not physically present through equipment such as a speaker-
  phone (see Ohio Attorney General Opinion No. 85-048). However, a
  provision of the Sunshine Law specifically requires an individual to
  be "present in person" in order to be considered as part of a quorum
  or vote.

- Are there situations in which the Sunshine Law does not apply?

  Yes, the Sunshine Law does not apply to an audit conference conducted by either the Bureau of Inspection and Supervision of Public
  Offices or by independent certified public accountants with officials
  of the school district. Collective bargaining meetings between the
  board and employee organizations are also not subject to the Sunshine Law.

- Can anyone sue a board, a committee, or a subcommittee claiming a
  Sunshine Law violation?

  Yes. Any person may bring an action in the court of common pleas
  to enforce the Sunshine Law. That person may seek an injunction to
  halt a violation or threatened violation of the law. Such a suit must be
  brought within two years of the violation or threatened violation.

- What happens if a board violates the Sunshine Law?

  Any action taken in executive session is void if the board has violated the Sunshine Law. So is any action taken in open session that
  has resulted from an unlawful executive session. A 1993 amendment
  to the Sunshine Law makes it clear that any board action is invalid if
  the board violated any of the notice provisions of the law. A court
  may issue an injunction compelling members of the board, a committee, or a subcommittee to comply with the Sunshine Law.

- What penalties may a court assess?

  If the court issues an injunction, it is required to assess a civil penalty of $500 against the board, a committee, or a subcommittee and require that entity to pay all court costs. The court is also to require the public body to pay the reasonable attorney's fees of the party who brought the suit, although such fees can be reduced if the court determines that the public body acted reasonably in believing that it was not violating the Sunshine Law and that its conduct served a public purpose.

- Can a board, a committee, or a subcommittee recover costs and attorneys fees if it was subjected to a nonmeritorious suit?

  Yes. However, the court must not only find in favor of the board, committee, or subcommittee but it must also determine that the bringing of the lawsuit by the plaintiff was "frivolous conduct."

- Is there any penalty that applies to individual board members?

  Yes. A board member who knowingly violates an injunction that has been granted by a court may be removed from office. The removal must be accomplished by a suit brought in common pleas court by the prosecuting attorney or attorney general.

The Importance of Board Minutes

The minutes of a board of education meeting are the official record of the proceedings. Therefore, a board of education speaks only through its minutes. This raises the question of, "What happens if erroneous minutes are approved by the board of education?" The answer is that the erroneous minutes would represent the official action of the board. Of course, once the error is discovered, it could be corrected by passing a new motion that reflects the original intent of the board. So long as there is no timeline or deadline connected with the motion, correction through new action could easily be achieved. However, a serious problem could arise from the approval of incorrect minutes if a deadline has passed that makes a new motion to correct the error impossible. For example, if the board intended to nonrenew a teacher but the minutes reflected that the renewal was granted, and the deadline for nonrenewing personnel passed before the board reconvened, it would not be possible to correct the mistake.

Therefore, it is very important for school administrators to read board minutes carefully to ensure that they reflect the true intent of the motion that was passed. Many boards of education have begun the practice of audiotaping meetings for review in case of controversy involving the accuracy of the clerk's minutes. Boards have also begun the practice of keeping electronic minutes. These are excellent safeguards to ensure the accuracy of minutes, but they do not replace the written and recorded minutes of the clerk-treasurer as the official record of board proceedings.

Abstentions by Board Members

Any time a motion or action of the board gives rise to a conflict of interest for a board member, that board member should abstain. A conflict of interest means that the board member could benefit in some way, mostly through monetary reward or increased influence, from an action taken by the board. Examples of conflicts of interest are the employment of relatives (in states with lenient nepotism laws) or the awarding of contracts to persons or companies in which the board member has a vested interest.

There are times when board members without a conflict of interest will choose to abstain on a motion. In those instances, there is case law to suggest that an abstention counts with the will of the majority. The court's rationale for this decision is that, barring a conflict of interest, a board member cannot abrogate his responsibility simply because he can't make up his mind, does not have an opinion, doesn't care enough to vote, or wishes to avoid controversy. Therefore, his abstention will count with the will of the majority.

For example, in the case of *Collins v. Janey*, 147 Tenn.477, 249 S. W. 801(1923), there was a motion to execute a contract before a school board consisting of seven members, and the vote was 3 for, 2 against, and 2 abstentions; the motion did not pass. However, when this action was challenged, the court ruled that the motion carried by a vote of 5 to 2. Those not voting were considered as assenting to the will of the majority.

Board Discretionary Authority

As was previously discussed, a board of education has discretionary power over the school district. However, this does not mean that the individual members of the board have legal authority in the school system outside the parameters established by board policy and procedures. For example, if a school board member, on his own initiative, visits a school building, he has no legal authority to exercise discretionary or ministerial authority. The visit would be no different, from a legal perspective, than any other citizen of the district. Board members only have legal authority within the context of the actions of an official board meeting.

Politically speaking, board members may exert pressure or influence by engaging in acts such as visiting school buildings and talking to school personnel. Most certainly, they will be treated differently than a citizen who visits the school. However, they have no legal authority to order school personnel to do anything. Such discretionary and ministerial authority must come from total board action.

STATE RELATIONSHIP WITH PRIVATE/PAROCHIAL SCHOOLS

The courts have traditionally held that as an aspect of its sovereignty a state has an inherent obligation to provide for the general welfare. This is referred to as the "police power." In pursuit of the police power, states have extensive regulatory authority over private and parochial schools. The extent of this power will vary from state to state depending upon the state's constitution and statutes. Generally, state regulatory authority is manifested in two ways: (a) incorporation or chartering, and (b) licensing of teachers and administrators. Some states exempt private and parochial schools from licensing requirements if they are approved under a regional or national accrediting agency. Private and parochial schools who receive any kind of state funds are subject to regulations so long as they do not interfere with the property rights of the private school or the First Amendment rights of the parochial school with regard to the free exercise of religion. Examples of required regulations are (a) proficiency testing, (b) zoning and construction regulations, and (c) building codes.

The U.S. Supreme Court, in the historic ruling in *Pierce v. Society of Sisters of the Holy Names of Jesus and Mary*, declared that parents have the right to direct the education and upbringing of their children. Therefore, states cannot require students to attend public schools. However, the state can exercise its police power to require private and parochial schools to follow regulations such as immunization laws to protect the general welfare of all citizens.

Teacher certification for private/parochial schools is generally handled in one or all of three ways:

1. Teachers in private/parochial schools be licensed by the state,
2. Teacher licensing not be required, but the nonpublic instruction must be equivalent to that offered in the public schools, and
3. Teacher licensing not be required but that nonpublic education conform to certain curriculum standards.

In the absence of state authority, the private/parochial schools operate as if their written policy books replace the state statutes. Their written policies will create a contract to educate with their parents and students. In cases of controversy, the courts will look to the clarity, fairness, and equality of application with regard to the school policies.

4

Church and State

The framers of the Declaration of Independence and the U.S. Constitution were interested in creating a nation that would allow the freedom of religion. The colonists knew the perils of mixing religion and state. The history of Europe had, for centuries, been dominated by religious wars and strife, both internally and externally. However, as the institutions of government and society emerged in the new nation called the *United States*, the belief in the presence of a supreme being and the desire to include such a belief in the cultural and societal activities of the nation permeated ceremonies, public and private alike. Therefore, even though religious freedom was specifically guaranteed in the U.S. Constitution, it seemed to be understood that God and religion would play a part in the fabric of the new nation. Thus, there has been a continual struggle to keep the separation of church and state within a society that has strong religious leanings.

THE EARLY ESTABLISHMENT OF RELIGIOUS FREEDOM

In 1786 the Virginia legislature passed the Jefferson Act to prevent the Anglican Church from being supported by public tax money. In the preamble to the act, Jefferson made four points.

1. God made man free, and deliberately chose that religion should be propagated by reason and not by coercion.

2. Legislators and rulers have impiously assumed dominion over faith, and have established and maintained false religions.
3. It is sinful and tyrannical to compel a man to furnish contributions for the propagation of opinions, which he disbelieves and abhors; and it is also wrong to force him to support this or that teacher of his own religious persuasion.
4. Our civil rights have no dependence on our religious opinion, and therefore imposing religious qualifications for civil office tends to corrupt religion by bribery to obtain purely external conformity. (See Leo Pfeiffer, *Church and State*, Boston: Beacon Press, 1967, pp. 113–14.)

James Madison, in his *Memorial and Remonstrance against Religious Assessments* in 1785, wrote what has become the most cited and quoted rationale for the separation of church and state. His points can be summarized essentially as follows:

1. Religion is wholly exempt from cognizance of civil society.
2. Since religion is exempt from the authority of the society at large, it cannot be subject to the will of a legislative body whose jurisdiction is both derivative and limited.
3. The same authority that can establish Christianity to the exclusion of other religions may establish, with the same ease, any particular sect of Christians to the exclusion of other sects, and the same authority that can force a citizen to contribute three pence only of his property for the support of any one establishment may force him to conform to any other establishment in all cases whatsoever.
4. All men are to be considered as entering into society on equal conditions and to retain equally their natural rights; state taxation for religious purposes denies equality to those who do not embrace, profess, or observe the religion, which we believe to be of divine nature.
5. Patrick Henry's Bill for Religious Assessments implies either that the civil magistrate is a competent judge of religious truth or that he may employ religion as an engine of civil policy. The first is an arrogant pretension; the second, an unhallowed perversion of the means of salvation.

6. The above bill is unnecessary because religion does not need the support of human laws; on the contrary, the bill fosters a suspicion that the friends of religion are too conscious of its fallacies to trust in its own merits.

7. Experience shows that ecclesiastical establishments, instead of maintaining the purity and efficacy of religion, have resulted in pride and indolence in the clergy; ignorance and servility in the laity; in both, superstition, bigotry, and persecution.

8. Since religion is not within the cognizance of civil government, it cannot be argued that it is necessary to legally establish it.

9. The bill degrades from the equal rank of citizen all those whose opinions in religion do not bend to those of the legislative authority.

10. The bill will add a fresh motive to migration by revoking the liberty that citizens now enjoy.

11. The bill will destroy that moderation and harmony which the forbearance of our laws to intermeddle with religion has produced among its several sects.

12. The many who have not accepted the truth of Christianity will be discouraged to do so.

13. The inevitable difficulty of enforcing a law obnoxious to so great a proportion of the citizens will tend to enervate the laws in general and to slacken the bonds of society.

14. It is not sufficiently clear that a majority of the citizens approve the bill.

15. Since the equal weight of every citizen to the free exercise of his religion is equal in weight to all other natural rights, acceptance of a legislative infringement of this right means that the legislature may likewise infringe the freedom of the press or abolish trial by jury. (Pfeiffer, pp. 112–13.)

CONSTITUTIONAL BASIS FOR THE
SEPARATION OF CHURCH AND STATE

The First Amendment to the U.S. Constitution guarantees "free exercise of religion" and prohibits the "establishment of religion" by the state.

Legal controversies in education concerning the separation of church and state involve either a person's claim that his free exercise rights have been denied, or that the state is attempting, through some legislative or executive act, to establish religion.

An effective way to study the historical relationship of church and state with regard to public and parochial education is to show how the wall of separation has been removed "brick by brick." Today, the wall of separation is less of a wall and more of a sieve, through which the relationship between church and state flows freely with far few barriers than originally existed.

Child Benefit Theory

In the historic *Cochran v. Louisiana* case in 1932, the Supreme Court held that a state statute that authorized the lending of textbooks to the parochial schoolchildren of Louisiana was constitutional. This was the first "brick" in the wall of separation to fall. The legal rationale of the court was that the textbooks were being loaned to the children and not to the parochial schools. Therefore, the statute was constitutional because it was the responsibility of the state legislature to provide for the general welfare and needs of all its citizens, regardless of where they attended school. The "child benefit theory" established by *Cochran* has been used as a precedent for upholding many subsequent acts of both the state and federal legislatures that provided aid to parochial and private schools. The court ruled that lending textbooks to parochial schoolchildren did not violate the establishment clause of the Constitution.

Public Purpose Theory

In 1947, the New Jersey legislature authorized the transportation of children "living remote from any schoolhouse," including transportation of nonpublic children. This statute was challenged as a violation of the establishment clause in the case of *Everson v. Board of Education.* The Supreme Court ruled that the legislative act was intended to facilitate the opportunity of children to get a secular education and that such intention served a "public purpose." Thus was born the public purpose theory. In its

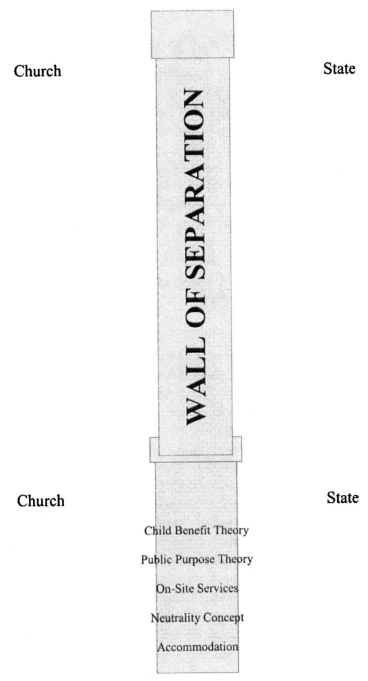

Church   State

WALL OF SEPARATION

Church   State

Child Benefit Theory

Public Purpose Theory

On-Site Services

Neutrality Concept

Accommodation

Figure 4.1. The Wall of Separation.

opinion, the Court made the following points, which have been used as precedent for subsequent decisions.

1. The establishment of religion clause of the First Amendment means that neither the state nor the federal government can set up a church, and neither can they pass laws that aid one religion, aid all religions, or prefer one religion over another.
2. No tax in any amount, large or small, can be levied to support any religious activities or institutions, whatever they may be called, or whatever form they may adopt to teach and practice religion.
3. Separation of church and state does not require that the state be an adversary to religion. State powers should not be used to handicap religions.
4. This decision also held that the use of tax money to pay bus fares for parochial children did not violate the Fourteenth Amendment by taking property without due process of law.

The public purpose theory initiated by *Everson* was the second "brick" to fall in the wall of separation. The position that a public purpose was served by transporting parochial children on public buses is grounded at least partly in the opinion that it provided safety for the parochial children, and that such safety served a public purpose. To eliminate parochial children walking on busy streets and intersections while public schoolchildren were riding in buses traveling the same route was, to the Court, serving a public purpose. In relation to the safety of the citizenry, such as fire and police protection, the religion of the person in need of safety protection was never in question. The Court felt that universal protection should also extend to parochial school transportation.

The *Everson* decision has led many states to pass statutes that provide public transportation to parochial students. Another far-reaching effect of the *Everson* decision was the statement by the Court that the state was not required to be an adversary to religion. This judicial philosophical stance set a precedent that has permeated U.S. Supreme Court decisions in recent decades. *Everson* was followed by the *Allen* case (*Board of Education of Central School District # 1 v. Allen*), which supported the lending of textbooks to parochial and private schoolchildren in New York.

The Lemon Test

Shortly after *Allen,* state legislatures entertained bills and enacted statutes to provide aid to parochial schools. Such plans took many forms. For example, there were statutes to provide salary supplements to parochial teachers of secular subjects, reimbursements to parochial teachers of secular subjects, textbooks, and instructional materials. In the case of *Lemon v. Kurtzman,* the Court enunciated a three-part test to determine whether or not the separation of church and state was breached by legislative action.

Does the law:

1. Have a secular legislative purpose?
2. Enhance or inhibit religion?
3. Create an excessive entanglement between church and state?

In the *Lemon* case, the court ruled the statute unconstitutional because of the significant amount of monitoring and supervision that would be required to ensure that annual appropriations were properly spent would create excessive entanglement.

In recent decades, the Lemon Test has been under attack from some Supreme Court members. Justice Sandra Day O'Connor has publicly stated that the test is flawed because, in order to ensure that the law in question has a secular purpose and does not either enhance or prohibit religion, the third prong, excessive entanglement, must be violated.

Gradually, the Lemon Test is being dismantled. In 1983, in the case of *Mueller v. Allen,* the Court took a major philosophical turn when it upheld a Minnesota law that permitted taxpayers to deduct expenses for tuition, textbooks, and transportation for their children attending parochial elementary and secondary schools. This reversed the Court's philosophy enunciated in *Nyquist, Sloan,* and *Meek,* and upheld the law even though it was clear that the law primarily benefited religious institutions. The Court stated, "Where aid to parochial schools is available only as a result of decisions of individual parents, no insinuation of state approval can be deemed conferred on any particular religion."

Auxiliary Services

Many states approached the aid to parochial and private schools through providing auxiliary services to the children in areas such as reading, speech pathology, and psychological testing. These services were defined and clarified through the following cases: *Nyquist*, *Meek v. Pittenger*, and *Wolman v. Walter*. These cases defined what services to the parochial schools were legal. A significant ruling was that the services could not be provided on parochial school grounds. Therefore, the parochial students had to be transported off parochial school grounds to receive the instruction. This required the public schools to build or rent facilities for instructional purposes because many of the parochial school buildings were a considerable distance from the public school building. This legal ruling, which created administrative costs, was challenged but upheld in 1985 in the *Aguilar* decision. However, in 1997, another major brick in the wall of separation fell when, in the case of *Agostini v. Felton*, the U.S. Supreme Court ruled that auxiliary services could be provided on parochial school grounds so long as the classroom or instructional facility that was being used did not contain religious symbols.

Mitchell v. Helms

In June 2000, a plurality of the Court, in a decision written by Justice Clarence Thomas, apparently removed all constitutional barriers that had previously prevented the flow of tax dollars to parochial schools. In this decision, Thomas introduced a new concept to the separation of church and state issue, and brought down another brick in the wall of separation through a "Concept of Neutrality toward Religion."

The essence of the decision is that if tax funds used do not benefit one religion group over another, and if they do not discriminate between religious factions, then the statute distributing the funds is constitutional. In addition, the Court ruled that whether or not the parochial school diverts the money for sectarian purposes is not an issue, and that such diversion does not violate the Constitution. The plurality of the justices appear to negate the argument that public funds could not be used for "pervasively sectarian" purposes. The plurality seem to be saying that so long as the funds are distributed neutrally, and do not discriminate benefiting one religion over another, that it does not matter whether the education program for which the funds are used is "pervasively sectarian." Thus, with respect to governmental aid to religious schools, the divertibility of such aid to religious indoctrination does not violate the establishment of religion clause of the federal Constitution's First Amendment, where (1) the government aid is not itself unsuitable for use in the public school because of religious content, and (2) eligibility for aid is determined in a constitutionally permissible manner.

The Court did not address the "excessive entanglement" issue, but by implication suggested it would be given little credence in the future. In delivering this decision, the Court reversed previous decisions that had been strong precedents for separation: *Meek v. Pittenger* and *Wolman v. Walter.*

Released Time for Religious Instruction

Attempts by religious groups to use public schools as a vehicle to promote religion has been a persistent conflict in church-state litigation. In 1948, in the *McCollum* case, the Court ruled that religious instruction on public school grounds during the school day enhanced religion and was, therefore, denied on the basis that it violated the establishment clause. In a later case, *Zorach v. Clauson*, the Court ruled that a New York law that allowed students to be released from school to go off campus for religious instruction was constitutional.

Prayer and Bible Reading during the School Day

Prayer and Bible reading in public schools is a perpetual political issue that has plagued the country for decades. In view of its continued advocacy in the halls of state legislatures, Congress, and the court systems, the controversy appears to be gaining momentum. Constitutional amendments have been offered to permit prayer and Bible reading in public schools. Thus far, those attempts have not been successful.

States have tried various ways to pass statutes that would be approved by the courts as constitutional. In the companion cases of *Abington v. Schempp* and *Murray v. Curlett*, laws in Pennsylvania and Maryland that provided for opening ceremonies in public schools embracing reading of the Bible or recitation of the Lord's Prayer were held unconstitutional, violating both the establishment and free exercise clause of the First Amendment. The Court's judgment could be summarized as follows:

1. The free exercise clause cannot be used by the majority to claim that their free exercise rights are being taken away when state-required Bible reading and prayer are prohibited. The majority cannot use the machinery of the state to practice and advance its religious beliefs.
2. The establishment clause prohibits the fusion of state and religious functions or "a dependency of one upon the other."
3. The establishment clause is not restricted to forbidding governmental preference of one religion over another.
4. These laws providing for prayer and Bible reading violate the establishment test of (a) Does the statute have a secular purpose, and (b) Is the primary effect that of advancing or inhibiting religion?
5. The fact that individual students could absent themselves from religious exercises in public schools upon parental request does not furnish a defense to constitutionality under the establishment clause.
6. The state may not establish a religion of secularism by opposing or showing hostility toward religion.
7. The study of the Bible for its literary and historic qualities is not inconsistent with the First Amendment.
8. The purpose of the free exercise clause is to secure religious liberty for the individual by prohibiting the invasion of civil authority. In order to invoke this clause, plaintiff must show that state action has a coercive effect. No such effect is required to show violation of the establishment clause.

In a later case, *Wallace v. Jaffree*, an Alabama statute authorizing a period of silence for meditation or volunteer prayer was struck down by the Supreme Court because it was an endorsement of religion lacking any clear secular purpose. The Court also raised the point that the First Amendment requires a statute must be invalidated if it is entirely motivated by a purpose to advance religion. The record showed that the sponsor of the bill wanted to return voluntary prayer to the schools. The sponsor had stated, "No, I did not have any other purpose in mind" except to return prayer to the schools.

This case marked a beginning of the change of direction by the Supreme Court toward more accommodations toward religion in applying the First Amendment in public school cases. In dissenting, Chief Justice Rehnquist stated, "The Establishment Clause has been expressly freighted with Jefferson's misleading metaphor for nearly forty years. . . . Our perception has been clouded not by the Constitution but by the mists of an unnecessary metaphor."

Justice Sandra Day O'Connor also dissented, stating that over twenty-five states permitted or required public school teachers to observe a moment of silence in their classrooms.

Prayer at School Events

Conflicts over prayer at school events pose the question, "Which shall prevail, free speech or the free exercise of religion?" There are two landmark cases that give public school guidance to this issue.

Lee v. Weisman

In this case, the Supreme Court held that the school could not provide for "nonsectarian" prayer to be given by a clergyman selected by the school at graduation ceremonies. Including clergy who offered prayers as part of an official public school graduation ceremony is forbidden by the establishment clause. Justice Kennedy wrote for the majority. The key points of the case are:

1. The question the Court addressed in this case was, "When does accommodation of free exercise of religion cross the line and become establishment of religion?"
2. The Court said that the principle that government may accommodate the free exercise of religion does not supersede the fundamental limitations imposed by the establishment clause, which guarantees at a minimum that a government may not coerce anyone to support or participate in religion or its exercise, or otherwise act in a way which "establishes a state religion or religious faith, or tends to do so."
3. In this situation, school principals, who are state officials, directed the performance of a formal religious exercise at graduation ceremonies. Therefore, the decision that prayer would be a part of the

ceremony and the selection of the religious participants were choices of the principal, thus attributable to the state.

4. The voluntary nature of the ceremony was not a determinant of constitutionality. A requirement that a student stand and remain silent during the giving of the nonsectarian prayer at a graduation ceremony in a public school violates the establishment clause, even though attendance at the ceremony was completely voluntary. According to the majority of the Court, a student should not be required to give up attendance at a ceremony, an important event in the life of a graduate, in order to avoid unwanted exposure to religion.

5. The Court rejected the defendants' argument that free speech justified the school's incursion on the religious freedom of the student.

6. The Court also stated that the inclusion of a nonsectarian prayer constituted an impermissible establishment of religion by requiring that the student stand and remain silent during the giving of the prayer, even though the student was not required to join in the message and was free to meditate on his own religion.

7. The Court also stated that the fact that the prayer only took two minutes was not a valid reason to make the prayer constitutional.

Santa Fe Independent School District v. Doe

In this case, the U.S. Supreme Court declared that a Texas school district's policy authorizing the delivery of an "invocation and/or message" before home varsity football games was unconstitutional. The Court made the following points:

1. Under the circumstances presented, a student invocation pursuant to the policy violated the establishment of religion clause because:
   a. Such invocations were not private student speech, but were public speech.
   b. Student participation in the process did nothing to protect minority views.
   c. The policy involved perceived an actual endorsement of religion.
   d. The student election mechanisms did not insulate the school from the coercive elements of the message.

e. The elections encouraged divisiveness along religious lines in a public setting.

f. Even if every high school student's decision to attend a home football game was regarded as purely voluntary, the delivery of a pregame prayer had the improper effect of coercing those present to participate in an act of religious worship.

2, The simple enactment of the policy was a constitutional violation, even if no student ever offered a religious message pursuant to the policy.

The clearest way to present the Court's view is to state that everyone who attended the football game was exposed to religious activity without an option to not participate. The crowd was a captive audience who came to see a football game. The fans that accompanied the visiting team probably had no idea that a pregame prayer was part of the spectacle. Therefore, coercion exists.

Even though the pregame prayer, conducted over the loudspeaker system, is not constitutional, the voluntary prayer conducted by a group of players in the privacy of their huddle would be constitutional because no one else is coerced into participating with them, and, it is not under the sponsorship of the school or the state.

Flag Salute

In the historic case *West Virginia Board of Education v. Barnette*, the Court held that the regulation making continued attendance in public schools contingent on a student's willingness to salute the American flag and give the pledge denied freedom of speech and freedom of worship. This precedent established that no public school could demand that any student pledge the flag. The freedom to worship, speech, assembly, and press (First Amendment rights) can only be restricted to prevent "grave and immediate" danger to interests, which the state may lawfully protect. The state and thus the public schools may require instruction and study in our history and political science, which may tend to inspire patriotism and love of country, but cannot require assertions of acts that violate religious beliefs.

Equal Access Act

The Equal Access Act, passed by Congress in 1984, states that if you have noncurricular activities in your school, you have created a limited open forum and must therefore allow any organized group to meet. This act applies to all public schools receiving federal funds. The act was further clarified in the case of the *Board of Education of the Westside Community Schools v. Mergens*. In this case, high school students belonging to a Christian club were denied the right to meet at school by the board on the grounds that it would violate the establishment clause of the First Amendment. They sued for equal access. The school was given the choice of escaping the Equal Access Act and giving up federal funding or allowing the Christian club to meet on school grounds. In rendering this decision, the Court declared that noncurricular clubs included chess, photography, Future Business Leaders of America, and the National Honor Society.

The Court declared that a "limited public forum" exists whenever a public secondary school grants an offering or opportunity for one or more noncurriculum-related student groups to meet on school premises during noninstructional time. The use of the term "limited public forum" by the Court seems to give the school more flexibility in deciding those activities for which they must open their premises. Had the Court used the term "public forum," the school would have no flexibility in denial of their facilities unless they completely closed their premises to all external groups.

ADMINISTERING THE ESTABLISHMENT CLAUSE IN SCHOOLS

In 1943, in the flag-salute case of *West Virginia v. Barnette*, the U.S. Supreme Court extended First Amendment protection to public school students. In this case, the majority of the Court held that the free speech and free exercise of religion provisions of the First Amendment guarantees the right of students to be excused from the flag salute on grounds of conscience. Justice Robert Jackson, writing for the majority, warned of the dangers of coercion by any governmental agency when he wrote, "If there is any fixed star in our Constitutional constellation, it is that no official, high or petty, can prescribe what shall be orthodox in politics, nationalism, religion, or other matters of opinion or force citizens to confess by word or act their faith therein."

In subsequent rulings the Court has been more strict in applying First Amendment establishment clause protection to public school students because of the impressionableness of young people and because compulsory attendance laws make them a captive audience of the state. Therefore, the school administrator must understand how the establishment clause is interpreted by the courts.

The Bill of Rights was ratified in 1791. The First Amendment read: "Congress shall make no law respecting an establishment of religion, or prohibiting the free exercise thereof; or abridging the freedom of speech, or of the press, or the right of the people peacefully to assemble, and to petition the government for the redress of grievances." In relation to the separation of church and state, the school administrator must understand the establishment and free exercise clauses.

In administering the establishment clause, keep the following legal principles and precedents in mind:

1. The court emphasizes the importance of "neutrality" in the acts of school officials toward religion. This means that school officials can neither promote nor inhibit religion, and cannot prefer one religion over another, or religion over nonreligion. However, this does not mean that school officials should try to keep religion out of the public schools. It does not mean that schools should be hostile or an adversary of religion. Neutrality means rejecting school endorsement or promotion of religion while simultaneously protecting the religious liberty rights of all students.

2. The establishment clause speaks to what one may or may not do. It does not include the private rights of speech that all students enjoy, which is their right because of the free exercise clause.

3. There are many school activities that are related to religion—for example, holiday activities in December. When planning and implementing these activities, school officials should consider the following:
   • Is there an educational or civic purpose to the activity?
   • Are you sure that the activity will not advance or inhibit anyone's religion?

- Is the activity in line with the mission of the school?
- Is there any chance that a student, teacher, or parent will feel this activity is exclusive of his or her religious beliefs?
- If the discussion of religion is a part of the activity, will that discussion be academic in nature, accurate, and balanced?

ADMINISTERING THE FREE EXERCISE CLAUSE

School officials should know that although the freedom to believe as one chooses is absolute in this country, the freedom to act on those beliefs within the school day is not. In deciding controversies where the student is claiming that the school (state) is violating his or her free exercise rights, the courts weigh that individual right against the school's compelling interest. This test, first articulated in the case of *Sherbert v. Verner* in 1963, consists of the following four questions:

1. Does the personal claim involve a sincere religious belief?
2. Does the government action create a substantial burden on the person's ability to act on that belief?
3. If these two elements are established, then there is a burden on the government (school) to prove that:
4. Their actions are furthering a "compelling state interest" and
5. That they have pursued their actions and interests in the least restrictive manner to religion.

However, in 1990 the Supreme Court weakened the *Sherbert* test by their ruling in *Employment v. Smith*. In that case, the Court held that the burden on free exercise no longer had to be justified by a compelling state interest. After this ruling, school policies or actions that were intended to prohibit the free exercise of religion or violated other constitutional rights were subject to the compelling interest test.

So the question for school officials is, "How do school officials determine when they must accommodate a religious liberty claim under the free exercise clause?" In trying to simultaneously protect this individual right and the compelling interests of the school, keep in mind the following legal principles and precedents:

- Always keep the spirit of the law in mind.
- Excuse students from certain parts of the curriculum (reading selections) so long as the intent is sincere and can be done without a disruption to the class. This principle applies to issues within the curriculum, but does include a student being excused from the entire course offering. Excusing a student from an entire curriculum offering could lead to serious disruption in the school.
- Be flexible in responding to requests for accommodation of religious practices during school days, such as excuses for religious holidays not included in the school calendar, or special clothing to observe religious holidays.
- Students are free to pray, individually or in groups, so long as such prayers are not disruptive and do not infringe upon the rights of others.
- Students may share their religious faith with other students so long as it is not disruptive or does not infringe upon the rights of others.
- Students may use their religious beliefs in completing classroom assignments so long as they do not attempt to compel a captive audience (their classmates) to listen. However, the incorporation of their belief must have been appropriate to the academic assignment.
- Many states have "moments of silence" at the start of school. Such a practice must be genuinely neutral. If it can be shown that the purpose is to allow state-sponsored prayer, it would not be constitutional (*Wallace v. Jaffree*).
- The Equal Access Act protects student religious clubs as extracurricular or noncurriculum-related groups. Teachers can be present for monitoring purposes only in a nonparticipatory capacity.

CONCLUSION

The public schools are currently presented with the difficult task of allowing "Permissible Accommodation without Impermissible Establishment." The U.S. Supreme Court has maintained the separation of church and state in instances where they feel certain parties have had either their free exercise or establishment rights violated as determined by the Lemon Test. However, they do not seem to feel that these barriers between church and state exist in relation to the flow of federal and state funds to private and parochial schools. In the area of funding, full accommodation seems to be the consensus of a majority of the U.S. Supreme Court.

CHURCH–STATE CASE SUMMARIES

Public School Law

U.S. Supreme Court
281 U.S. 370
Cochran et. al. v Louisiana State Board of Education
No. 468

Argued April 15, 1930   **Decided April 28, 1930**

Topic: The use of public funds to provide textbooks for private school children in the state of Louisiana.

Issue: Does the purchase of schoolbooks for private school use with public tax money violate provisions of Louisiana Constitution, Section f 4 of Article IV, and/or the Fourteenth Amendment?

Facts: Messers Challen B. Ellis and Wade H. Ellis were attempting to bring an injunction against the state of Louisiana for a group of "citizens and taxpayers" to restrain the Louisiana State Board of Education from *using money from a severance tax fund to purchase schoolbooks and supplying them free of charge to private school children.*

The trial court refused to issue an injunction on the grounds that it did not violate provision in the state constitution, Section 4 of Article IV, or the Fourteenth Amendment of the federal Constitution. The state supreme court upheld the ruling of the Louisiana courts not to issue an injunction. The board of education was directed to provide the books for all of the state's children free of cost.

Findings of the Court: It was held that there was no federal question to be settled in response to the plaintiff's charge to Section 4 of Article IV or the Fourteenth Amendment. Its guarantees are political and not judicial in nature. No funds were used to aid "private, religious, sectarian, and other schools not embraced in the public educational system of the state." The textbooks were for the benefit of private schoolchildren. The judgment was affirmed.

Rationale: Using the child benefit theory, the books were purchased for the children of the state, free of cost to them. The schools did not benefit from the purchases—the children did and, thus, the state. The books could be purchased if they were books that could be used by any public schoolchildren. None were nor were able to be adapted for religious instruction, nor were the books given to the children. Legislation is not intended to segregate private schools or their pupils. By purchasing the books for the students, the state of Louisiana benefited as much as the students and thus the common interest was safeguarded. Not related to the federal question, but a part of the opinion of Judge Hughes, was that the books were not given to the children, but lent to them.

Historical Framework: The country was well into the Depression at the time of this ruling. Herbert Hoover was soon to be voted out of office. Chief Justice Charles Evans Hughes led the Court at the time. He had originally been appointed to the Court by William Howard Taft and quit to run for the presidency in 1916. He was appointed Chief Justice by Hoover. He followed the conservative Court of Chief Justice Taft and inherited many of those justices. He tended to be autocratic, and his Court did not include much conferencing. His "reign" could be said to be divided into two parts: the initial conservative years (during which this ruling took place) and the years of radical reform under Roosevelt with hostile division.

330 U.S. 1
Everson v. Board of Education of the Township of Ewing et al.
No. 52
Argued November 20, 1946　　　　　**Decided February 10, 1947**
133
N.J.L. 350, 44 A.2D 333
Affirmed

Topic: This was a case known as the "New Jersey School Bus Case," which concerned the reimbursement of parents for bus fare necessary to send their children to private schools. The argument arose from the fact that the government used public funds to subsidize these children's education at private religious institutions. The plaintiff in this case argued that this practice represented the support of religion and was strictly prohibited in the Constitution under the First Amendment clause separating church and state.

Issue: Pursuant to a New Jersey statute authorizing district boards of education to make rules and contracts for the transportation of children to and from schools other than private schools that operate for profit. A board of education by resolution authorized the reimbursement of parents for fares paid for the transportation by public carrier of children attending public and Catholic schools. The Catholic schools operated under the superintendency of a Catholic priest and, in addition to secular education, gave religious instruction in the Catholic faith. A district taxpayer challenged the validity under the federal Constitution of the statute and resolution, so far as they authorized reimbursements to parents for the transportation of children attending sectarian schools. No question was raised as to whether the exclusion of private schools operated for profit denied equal protection of the laws; nor did the record show that there were any children in the district who attended, or would have attended but for the cost of transportation, any but public or Catholic schools.

Facts: A New Jersey school district had passed a plan allowing the reimbursement of schools for the transportation of students to private schools. The district was acting under a statute allowing schools to regulate the transportation of students. A state court had ruled the plan unconstitutional, but the New Jersey Court of Errors and Appeals reversed the decision, ruling in favor of the defendant and stating that the payments represented assistance to the families and not the religious institution. However, the court did state vehemently that the separation between church and state is a wall, which must be kept "high and impregnable."

Findings of the United States Supreme Court: The Court voted 5-4 in favor of upholding the New Jersey plan. The finds were:

1. The expenditure of tax-raised funds thus authorized was for a public purpose, and did not violate the due process clause of the Fourteenth Amendment.
2. The statute and resolution did not violate the provision of the First Amendment prohibiting any "law respecting an establishment of religion."

Rationale: Justice Black gave the majority opinion, stating paying for the busing of parochial school students does not breach the establishment clause. Even though the assistance might make parents more likely to send their children to such schools, the authorization does not unduly assist the schools. The policy is general because it applies to public and private school students and does not single out those attending religious schools. The funding of busing is similar to the public payment of policeman and fireman who protect parochial school students.

Although the Court favored a broad interpretation of the establishment clause, in the same decision the Court adopted Thomas Jefferson's view that the establishment clause was intended to erect "a wall of separation between church and state." Justice Black's majority opinion outlines a number of principles (broken into sections for clarification) that have evolved into the establishment clause legal precedent: The "establishment of religion" clause means at least this:

1. Neither a state nor a government can set up a church.
2. Neither can pass laws that aid one religion, aid all religions, or prefer one religion to another.
3. Neither can force or influence a person to go or to remain away from church against his will or force him to profess a belief or disbelief in any religion.
4. No person can be punished for entertaining or professing religious beliefs or disbeliefs, for church attendance or nonattendance.
5. No tax in any amount, large or small, can be levied to support any religious activities or institutions, whatever they may be called, or whatever form they may adopt, to teach or practice religion.
6. Neither a state nor a federal government can, openly or secretly, participate in the affairs of any religious organization or groups and vice versa.

Justice Rutledge gave the dissenting opinion, stating the plan supports religious training and belief through the use of government funds. The funds for the plan are taken from taxes levied on citizens of all faiths and should not be used to further the religious education of children of other faiths, thereby violating the establishment clause. If it is permissible to pay for the transportation to private religious school on the grounds it promotes education, then why not pay for the entire costs of the schooling on these same grounds?

Agreeing in dissenting were Justice Frankfurter, Justice Jackson, and Justice Burton.

Significance: Using the Fourteenth Amendment, the Court applied the establishment clause to the states. However, it was not violated so long as money was not given directly to religious schools or gave them specific benefits.

Supplement Information: The statute reads:

> Whenever in any district there are children living remote from any schoolhouse, the board of education of the district may make rules and contracts for the transportation of such children to and from school . . . other than a public school, except such school as is operated for profit in whole or in part.
>
> When any school district provides any transportation for public school children to and from school, transportation from any point in such established school route to any other point in such established school route shall be supplied to school children residing in such school district in going to and from school other than a public school, except such school as is operated for profit in whole or in part. (Laws of New Jersey 1941, c. 191, N.J.S.A 18:14-8)

Lemon v. Kurtzman
Appealed from the United States District Court
for the Eastern District to
the Supreme Court of the United States
Heard on March 3, 1971 and Filed on June 28, 1971

History:

No. 569, Rhode Island, *Earley et al. v. DiCenso et al.* and Case No. 570, *Robinson, Commissioner of Education of Rhode Island, et al. v DiCenso et al.* on appeal from United States District Court for the District of Rhode Island.

No. 89, Pennsylvania, Lemon v. Kurtzman, on appeal from the United States District Court for the Eastern District of Pennsylvania.

Topic: Statutes that provide state funding to church-affiliated schools.

Issue: Can Rhode Island and Pennsylvania adopt state statutes that give portions of state funds to elementary and secondary schools that are affiliated with churches? Does this violate the religious clauses of the First Amendment? Can states provide funding if it is only for secular education?

Facts:

- In 1969 Rhode Island enacted the Rhode Island Salary Supplement Act. They adopted this statute because it was difficult for nonpublic schools to compete for the most qualified teachers because they were unable to offer competitive salaries due to lack of funds. The statute said that nonpublic elementary schools could get a supplement to their contracts of up to 15 percent of their salary.
- There were restrictions placed on this funding. The per-student spending in the nonpublic school had to be less than the state's average per-student spending. Also, the nonpublic teacher's salary was not allowed to go over the top of the pay scale for the state's public schools. In addition, teachers who received the supplement were only allowed to teach secular subjects.
- The district court found the statute to violate the establishment clause of the First Amendment because it gave rise to "excessive entanglement" of church and state. Also it was aiding in the advancement of a religion.
- The Pennsylvania Nonpublic Elementary and Secondary Education Act was enacted in 1968. It was passed because of the increasing cost of education. Based on this statute, the state gave nonpublic schools money to help with salaries, books, and teaching materials. Five million dollars was spent every year because of this statute.
- The school that gets the funding must prove in an audit that they are keeping these funds separate from religious funds. The statute also limits what courses the funds can be used for. They can only be used for certain secular subjects. The state superintendent of public instruction must approve the materials and books.
- The district court dismissed the case and said that they did not feel that the act went against the establishment or free exercise clauses.

Findings of the U.S. Supreme Court: Mr. Chief Justice Burger wrote the majority opinion on this case. Five other justices joined him in his decision. One of these justices took part in only one of the two decisions. Another justice wrote a concurring opinion and was joined by another justice. One justice partially concurred and partially dissented.

The Court found that the statutes in Rhode Island and Pennsylvania were not constitutional because they violated the religious clauses of the First Amendment. Both statutes cause excessive entanglement of government and religion. It upheld the decision in the Rhode Island case and reversed the Pennsylvania decision.

The Court established a Lemon Test to determine if a statute violates the First Amendment. The Lemon Test has three parts. The statute must have a secular purpose, the statute must not promote or prevent religion, and the state must not get excessively entangled with religion because of the statute.

Rationale:

- The statutes violated the First Amendment because they could show favoritism to one religion and thus violated the part of the amendment that prohibits the making of a law "respecting an establishment of religion." Funding religious schools could lead to establishing a state religion. The Constitution doesn't specifically prohibit the funding action. However, the establishment clause is meant to prevent states from giving "sponsorship, financial support, and active involvement" of the state in church activities. The Court used the decision *Walz v. Tax Commission*, 397 U.S. 664, 668, 90 S. Ct. 1409, 1411, 25 L.Ed.2d 697 (1970) to aid them in making this point.
- The Court found that because of the purpose of religious schools they were becoming entangled by giving those schools money. Based on the proximity of these parochial schools to churches, it was easy for them to give lessons in religion. Religion is also part of the whole package offered at nonpublic schools. These schools also have religious symbols within them, as well as extracurricular activities that are religious, and nuns teaching classes. Also, children of school age are easily influenced by teachers and it is hard for teachers to separate out the religious parts of the curriculum. By giving money to the parochial schools, the state is contributing to the mission of the church. Because of this, states may only provide funding for public, secular education.
- States also become entangled with churches through monitoring the school. In order to monitor the schools to ensure that they are com-

plying with the restrictions placed on them by the statute, the state would have to visit the nonpublic schools frequently and make judgments as to whether or not they were using funds meant for secular education for religious education. It is impossible to monitor teachers constantly to see if they are teaching religion when they have agreed not to. They cannot be evaluated a single time because they may change their practices. This causes the government to have a continuing relationship with the religious schools.

• The practice of providing funding for parochial schools brings up yet another entanglement issue. It could cause political divisions, which was one of the sole reasons that the First Amendment was put in place. There will be divisions between those candidates who want to fund religious education and those who do not. There is concern that people will vote based on their religious beliefs.

• The Court did note that it is permissible to give funding to students and parents as was done in the *Everson* and *Allen* cases. It is not permissible to give funds directly to a school affiliated with a church. They pointed out that they warned against giving money to religious institutions in the *Walz v. Tax Commission* case.

• Additionally, the Court cautioned that this action cannot be compared to the decision of *Walz v. Tax Commission*, which allowed churches to remain tax exempt. Because there was a historical precedent of allowing churches to abstain from paying taxes, and there is no history of giving money to religious schools, the two cannot be compared.

• The Court added that the states were not trying to advance or prohibit religion. They thought that the religious and secular parts of education could be separated. The states were only trying to live up to their obligation to uphold minimum standards in all schools.

Agostini et al. v. Felton et al.
Certiorari to the U.S. Court of Appeals for the Second Circuit
No. 96-552

Argued April 15, 1997 **Decided June 23, 1997**

Topic: Does the federal funding of public school employees to teach special education programs in parochial schools violate the establishment clause of the First Amendment, "Congress shall make no law respecting an establishment of religion, or prohibiting the free exercise thereof."

Issue: A New York parochial school board challenged the district court's upholding of a twelve-year-old decision in *Aguilar v. Felton*, which prohibited public school teachers from teaching in parochial schools. The current proposal offered help to needy students in private schools by sending public school teachers to tutor them after school. New York was forced to offer remedial help to students through "local educational agencies." Students did not need to attend public schools in order to be eligible for the assistance.

Those who were to receive tutoring were students who:

- reside in low income areas or
- failed or were at risk of failing the state's student performance standards

Facts: The *Aguilar v. Felton* case, which was made up of six federal taxpayers, sued their local board on the grounds of "excessive entanglement of Church and State in the administration of Title (I) benefits" in 1978.

Local boards initially provided Title I services to private school children after school without allowing public employees on private school property. They would transport parochial/private school children to the public school after school hours for Title I services. Due to its low attendance and overall lack of success, local education agencies started to provide Title I service on private school property during school hours.

Aguilar's case pushed the local boards back into the unsuccessful and costly practice of providing Title I services on public, leased private property or even mobile vans parked near, yet off, school property.

Next, *Aguilar* ensured that public or state representation through teachers during regular school hours caused "conformity" or a "graphic symbol" of "conjoined church and state." Also that "shared time" as in the case of *Ball*, which was unconstitutional allowing "state financed religious indoctrination." In the case of *Aguilar*, the Court based its decision on three main discrepancies:

- That public employees would "inculcate religion" in the work.
- "Symbolic unions" of church/state.
- Aid to religious school was aid for "religious indoctrination."

The establishment clause was reevaluated by the new Court. The first case evaluated was *Zoberst*, a deaf student who needed a publicly funded translator for class, even though the translator would be translating Catholic ideology. The decision allowing the use of the translator was based on a "private decision of individual parents." Rehnquist felt the establishment clause is to "prohibit a national religion." He felt it did not intend to establish a "government neutrality between religion and irreligion, nor did it prohibit the Federal Government from providing non-discriminating aid to religion." The second example is *Witters v. Washington*, whereby they did not stop vocational funds for a blind person from entering a Christian college to become a minister.

Finding: On June 23, 1997, in a 5-4 court decision, the Court allowed public school teachers to tutor private school students in their private schools, even if the schools were primarily religious in nature.

Justice Sandra Day O'Connor stated in her majority opinion that the Court had already effectively overruled the 1985 *Aguilar* case, citing two later Court decisions: *Witters v. Washington* (1986) and *Zoberst v. Catalina Foothills School District* (1993).

First, the ruling in *Zoberst* did not permit a ban on placing all public employees in sectarian schools (a sign language interpreter had been provided for a deaf student). Since there is little difference between providing a sign language interpreter, which the Court already allowed, and a tutor, then interaction that would result between the state and church is allowable.

Second, the Court held that not all government aid that directly assists in the educational function of religious schools would also be promoting religion. The location of the classroom (either in public or religious schools) should not be relevant.

Third, O'Conner decided that school boards were capable of creating administrative rules ensuring that teachers acted in a religiously neutral fashion, neither promoting nor hindering sectarian religious views.

Finally, O'Connor found that there was no reason to presume that the parents of students attending secular public schools would get the impression that the city government approved of religious education merely because government employees were also working in religious schools.

The interaction that would result between the state and church is allowable because a relationship between the two is inevitable. The decision reinforced the belief that the state can conduct public programs in religious schools without becoming excessively entangled with the religion. This is contrary to the earlier attitude that there must be an absolute wall between public and religious schools.

Dissenting: Justice Ginsberg stated in her dissenting opinion that the case should not be returned, or overturned, because it is essentially the same case that was ruled on twelve years earlier and the Court does not rehear cases.

Arguments that subsequent decisions at lower level courts go against the prior decision, thereby mandating that this new case be heard, are not persuasive because "lower courts lack the authority to determine whether adherence to a judgment of this court is inequitable."

McCollum v. Board of Education School District No. 71
Champaign County, Illinois
Argued December 8, 1947   **Decided March 8, 1949**

Precedent: Everson v. Board of Education (1946). This case reinforced the precedent of government money financing portions of religious, sectarian education by having those funds applied to activities other than direct religious education.

Topic: Offering voluntary classes in religion to public school students during the school day. Released time for religious instruction on public school premises is unconstitutional.

Issue: Did the use of the public school system for religious classes violate the First Amendment's establishment clause? Is the school using tax-established and tax-supported public schools to teach religion to students? The establishment clause was intended to prohibit the federal government from declaring and financially supporting a national religion, such as existed in many other countries at the time of the nation's founding. Thomas Jefferson and James Madison suggested the need to establish "a wall of separation" between church and state.

Fact: With the permission of the school board (granted under its general supervisory powers over the use of public school buildings), religious teachers employed by the school (from private religious groups) gave religious instruction in the public school building once each week. The voluntary association was called the Champaign Illinois Council on Religious Education and it represented the Catholic, Protestant, and Jewish faiths. The religion teacher was not paid by the state but was subject to the approval and supervision of the school superintendent. The "release time" program allowed students in grades 4 through 9 the option of attending the religion class of their choice or go elsewhere in the building to pursue secular studies. In order for a student to participate in the religious instruction, a permission slip had to be signed by a parent. Mrs. McCollum (who was an atheist) was a parent of a child enrolled in the Champaign public schools. She charged that the joint public school/religious group program violated the First and Fourteenth Amendments of the U.S. Constitution. She wanted the school board to "adopt and enforce rules and regulations prohibiting all instruction in and teaching of all religious education in all public schools in Champaign District Number 71." She lost in the Illinois courts, but the Supreme Court ruled 8 to 1 that the "released time" program violated the ban on establishment. This demonstrates that use of tax-supported property for religious instruction and the close cooperation between the school authorities and the religious council in promoting religious education violates the establishment clause of the First Amendment. The operation of the state's compulsory education system thus assists and is integrated with the program of religious instruction carried on by separate religious sects. Students compelled by law to go to school for secular education are released in part of their legal duty upon the condition that they attend the religious classes.

The Supreme Court went on to say the following. To hold that a state cannot, consistent with the First and Fourteenth Amendments, utilize its public school system to aid any or all religious faiths or sects in the dissemination of their doctrines and ideals does not, as counsel urge, manifest a governmental hostility to religion or religious teachings. A manifestation of such hostility would be at war with our national tradition as embodied in the First Amendment's guarantee of the free exercise of religion. The First Amendment rests upon the premise that both religion and government can work best to achieve their lofty aims if each is left free from the other within its respective sphere. The state also affords sectarian groups an invaluable aid in that it helps to provide pupils for their religious classes through the use of the state's compulsory public school machinery. This is not separation of church and state.

Solitary Dissent by Justice Stanley Reed:

- When actual church services have always been permitted on government property, the mere use of the school buildings by a nonsectarian group for religious education ought not be condemned as an establishment of religion.
- For a nonsectarian organization to give the type of instruction here offered cannot be said to violate our rule as to the establishment of religion by the state.
- Devotion to the great principle of religious liberty should not lead us into a rigid interpretation of the constitutional guarantee that conflicts with accepted habits of our people.
- The opinions don't say in words that the condemned practice of religious education is a law respecting an establishment of religion contrary to the First Amendment.
- As no issue of prohibition upon the free exercise of religion is before us, we need only examine the school board's action to see if it constitutes an establishment of religion.

Conclusion: The Court held that the use of public school facilities during the instructional day for religious instruction and the close cooperation between the school authorities and the religious council violated the establishment clause. Because students were required to attend school and were released in part from this legal duty if they attended religious classes, the Court found that the Champaign system was "beyond question a utilization of the tax-established and tax-supported public school system to aid religious groups and to spread the faith." Any act by the government to assist religion broaches the wall that must separate church and state.

Engle et al. v. Vitale et al.
No. 468
Supreme Court of the United States
Argued April 3, 1962   **Decided June 25, 1962**

Topic: Prayer in public schools.

Issue: Whether the Board of Regents of the State of New York has the power/right to construct a prayer that is used daily at the start of the school day. Whether said prayer, nondenominational and voluntary, violated the establishment clause of the First Amendment. Whether the Union Free School District No. 9, New Hyde Park, New York, could adopt this prayer and instruct the principal to cause the following prayer to be said aloud by each class in the presence of a teacher at the beginning of each school day:

> Almighty God, we acknowledge our dependence upon Thee, and we beg Thy blessings upon us, our parents, our teachers and our Country.

Fact: Case brought by the parents of ten children shortly after the practice of reciting the regents' prayer, insisting that use of this official prayer in public schools was contrary to the beliefs, religions, or religious practices of both themselves and their children. Among other things, these parents challenged the constitutionality of both the state law authorizing the school district to direct the use of prayer in public schools and the school district's regulation ordering the recitation of this particular prayer on the ground that these actions of official governmental agencies violate that part of the First Amendment of the federal Constitution, which commands that "Congress shall make no law respecting an establishment of religion" —a command that was "made applicable to the State of New York by the Fourteenth Amendment of the said Constitution."

Findings: The Court held that neither the fact that the prayer was denominationally neutral nor the fact that it was voluntary can serve to free it from the limitations of the establishment clause of the First Amendment. The law did, in fact, establish an official state religion even if coercion was not present.

Robert E. Lee, individually and as principal of Nathan Bishop Middle School, et al., petitioners v. Daniel Weisman etc.
Supreme Court of the United States
1992 505 U.S. 577, 112 S. Ct. 2649

Topic: Constitutionality of nonsectarian prayer at a public school graduation ceremony.

Issue: Is it constitutional for a public school official to ask a member of the clergy to recite a prayer at a graduation ceremony? Is it relevant that the school official (in this case, principal Robert E. Lee of Nathan Bishop

Middle School) asked the clergy member, a local Jewish rabbi, to keep the prayer nonsectarian?

Facts: Deborah Weisman graduated from Nathan Bishop Middle School, a public school in Providence, Rhode Island, at a formal ceremony in June 1989. For years, the policy of the Providence School Committee and the superintendent of schools had been to permit principals to invite members of the clergy to give invocations and benedictions at middle school and high school graduations. Many, but not all, of the principals elected to include prayers as part of the graduation ceremonies. Acting for himself and his daughter, Deborah's father, Daniel Weisman, objected to any prayers at Deborah's middle school graduation, but to no avail. The school principal, petitioner Robert E. Lee, invited a rabbi to deliver prayers at the graduation exercises for Deborah's class. Rabbi Leslie Gutterman, of the Temple Beth El in Providence, accepted.

It had been the custom of Providence school officials to provide invited clergy with a pamphlet entitled "Guidelines for Civic Occasions," prepared by the National Conference of Christians and Jews. The guidelines recommend that public prayers at nonsectarian civic ceremonies be composed with "inclusiveness and sensitivity," though they acknowledge prayer of any kind may be "inappropriate on some civic occasions." The principal gave Rabbi Gutterman the pamphlet before the graduation and advised him that the invocation and benediction should be nonsectarian.

Rabbi Gutterman's prayers were as follows:

[Invocation] God of the Free, Hope of the Brave, for the legacy of America where diversity is celebrated and the rights of minorities are protected, we thank You. May these young men and women grow up to enrich it.

For the liberty of America, we thank You. May these new graduates grow up to guard it.

For the political process of America in which all its citizens may participate, for its court system where all may seek justice, we thank You. May those we honor this morning always turn to it in trust.

For the destiny of America, we thank You. May the graduates of Nathan Bishop Middle School so live that they might help to share it.

May our aspirations for our country and for these young people, who are our hope for the future, be richly fulfilled.

Amen.

[Benediction] O God, we are grateful to You for having endowed us with the capacity for learning which we have celebrated on this joyous commencement.

Happy families give thanks for seeing their children achieve an important milestone. Send your blessings upon the teachers and administrators who helped prepare them.

The graduates now need strength and guidance for the future, help them to understand that we are not complete with academic knowledge alone. We must each strive to fulfill what You require of us all: To do justly, to love mercy, to walk humbly.

We give thanks to You, Lord, for keeping us alive, sustaining us, and allowing us to reach this special, happy occasion.

Amen.

Shortly before the ceremony, the district court denied the motion of Deborah's father for a temporary restraining order to prohibit school officials from including the prayers in the ceremony, and the prayers above were indeed recited by Rabbi Gutterman. Subsequently, Weisman sought a permanent injunction barring Lee and other petitioners, along with various Providence public school officials, from inviting clergy to deliver invocations and benedictions at future graduations (since it appeared quite likely that such prayers would be conducted at Deborah's high school graduation). The district court enjoined petitioners from continuing the practice at issue on the ground that it violated the establishment clause of the First Amendment. The court of appeals affirmed this finding.

Findings of the Supreme Court of the United States: The Supreme Court found Principal Lee's and the school district's tradition of opening and closing graduation ceremonies with prayer unconstitutional. Delivered by Justice Kennedy, the opinion stated that the principle that government may accommodate the free exercise of religion does not supersede the fundamental limitations imposed by the establishment clause of the First Amendment, which guarantees at a minimum that a government may not coerce anyone to support or participate in religion or its exercise, or otherwise act in a way which "establishes a [state] religion or religious faith, or tends to do so" (*Lynch v. Donnelly*, 465 U.S. 668).

The fact that Principal Lee requested a "nonsectarian" prayer to make the prayers acceptable to most persons, though done most probably in good faith, was declared irrelevant by the Court. It did not resolve the dilemma caused by the school's involvement, since "the government may not establish an official or civic religion as a means of avoiding the establishment of a religion with more specific creeds."

The Court's opinion offered that the establishment clause was inspired by the lesson that in the hands of government, what might begin as a tolerant expression of religious views may end in a policy to indoctrinate and coerce. Prayer exercises in elementary and secondary schools carry a particular risk of indirect coercion (*Engel v. Vitale*, 370 U.S. 421; *Abington School District v. Schempp*, 374 U.S. 203).

The petitioners' argument that students are not required to be at the ceremony, therefore relieving the district of coerced religious prayer was rejected, as the Court stated that school graduations are some of "life's most significant occasions, and a student is not free to absent herself from the exercise in any real sense of the term 'voluntary.'"

Lastly, the Court affirmed that inherent differences between the public school system and a session of a state legislature distinguish this case from *Marsh v. Chambers*, 463 U.S. 783, which condoned a prayer exercise. "The atmosphere at a state legislature's opening, where adults are free to enter and leave with little comment and for any number of reasons, cannot compare with the constraining potential of the one school event most important for the student to attend."

In his dissent, Justice Scalia included, among other things, that the "history and tradition of our Nation are replete with public ceremonies featuring prayers of thanksgiving and petition." He continued that the Court's opinion was "oblivious to our history as to suggest that the Constitution restricts 'preservation and transmission of religious beliefs . . . to the private sphere . . . citing that our own Declaration of Independence, the document marking our birth as a separate people," appealed to the "Supreme Judge of the world for the rectitude of our intentions," and avowed "a firm reliance on the protection of divine Providence."

Justice Scalia was joined by Justices Rehnquist, White, and Thomas in dissent. Justice Kennedy delivered the opinion of the Court, in which Blackmun, Stevens, O'Connor, and Souter joined. Blackmun and Souter filed concurring opinions, in which Stevens and O'Connor joined.

Santa Fe Independent School District
v.
Jane Doe, individually and as next friend for her minor children, Jane and John Doe, et al.
On a writ of certiorari to the United States court of appeals for the fifth circuit United States Supreme Court (99-62) 530 US 290 (2000) 168 F.3d 806 affirmed

Argued: March 29, 2000   **Decided: June 19, 2000**

Topic: Separation of church and state, regarding school prayer.

Issue: Is a school district's policy permitting student-led, student-initiated prayer at football games a violation of the establishment clause of the First Amendment?

Facts: Prior to 1995, a student elected as Santa Fe High School's student council chaplain delivered a prayer over the public address system before each home varsity football game. In April 1995, two sets of Mormon and Catholic students or alumni and their mothers filed a suit challenging this practice and others under the establishment clause of the First Amendment. While the suit was pending, the Santa Fe Independent School District adopted a series of different policies in May, July, August, and October regarding prayer at school events, including one that authorized two student elections: the first to determine whether "invocations" should be delivered at games, and the second to select the spokesperson to deliver them. After the students held elections authorizing such prayers and selecting a spokesperson, the U.S. District Court entered an order modifying the policy to permit only nonsectarian, nonproselytizing prayer. The Fifth Circuit Court of Appeals held that, even as modified by the U.S. District Court, the football prayer policy was invalid. The "October Policy" was the policy in question before the U.S. Supreme Court.

Finding of the U.S. Supreme Court: In its 6-3 vote, affirming the decision of the Fifth Circuit Court of Appeals, the U.S. Supreme Court held that the district's policy permitting student-led, student-initiated prayer at football games violates the establishment clause. Justice Stevens gave the opinion of the majority.

Rationale: Using *Lee v. Weisman* as the primary guide (a 1992 case in which the Court held that a prayer delivered by a rabbi at a graduation ceremony violated the establishment clause), the Court rejected the district's argument on three grounds. First, the student's invocation was district-endorsed public speech, not private speech. Second, the district's policy coerced students into making the choice between attending games or participating in a religious ritual. Third, despite the fact that no invocation had actually taken place yet under the new policy, the policy itself has the purpose of establishing religion. The Court declared all of these behaviors to be in violation of the establishment clause of the First Amendment.

First, the district argued that the precedent of *Lee* was not applicable in this case because in Santa Fe's policy the government (district) is not speaking in endorsement of religion but is neutral. They argued that the student speech is private speech forum and may therefore endorse religion under the free exercise and free speech portions of the First Amendment. The Court rejected this four ways:

1. "These invocations are authorized by a government policy and take place on government property at government-sponsored school-related events" with no intention, in policy or practice, to open the microphone to other students/members of the public other than the student chosen by the election who must follow the policy prescribed "appropriate" speech guidelines, and will be the only invocation giver all season. Therefore, the district is not neutral and the speech is not private.
2. The "student election system['s] . . . majoritarian process implemented by the District guarantees, by definition, that minority candidates will never prevail and that their views will be effectively silenced." By definition, for a forum to be public, the opportunity to speak cannot be dependent upon the consent of the majority—for example, an election process. Therefore, the district is not neutral and the speech is not private.
3. The Court indicated that the district policy involves both perceived and actual endorsement of religion.
   a) The Court saw the district as "entangled" in the religious message of the invocation through their chosen process and in the invocation guidelines, which mandate that the student's words be

consistent with the goals of the policy, one of which is "to solemnize the event." In using the term *invocation*, the policy required an appeal for divine assistance (which had also been the routine practice of the student chaplain previously), demonstrating an endorsement of religion.

b) The invocation is delivered to a large audience assembled as part of a regularly scheduled, school-sponsored function conducted on school property, therefore demonstrating an endorsement of religion.

c) The message is broadcast over the school's public address system, which is under the control of school officials. The pregame show, at which the invocation takes place, is filled with the school's logo: on the team, cheerleaders, band members, across the playing field, on banners/flags, on the crowd's attire, and on signs they may hold. In this setting, the district has chosen to permit the selected student to give the invocation, a setting in which even the most objective observer would view as a state (district) endorsement of prayer in public school, violating the precedents of *Lee* and *Engle v. Vitale*.

4. Although the district claims secular purposes with their policy—such as fostering free speech, solemnizing the event, promoting good sportsmanship and student safety, and establishing an appropriate environment for competition—the Court said, "it is the duty of the courts to distinguis[h] a sham secular purpose from a sincere one." The Court saw the district's purposes as a "sham" due to the following:

a) Only one kind of message was promoted, an invocation.

b) One student is permitted to give a content-limited message.

c) Solemnizing an event would be fine without government-endorsed prayer.

d) The policy evolved from an overt practice of invocations led by the "student chaplain" under a regulation titled "Prayer at Football Games." The attempt to preserve this "state-sponsored religious practice" is also demonstrated in the fact that the October Policy was not implemented when established, even though the student selection had occurred under the previous "August" policy.

Therefore, the sending of this message in this context is not "public speech," but is government endorsed school prayer, which violates the First Amendment.

Second, the district argued that the precedent of *Lee* was not applicable in this case because the district did not coerce anyone to participate, but rather the messages evolved from "student choices," and attendance at extracurricular events is voluntary. The Court rejected this in several ways:

1. The two-step student choice process revealed that the students were not unanimous on the issue of whether prayer should be held at games, resulting in the religious will of the majority being imposed upon the minority in a process chosen and conducted by the district. In *Lee*, the Court established that the "preservation and transmission of religious beliefs and worship is a responsibility and a choice committed to the private sphere" (505 U. S., at 589).
2. Attendance at games is not voluntary for the players, cheerleaders, and band members. Their participation in addition to the fans' is part of a "complete educational experience."
3. In *Lee*, the Court acknowledged the significance of strong social pressure on students to conform. Attendance at high school football games in the United States, the Court decided, also falls prey to that influence, making it less voluntary. In this context, the district is forcing students to choose between attending the game and participating in a religious ritual. According to the Court's interpretation of the First Amendment, this is not a decision the government (district) can require students to make.

Therefore, the Court indicated that the district's policy forces students into a choice, which is not the government's place to do under the establishment clause of the First Amendment. This does not prohibit students from praying; it prevents the government (district) from sponsoring or endorsing it.

Third, the district argued that the case against them had to fail because the current policy to which the Jane Does objected had not actually been put into practice. The Court rejected this argument on the following grounds:

1. The policy itself was a constitutional violation through its purpose of government established religion, for which the Court did not have to wait to go into action for confirmation of that fact, and further injury. *Wallace v. Jaffree* served as the Court's precedent, as well as the standard established through *Lemon v. Kurtzman* of invalidating a statute that "lacks a secular legislative purpose."
2. The policy grants the majority of students power to subject students with the minority view to unconstitutional messages; a transfer of power whether used or unused is itself unconstitutional. As the Court stated in its decision, "Simply by establishing this school related procedure, which entrusts the inherently non-governmental subject of religion to a majoritarian vote, a constitutional violation has occurred."

Dissent: Chief Justice Rehnquist, Justice Scalia, and Justice Thomas dissented. These justices perceived both the content of the majority opinion and its tone to be objectionable. Their own points included:

- It is not inevitable that the policy will lead to a violation of the establishment clause. This is too rigid a *Lemon* application, which itself has had a "checkered career." The ultimate speech that will result from the "district's student-message policy" is private speech of the elected student's choice.
- The policy has plausible secular purposes, indicating it is possible to solemnize an event like a game without prayer; for example "urging that a game be fought fairly" or a "solemn rendition of our national anthem."
- The important "context" to consider is the district's willingness to follow the district court's guidelines, and even go further than required in allowing the chosen student to select either an "invocation" or a "message."
- *Lee v. Weisman* does not apply to this case because this is private speech. Students may choose the speaker based on secular criteria, but then the chosen student selects to give a religious speech; therefore this is not government endorsement of religion, but the student's protected free speech and free exercise.

- The establishment clause does not mandate "content neutrality" — that's for speech cases, not religion cases.
- Schools can restrict student speech to certain categories and solemnize an event without prayer, such as with a "favorable introduction to the guest speaker."

Westside Community Board of Education v. Mergens
496 U.S. 226 (1990)
Certiorari to the U.S. Court of Appeals for the 8th Circuit
No. 88-1597

Argued January 9, 1990   **Decided June 4, 1990**

Topic: Prayer groups in school.

Issue: Should students have the right to create and participate in religious clubs on school grounds? Should the religious clubs that are created have the same privileges and rights as other noncurriculum school clubs?

Facts: Westside High School is a public secondary school located in Nebraska that receives federal financial assistance. The school allows its students to voluntarily join a variety of different groups and clubs, all of which meet after school on school grounds. The school board policy states that the approximately thirty clubs at the school further the "total education" program. The policy requires faculty sponsorship for all clubs, but the clubs cannot be sponsored by political or religious organizations. No one can be denied membership to these clubs on the basis of race, creed, sex, or political beliefs. Students who want to create a club must present their request to school officials to determine if the club is consistent with the policies of the district's goals.

In January 1985, Bridget Mergens requested permission to form a Christian club, which would have voluntary membership and would be open to all students, regardless of religious affiliation. In addition, no faculty sponsor would be required. School officials denied permission to create the Christian club. After the board denied Mergens permission, former and current students filed suit, arguing that the denial of their request violates the Equal Access Act and their First and Fourteenth Amendment Rights. School officials argued that the act does not apply to Westside High School because it violates the establishment clause of the First Amendment, which is unconstitutional.

Findings of the Courts: The Court of Appeals for the Eighth Circuit ruled for the students; the U.S. Supreme Court affirmed the ruling. The Supreme Court finds that the Equal Access Act does not violate the establishment clause. Justice O'Connor delivered the opinion that the school officials violated the Equal Access Act by denying students permission to form a Christian club.

Rationale: The act requires that if the school receiving assistance has a "limited open forum" for one or more noncurriculum-related student groups and allows the groups to meet on school grounds, then the school cannot deny "equal access" to any group. A "limited open forum" exists if the club's subject matter is not being taught in a regularly offered course and does not require participation for academic credit. Some of Westside's clubs already in existence include noncurriculum-related groups such as a chess club and a club for students interested in scuba diving. Since a "limited open forum" exists, Westside cannot prohibit "equal access" to student clubs that want to meet during noninstructional time on school premises. In addition, the school cannot prohibit the club from being part of the student activities program, giving students access to the school newspaper, PA announcements, bulletin boards, and club fairs.

O'Connor, along with Justice White and Justice Blackmun, also conclude that the act does not violate the establishment clause. First of all, the act grants access to both religious and secular speech. In addition, the act does not allow participation by school officials but does allow a faculty monitor to be present for "custodial purposes" only. The act requires that meetings must take place during noninstructional time. Also, "nonschool" persons may not direct, control, or regularly attend meetings.

Justice Marshall and Justice Brennan agree that the act does not violate the establishment clause, but the creation of the club will not ensure government neutrality regarding religion. They believe that the current student groups at Westside do not advocate controversial topics but adding a controversial group to the "total education" program may create peer pressure and even show that Westside endorses religious activity. They believe that Westside should either discontinue participation in all clubs or completely dissociate itself from endorsement of the Christian club.

Similarly, school officials argue that the Court's reading of the act interferes with local control over schools and their activities. The Court, however, holds that the school districts still maintain authority over recognized activities in which students participate and restates that the act preserves the school's right to uphold order and discipline, protect the well-being of students, and ensure attendance at club meetings is voluntary. The Court also states that the act only applies to schools that receive federal funding. To avoid obligations made by the statutes, the school could forego its funding.

O'Connor states that if the school refuses to allow religious groups to use its facility, the school would demonstrate "hostility" toward the group, not neutrality, which may cause more problems. Also, because students have freedom to participate in any club, the school does not appear to endorse a particular religious belief.

Since the Court has found that the school has violated the Equal Access Act, it is not necessary to determine if the First Amendment was also violated.

Wallace v. Jaffree
472 U.S. 38 (1985)
U.S. Supreme Court
471: U.S. 38
Wallace, Governor of Alabama, et al. v. Jaffree et al.
Appeal from the U.S. Court of Appeals for the Eleventh Circuit
No. 83-812

Argued December 4, 1984   **Decided June 4, 1985**

Topic: Appellees challenged the constitutionality of a 1981 Alabama statue (16-1-20.1) authorizing a one-minute period of silence in all public schools for "meditation or voluntary prayer."

Issue: The Alabama statute stated that the moment of silence was for the purpose of meditation/prayer; was this violating the First Amendment's establishment clause?

Facts: The parent of students sued, claiming that the law violated the establishment clause by compelling students to pray, therefore exposing them to religious indoctrination. Appellee Ishmael Jaffree filed a complaint on behalf of three of his minor children. The complaint named members of the Mobile County School Board, various school officials, and the minor plaintiff's three teachers as defendants. The complaint also further alleged that two of the students had been subjected to various acts of religious indoctrination (saying prayers in unison), and were exposed to ostracism from the class members if they did not participate. Jaffree also said that he had repeatedly but unsuccessfully requested that the devotional services be stopped.

Initial Findings of the District Court and Court of Appeals: Senator Donald Holmes testified that he was the "main sponsor" of the bill to return voluntary prayer to the schools. There were actually three statutes: one mentioning meditation, one mentioning voluntary prayer, and one mentioning teacher-directed prayer. They held that the establishment clause of the First Amendment does not prohibit a state from establishing a religion.

Findings of the Supreme Court: The U.S. Supreme Court reversed the decision. Justice Stevens wrote the majority opinion; the court decided 6-3 that the Alabama law was unconstitutional. The Court found that the statute was invalid because it was entirely motivated to advance religious beliefs (*Lemon v. Kurtzman*). The First Amendment requires that a statute must be invalidated if it is entirely motivated by a purpose to advance religion.

One important aspect to this case is that the authors of the majority opinion (Brennan, Marshall, and Blackmun), two concurring opinions (O'Connor and Powell), and all three dissents (Burger, White, and Rehnquist) agreed that a moment of silence at the beginning of the school day would be acceptable. Justice O'Connor stated, "A state-sponsored moment of silence in the public schools is different from the state-sponsored prayer or Bible reading."

Rationale: Senator Donald Holmes admitted that he wanted to return voluntary prayer to the schools. So two conclusions are apparent:

1. The statute was enacted to convey a message of state endorsement and prayer; and
2. The statute was enacted for a religious, not a secular, reason.

Such an endorsement is not consistent with the established principle that the government must pursue a complete course of neutrality toward religion.

5

Attendance Law

As public schools evolved in America, all states eventually passed compulsory attendance laws. A large part of the public motivation for these laws is found in the political nature of democracy, which relies upon public participation for its success and longevity. It was felt by many that an educated populace was necessary to preserve the American form of government. The best way to ensure an educated populace is through compulsory school attendance funded by public taxation.

THE COMMON LAW DOCTRINE OF *PARENS PATRIAE*

The legality of compulsory school attendance is based upon the principle of *parens patriae*, which is a Latin term meaning "father of the country" or "father of the state." States have what is called police power, which means that the state is responsible for seeing to the safety and welfare of its citizenry. Among these police powers is the responsibility to see to the safety and welfare of children who, for whatever reasons, are not provided for properly by parents or guardians. *Parens patriae* justifies state control over the exercise of certain parental choices. The premier case in enunciating and justifying state control over certain parental choices is the 1943 case, *Prince v. Massachusetts*, in which a legal guardian was found guilty of contributing to the delinquency of a minor by permitting her nine-year-old ward to sell Jehovah's Witnesses publications on a public street. The act was found to be in violation of Massachusetts's child labor law. The Supreme Court addressed the conflicting claims of parent and state by stating, "The family itself is not beyond regulation in the public interest. . . . Acting to guard the general interest in youth's well being, the state as parens patriae may restrict the parent's control by requiring school attendance, regulating or prohibiting the child's labor and in many other ways."

Parens patriae is a common law doctrine that maintains that the state, as a parent of all persons, has the inherent prerogative to provide for the commonwealth and individual welfare. As guardian over everyone in the state, the state has the authority to protect those who are not legally competent to act on their own behalf. This protection extends to children who, because of their age, are not able to care for themselves. Children have a right to be protected not only from parental abuse but also against the ignorance of their parents. If the parents are unwilling or unable to see the benefits of education, the state may force compulsory attendance in order to protect the child against the shackles of unfit parents.

The protection of a child from a parent requires statutory action. A child has no constitutional protection from its parents. Among those statutory actions are compulsory school attendance laws and required curriculum. These statutes must be supported by a compelling, rational state interest before the rights of either parents or children can be restricted or infringed upon.

LEGAL ISSUES IN SCHOOL ATTENDANCE LAW

1. Does a child have the constitutional right to attend public school tuition free?

   A precedent-setting case over this issue is *Plyler v. Doe*, a Texas case involving the legislature's attempt to stop the public education of illegal aliens.

2. Can a child be compelled to attend public school to meet compulsory attendance law?

   Although all states currently provide for meeting compulsory attendance laws in a variety of ways, such flexibility has not always been present. It has been an evolving process. The issue was first addressed in the 1920s in the case of *Pierce v. Society of the Sisters of the Holy Names of Jesus and Mary*.

3. What is the definition of bona fide residence?

Bona fide residence has traditionally had a two-part definition: (a) physical presence, and (b) the intent to stay or remain (see *Martinez v. Bynum*).

This definition implies that a state may institute geographical boundaries for school districts and thus create the elements necessary to determine physical presence. The intent to stay is sometimes more difficult to ascertain. The rationale for this aspect of the definition is to protect school districts from students who reside in the district apart from parents or legal guardians solely for the purpose of attending school tuition free.

Needless to say, the development of voucher programs changes the definition of bona fide residence. The paradigm shift is from geographical boundaries to parental choice. Thus physical presence will be defined by the scope of the voucher. For example, if the state adopts a voucher program that includes every school district in the state, then physical presence would mean that the parent or guardian must live within the physical boundaries of the state. If the voucher program includes a city, then any parent or guardian who lives within those city limits could send his or her children tuition free to any city school. Although voucher programs provide for more parental choice, physical presence within the geographical boundaries of that choice would still be applicable, as would the intent to remain requirement.

The legal rationale for bona fide residence is an obvious one. Without some prior knowledge of potential enrollment, it would be impossible for school officials to plan for current and future needs with regard to facilities, transportation, staffing, and other significant budgetary considerations. Voucher plans which provide for a wide range of choices for parents, involving multiple school districts, will have to include sufficient lead time for these issues to be addressed.

4. What are the exceptions to compulsory attendance?

   a. Religious Freedom

      There have been times when compulsory attendance laws and an individual's First Amendment rights to the free exercise of religion have come into conflict. A precedent-setting case for this conflict is the famous *Yoder v. Wisconsin*. Since the ruling in this case, other individuals and groups have attempted to claim the Amish Exception that was granted in the *Yoder* case. Keep in mind that the Amish Exception was granted based on the unique nature of the Amish religion and culture and was not intended to be a blanket permission to any person to exempt himself from compulsory attendance laws based on religious beliefs.

b. Homeschooling

In recent years many states have passed homeschooling statutes that allow parents to homeschool their children. These laws vary from state to state but usually include some kind of monitoring role for the public school of residence. In most instances, the parent has to submit some form of evidence or data that demonstrates that the child is making satisfactory progress in the basic subjects. It should be noted that, in some instances, such as Ohio, the statute clearly states that if there is a conflict between the compulsory attendance law and the sincerely held religious beliefs of the parents, the compulsory attendance law must give way.

Homeschooling has produced the question of partial attendance by homeschoolers. Homeschooling parents have, in some instances, demanded that their child be allowed to attend the public school on a part-time basis to take subjects that the parent does not feel comfortable teaching. The answer to this demand varies from state to state and district to district. It is being done in some areas and prohibited in others. Thus far the courts have refused homeschool parents' claim to "hybrid rights" theory. This theory claims that to deny part-time attendance rights to homeschooled children is to deny them their free exercise of religion, First Amendment rights, and to deny the parents their rights to direct their child's education as they please.

5. Who are the stakeholders in attendance law cases?

In court cases involving attendance, the courts have to determine whose interest is best served—the state, the parent, or the child? The state was well served in the cases of *Prince v. Massachusetts* and *Martinez v. Bynum*, the parents in *Pierce v. Society of the Holy Names of Jesus and Mary* and *Yoder v. Wisconsin*, and the child in *Yoder v. Wisconsin*.

SCHOOL VOUCHERS

The advent of school voucher programs in many states has had a profound impact on compulsory attendance law. These various state laws differ in specifics but have basically replaced bona fide residence principles. As defined in *Martinez v. Bynum*, bona fide residence consists of two elements: (a) physical presence, and (b) intent to remain. Under voucher plans, this two-part definition of legal residence is replaced by parental choice. However, geographical barriers may be taken into account establishing the rules for the voucher system. For example, the statute may limit the parental choice to contiguous school districts. Or it might not. So long as the parental choice is limited to public schools, the courts have left little doubt that such plans are constitutional. If, however, private and parochial schools are included in the voucher system, the separation of church and state, and thus the First Amendment, become the center of the debate. The following discussion, based on the U.S. Supreme Court ruling on the constitutionality of the Ohio statute that created a voucher plan for the Cleveland area, presents the legal and educational issues of parental choice and religion.

Amendment I to the U.S. Constitution

Congress shall make no law respecting an establishment of religion, or prohibiting the free exercise thereof; or abridging the freedom of speech or of the press, or the right of the people peaceably to assemble, and to petition the Government for a redress of grievances.

An Example of a Voucher Plan

The following is an example of a voucher plan that includes the private and parochial sector (Table 5.1).

Pilot Project Scholarship Program Summary

The program provides financial assistance to families in any Ohio school district that is or has been "under federal court order requiring supervision and operational management of the district by the state superin-

Table 5.1.

For Vouchers: Clint Bolick Institute for Justice Providing parents a necessary choice	Against Vouchers: Barry Lynn Americans United for Separation of Church and State A bite out of public education
Main Points	
• Children are not receiving an equal educational opportunity in Cleveland Public Schools. • Vouchers offer parents choice of religious and nonreligious schools. • Similar programs include GE Bills, day-care vouchers for religious providers, disabled student can go to private schools at public expense. • Not allowing choice will continue status quo in the inner cities. Focus should be on student learning.	• Integrity, strength, and vitality of religious institutions best served when not dependent on government dollars. • All studies performed with voucherized students shows minimal increase in academic performance. • Many private religious schools practice discriminatory admission policies, teach religious dogma as fact, and have little to answer to public scrutiny.
Constitutionality	
Constitutional: Vouchers allow parents to use public funds to make free choice for themselves.	Unconstitutional: Direct payment of tax dollars to private religious schools.
Precedents	
Brown vs. Board of Ed. et al.: Every child will receive an equal educational opportunity	Establishment Clause Interpretation: Means more than not setting up a national religion, but also that government cannot promote or disparage religion in public institutions or fund religious institutions

tendent." Cleveland is the only Ohio school district to fall within that category.

Types of Assistance

1. Tuition aid for students in kindergarten through third grade, expanding each year through eighth grade, to attend a participating public or private school of their parent's choosing.
2. Tutorial aid for students who choose to remain enrolled in public school.

Participating Schools

1. Any private school, whether religious or nonreligious, may participate in the program and accept program students so long as the
   school is located within the boundaries of a covered district and
   meets statewide educational standards.
2. Participating private schools must agree not to discriminate on the
   basis of race, religion, or ethnic background, or to "advocate or foster unlawful behavior or teach hatred of any person or group on the
   basis of race, ethnicity, national origin, or religion."
3. Any public school located in a school district adjacent to the covered
   district may also participate in the program. Adjacent public schools
   are eligible to receive a $2,250 tuition grant for each program stu-
   dent accepted in addition to the full amount of per-pupil state funding attributable to each additional student.
4. All participating schools, whether public or private, are required to
   accept students in accordance with rules and procedures established
   by the state superintendent.

Tuition Aid

1. Families with incomes below 200 percent of the poverty line are
   given priority and are eligible to receive 90 percent of private school
   tuition, up to $2,250. For these lowest-income families, participat-
   ing private schools may not charge a parental copayment greater
   than $250.
2. For all other families, the program pays 75 percent of tuition costs,
   up to $1,875, with no copayment cap. These families receive tuition
   aid only if the number of available scholarships exceeds the number
   of low-income children who choose to participate.

The program has been in operation within the Cleveland City School District since the 1996–1997 school year. In the 1999–2000 school year, fifty-
six private schools participated in the program, forty-six (or 82 percent)
of which had a religious affiliation. None of the public schools in districts
adjacent to Cleveland have elected to participate. More than 3,700 students participated in the scholarship program, most of whom (96 percent)

enrolled in religiously affiliated schools. Sixty percent of these students were from families at or below the poverty line. In the 1998–1999 school year, approximately 1,400 Cleveland public school students received tutorial aid. This number was expected to double during the 1999–2000 school year.

This Ohio statute was challenged on the grounds that it violates the establishment clause of the First Amendment to the Constitution. In the legal challenge, *Zelman v. Simmons-Harris*, the U.S. Supreme Court issued the following ruling. We can conclude from the ruling that the current Supreme Court will look with favor upon voucher plans that include the private and parochial sector.

Supreme Court Ruling

Zelman v. Simmons-Harris, No. 00-1751; *Hanna Perkins School v. Simmons-Harris*, No. 00-1777; and *Taylor v. Simmons-Harris*, No. 00-1779.

The U.S. Supreme Court upheld the constitutionality of the school voucher program 5-4 in an unprecedented case decided June 27, 2002.

Held: The program does not offend the establishment clause. The Court's ruling says the Constitution permits state legislatures to pass voucher laws similar to Ohio's—not that they are required to do so. Besides Ohio, Wisconsin and Florida have enacted voucher programs.

Majority Opinion: Justice Rehnquist, concurring:

> We continue to ask whether the government acted with the purpose of advancing or inhibiting religion [and] whether the aid has the "effect" of advancing or inhibiting religion. There is no dispute that the program challenged here was enacted for the valid secular purpose of providing

Table 5.2.

Vote	
For	*Against*
Rehnquist (Majority Opinion)	Stevens
O'Connor	Souter
Scalia	Ginsburg
Kennedy	Breyer
Thomas	

educational assistance to poor children in a demonstrably failing public school system. Thus, the question presented is whether the Ohio program nonetheless has the forbidden "effect" of advancing or inhibiting religion.

We believe that the program challenged here is a program of true private choice, consistent with Mueller, Witters, and Zobrest, and thus constitutional. As was true in those cases, the Ohio program is neutral in all respects toward religion. It is part of a general and multifaceted undertaking by the State of Ohio to provide educational opportunities to the children of failed school districts. It confers educational assistance directly to a broad class of individuals defined without reference to religion, i.e., any parent of a school-age child who resides in the Cleveland City School District. The program permits the participation of all schools within the district, religious or nonreligious. Adjacent public schools also may participate and have a financial incentive to do so. Program benefits are available to participating families on neutral terms, with no reference to religion. The only preference stated anywhere in the program is a preference for low-income families, who receive greater assistance and are given priority for admission at participating schools.

There are no "financial incentive[s]" that "ske[w]" the program toward religious schools. Such incentives "[are] not present . . . where the aid is allocated on the basis of neutral, secular criteria that neither favor not disfavor religion, and is made available to both religious and secular beneficiaries on a nondiscriminatory basis." The program here in fact creates financial disincentives for religious schools, with private schools receiving only half the government assistance given to community schools and one-third the assistance given to magnet schools. Adjacent public schools, should any choose to accept program students, are also eligible to receive two to three times the state funding of a private religious school. Families too have a financial disincentive to choose a private religious school over other schools. Parents that choose to participate in the scholarship program and then to enroll their children in a private school (religious or nonreligious) must copay a portion of the school's tuition. Families that choose a community school, magnet school, or traditional public school pay nothing. Although such features of the program are not necessary to its constitutionality, they clearly dispel the claim that the program "creates . . . financial incentive[s] for parents to choose a sectarian school."

Justice Thomas, concurring:

Although one of the purposes of public schools was to promote democracy and a more egalitarian culture, failing urban public schools disproportionately affect minority children most in need of educational opportunity. At the time of Reconstruction, blacks considered public education "a matter of personal liberation and a necessary function of a free society." Today, however, the promise of public school education has failed poor inner-city blacks. While in theory providing education to everyone, the quality of public schools varies significantly across districts. Just as blacks supported public education during Reconstruction, many blacks and other minorities now support school choice programs because they provide the greatest educational opportunities for their children in struggling communities.

While the romanticized ideal of universal public education resonates with the cognoscenti who oppose vouchers, poor urban families just want the best education for their children, who will certainly need it to function in our high-tech and advanced society. As Thomas Sowell noted 30 years ago: "Most black people have faced too many grim, concrete problems to be romantics. They want and need certain tangible results, which can be achieved only by developing certain specific abilities," The same is true today. Staying in school and earning a degree generates real and tangible financial benefits, whereas failure to obtain even a high school degree essentially relegates students to a life of poverty and, all too often, of crime. The failure to provide education to poor urban children perpetuates a vicious cycle of poverty, dependence, criminality, and alienation that continues for the remainder of their lives. If society cannot end racial discrimination, at least it can arm minorities with the education to defend themselves from some of discrimination's effects.

Dissenting Opinions: Justice Stevens, dissenting:

Is a law that authorizes the use of public funds to pay for the indoctrination of thousands of grammar school children in particular religious faiths a "law respecting an establishment of religion" within the meaning of the First Amendment?

First, the severe educational crisis that confronted the Cleveland City School District when Ohio enacted its voucher program is not a matter that should affect our appraisal of its constitutionality. In the 1999–2000 school year, that program provided relief to less than five percent of the students enrolled in the district's schools. The solution to the disastrous conditions that prevented over 90 percent of the student body from meeting basic proficiency standards obviously required massive improvements unrelated to the voucher program. Of course, the emergency may have given some families a powerful motivation to leave the public school system and accept religious indoctrination that they would otherwise have avoided, but that is not a valid reason for upholding the program.

Second, the wide range of choices that have been made available to students within the public school system has no bearing on the question whether the State may pay the tuition for students who wish to reject public education entirely and attend private schools that will provide them with a sectarian education. The fact that the vast majority of the voucher recipients who have entirely rejected public education receive religious indoctrination at state expense does, however, support the claim that the law is one "respecting an establishment of religion." The State may choose to divide up its public schools into a dozen different options and label them magnet schools, community schools or whatever else it decides to call them, but the State is still required to provide a public education and it is the State's decision to fund private school education over and above its traditional obligation that is at issue in these cases.

Third, the voluntary character of the private choice to prefer a parochial education over an education in the public school system seems to me quite irrelevant to the question whether the government's choice to pay for religious indoctrination is constitutionally permissible. Today, however, the Court seems to have decided that the mere fact that a family that cannot afford a private education wants its children educated in a parochial school is a sufficient justification for this use of public funds.

We have been influenced by my understanding of the impact of religious strife on the decisions of our forbears to migrate to this continent, and on the decisions of neighbors in the Balkans, Northern Ireland, and the Middle East to mistrust one another. Whenever we remove a brick from the wall that was designed to separate religion and government, we increase the risk of religious strife and weaken the foundation of our democracy.

Justice Souter, dissenting:

Religious teaching at taxpayer expense simply cannot be condoned from taxpayer politics, and every major religion currently espouses social positions that provoke intense opposition. Not all taxpaying Protestant citizens, for example, will be content to underwrite the teaching of the Roman Catholic Church condemning the death penalty. Nor will all of American's Muslims acquiesce in paying for the endorsement of the religious Zionism taught in many religious Jewish schools, which combines "a nationalistic sentiment" in support of Israel with a "deeply religious" element. Nor will every secular taxpayer be content to support Muslim views on differential treatment of the sexes, or, for that matter, to fund the espousal of a wife's obligation of obedience to her husband, presumably taught in any schools adopting the articles of faith of the Southern Baptist Convention. Views like these, and innumerable others, have been safe in the sectarian pulpits and classrooms of this Nation not only because the Free Exercise Clause protects them directly, but because the ban on supporting religious establishment has protected free exercise, by keeping it relatively private. With the arrival of vouchers in religious schools, that privacy will go, and along with it will go confidence that religious disagreement will stay moderate.

ATTENDANCE CASE SUMMARIES

Plyler, Superintendent, Tyler Independent School District, et al. v. Doe, Guardian, et al.
457 U.S. 202 (1982)

Topic: Undocumented children of alien parents cannot be denied a public education.

Issue: The question presented is whether consistent with the equal protection clause of the Fourteenth Amendment, Texas may deny to undocumented school-age children the free public education that it provides to children who are citizens of the United States or legally admitted aliens.

Facts: In May of 1975 the Texas legislature revised its education laws to withhold from local school districts any state funds for the education of children who were not "legally admitted" into the United States and authorized local school districts to deny enrollment in their public schools to children not legally admitted to the country. In September of 1977 *Plyler v. Doe*, a class action suit, was filed in the U.S. District Court for the Eastern District of Texas on behalf of certain school-age children of Mexican origin residing in Smith County, Texas, who could not establish that they had been legally admitted into the United States. The action complained of the exclusion of plaintiff children from the public schools of the Tyler Independent School District. The district court held that illegal aliens were entitled to protection of the equal protection clause of the Fourteenth Amendment and that Texas law 21.031 violated that clause. The Court of Appeals for the Fifth Circuit upheld the district court's injunction.

Findings of the Supreme Court: The Supreme Court held in a 5-4 decision that the Texas law was unconstitutional based on the equal protection provisions of the Fourteenth Amendment to the U.S. Constitution. Justice Brennan delivered the opinion of the Court, in which Justices Marshall, Blackmun, Powell, and Stevens joined. Marshall, Blackmun, and Powell filed concurring options. Burger filed a dissenting opinion in which White, Rehnquist, and O'Connor joined.

Rationale: Majority opinion, Justice Brennan

- The Fourteenth Amendment says that "No State shall . . . deny to any person within its jurisdiction the equal protection of the laws." Aliens, even aliens whose presence in the country is unlawful, have long been recognized as persons guaranteed due process of law by the Fifth and Fourteenth Amendments.
- Children of undocumented workers do not choose the conditions under which they enter the United States. They should not be punished for the misconduct of their parents.
- While there is no federal constitutional right to an education, it is recognized that economic opportunity is severely limited for those unable to obtain one. Denying children access to education will not eliminate illegal immigration, and places a lifetime of hardship on the children of undocumented parents. It also places social and economic costs on other citizens if these children grow up to be unproductive members of society.

Dissenting opinion, Justice Burger

- Undocumented people, as opposed to legal residents, are not a group receiving special judicial protection according to past decisions, and the Court has never held that education is a fundamental right. Therefore, we should not be tempted to substitute our wisdom for that of the representatives elected by the state's citizens. Our precedents require that only state laws not violate the constitution. In this case the law must have a rational basis. It is certainly not irrational for the state to conclude, as it apparently has, that it does not have the responsibility to provide benefits for persons whose presence in this country is illegal.

Pierce, Governor of Oregon, et al. v.
Society of the Sisters of the Holy Names of Jesus and Mary
U.S. Supreme Court
268 U.S. 510 (1925)
No. 583, 584

Argued March 16 and 17, 1925   **Decided June 1, 1925**

Topics: Deprivation of property without due process, school attendance.

Issue: Did Oregon's Compulsory Education Act of 1922 violate the due process clause of the Fourteenth Amendment by unreasonably interfering with the liberty of parents and guardians to direct the education of their children?

Facts: Petitioners (Society of Sisters and Hill Military Academy) challenged Oregon's Compulsory Education Act, effective September 1, 1926, which required parents of children between the ages of eight and sixteen to send their children to a public school in the district where the children resided for the period of time a public school was held during the school year. There were exceptions to the act for children who were not normal, or who completed the eighth grade, or whose parents or private teachers resided at considerable distances from any public school, or who held special permits from the county superintendent. The purpose of the act was to compel general attendance at public schools by normal children between eight and sixteen years of age who had not completed the eighth grade.

The Society of Sisters was an Oregon corporation that provided care for orphans, educated youths, and established and maintained academies or schools that gave students moral training according to the teachings of the Roman Catholic Church. Established in 1880, the Society of Sisters had acquired the valuable goodwill of many parents and guardians. The Compulsory Education Act, even before its effective date, led to students withdrawing from the religious schools—costing it a portion of its income. The business was remunerative, requiring longtime contracts with teachers and parents. Enforcement of the statute would seriously impair, and possibly destroy, the profitable features of private schools and diminish the value of their property.

This case was decided together with that of the Hill Military Academy, which closely paralleled the Society of Sisters' argument.

Findings of the U.S. Supreme Court: By unanimous decision the Court ruled that Oregon's Compulsory Education Act of 1922 violated the deprivation of property without due process clause of the Fourteenth Amendment by interfering with the free choice of parents and guardians. Mr. Justice McReynolds delivered the opinion of the Court.

Rationale: Argument was made that:

1. To conduct schools was property and that parents and guardians, as a part of their liberty, might direct the education of children by selecting reputable teachers and places.
2. That appellees' schools were not unfit or harmful to the public, and that enforcement of the challenged statute would unlawfully deprive them of patronage and thereby destroy appellees' business and property.
3. The threats to enforce the act would continue to cause irreparable injuries and the suits were not premature.

Points:

1. No question is raised concerning the power of the state to reasonably regulate all schools, to inspect, supervise, examine, and so forth.
2. The inevitable result of enforcing this act would be destruction of possibly all private primary schools for normal children within the state of Oregon.
3. The fundamental theory of liberty excludes any general power of the state to standardize its children by forcing them to accept instruction from public teachers only. The child is not the mere creature of the state; those who nurture him and direct his destiny have the right, coupled with the high duty, to recognize and prepare him for additional obligations.

Decrees were affirmed and attached as footnotes to Justice McReynolds' opinion. These decrees added private instruction as an exemption to Oregon's Compulsory Education Act, thus securing the future of private school education.

The Unanimous Court: Oliver W. Holmes Jr., Willis Van Devanter, James C. McReynolds, Louis D. Brandeis, William Howard Taft, George Sutherland, Pierce Butler, Edward T. Sanford, and Harlan Fiske Stone.

Martinez v. Bynum
U.S. Supreme Court
461 U.S. 321
January 10, 1983

History: The district court held that Texas law 21.031 was justified by the state's legitimate interests in protecting and preserving the quality of its educational system and the right of its bona fide residents to attend state schools on a preferred tuition basis.

Topic: The public school residency requirements.

Issue: This case involves a challenge to the constitutionality of the Texas residency requirement (21.031(d)) governing minors who wish to attend public schools tuition free while living apart from their parents or guardians.

Facts: Roberto Morales was born in McAllen, Texas, and is a U.S. citizen by birth. His parents are Mexican citizens and live in Reynosa, Mexico. Roberto left Reynosa and returned to McAllen, Texas, to live with his sister for the primary purpose of attending school in the McAllen Independent School District. His sister, Oralia Martinez, was his custodian but did not want to be his legal guardian. As a result, Morales was not entitled to tuition-free admission to the McAllen schools.

Findings: Justice Powell delivered the opinion of the Court. In the case *of Inhabitants of Warren v. Inhabitants of Thomaston*, it was stated that when a person takes up his place of abode in a given place, without any present intention to remove therefrom, such place of abode becomes his residence. This two-part definition of residence has been recognized as a minimum standard in a wide range of contexts.

In the case of *Vladis v. Kline* a more rigorous domicile test was approved by the Court. In general, the domicile of an individual is his true, fixed, and permanent home and place of habitation. It is the place to which, whenever he is absent, he has the intention of returning.

The Court found section 21.031 more generous than the traditional residency standards. It requires a school district to permit a child to attend school tuition free if he has a bona fide intention to remain in the school district indefinitely and he would have a reason for being there other than the desire to attend school. As long as the child is not living in the district for the sole purpose of attending school, he satisfies the statutory test. Section 21.031 grants the benefit of residency to everyone who satisfies the traditional residence definition and to some who legitimately could be classified as nonresidents. Since there is no indication that this extension of the traditional definition has any impermissible basis, the Court cannot say that 21.031 violates the Constitution.

The Constitution permits a state to restrict eligibility for tuition-free education to its bona fide residents. The Court holds that 21.031 is a bona fide residence requirement that satisfies constitutional standards.

Concurring Opinion: Justice Brennan stated that the Court does not decide whether the statute is constitutional as applied to Roberto Morales, a U.S. citizen whose parents are nonresident aliens. He believed that if this question were before the Court, the constitutionality of the statute might be affected.

Dissenting Opinion: Justice Marshall wrote the dissenting opinion. In his view, the statutory classification, which deprives some children of an education because of their motive for residing in Texas, is not adequately justified by the asserted state interests. He holds the statute unconstitutional under the equal protection clause. He also argued that even if it were permissible to provide free public education only to those residents who intend to remain in the state, the Texas statute does not impose that restriction uniformly.

Justice Marshall pointed out the difference between residence and domicile. A person is generally a resident of any state with which he has a well-settled connection. Residence generally requires some condition greater than mere lodging. An intent to remain indefinitely in the state does not need to be shown to determine residency. The concept of domicile has typically been reserved for purposes that clearly require general recognition of a single state with which the individual, actually or presumptively, is most closely connected. Justice Marshall stated that residence, not domicile, is the traditional standard of eligibility for lower education.

The state provides free education to all lawful residents whether they intend to reside permanently or temporarily. The only exception is children who live apart from their parents or legal guardians for purposes of education. Those children must intend to remain indefinitely in a particular school district in the state in order to attend its schools. Because the intent requirement is applied to only one class of children, it cannot be characterized as a bona fide residence requirement.

Justice Marshall also stated that when the state provides a free education to some and denies it to others, it creates class distinctions inconsistent with the equal protection clause.

Wisconsin v. Yoder et al.
406 U.S. 205 (1972)

Topic: Compulsory attendance.

Facts: Jonas Yoder and Wallace Miller, members of the Old Order Amish religion, and Adin Yutzy, member of the Conservative Amish Mennonite Church, declined to send their children, ages fourteen and fifteen, to school after they completed the eighth grade. Wisconsin's compulsory-attendance law requires attendance in public or private school until reaching age sixteen. Respondents' defense stood on the grounds that the compulsory-attendance law violated their rights under the First and Fourteenth Amendments. Respondents lost in Green County Court and were fined $5 each. The Wisconsin Circuit Court affirmed the decision of the lower court. The Wisconsin Supreme Court reversed the lower court's decisions and found that the respondents' claim under the free exercise clause of the First Amendment was valid. This decision was appealed to the Supreme Court and certiorari was granted.

Findings of the Supreme Court: The Supreme Court affirmed the decision of the Wisconsin Supreme Court. In a 6-1/2 to 1/2 decision, written by Chief Justice Burger, they determined a state must balance its interest in universal education with the legitimate claims of special groups of constituents.

Majority Rationale: The Court based its decision on four main points.

1. The state's right to educate is not free from a balancing process when it impinges on other fundamental rights, such as those protected by the free exercise clause and the traditional interest of parents with respect to religious upbringing.
2. The respondents provide strong evidence that enforcement of the state's compulsory-attendance law after eighth grade would endanger the free exercise of their beliefs.

3. The 300-year Amish history and tradition has been self-sufficient in society and has demonstrated that their religious beliefs are integral to their way of life. Because of this, the difference between what the Amish now accept and what the state would require is minimal.

4. The state's claim as *parens patriae* to extend the benefit of secondary education regardless of the parent's wishes cannot be sustained against a claim of free exercise in this case. Foregoing the additional year or two of education would not impair the mental or physical health of the child or result in an inability to be a self-supporting citizen.

Dissenting Rationale: Dissenting in part was Justice Douglas. He states,

The argument for religious freedom was for the parents on behalf of the children, not the religious freedoms of the children themselves. The children may have their own views that the Court did not consider in the decision. Additionally, children should be given a voice when it comes to their own education. The wishes of their parents do not always coincide with their own. Finally, the emphasis on the law and order record of the Amish people is irrelevant to the case. Actions deeply rooted in religious convictions subversive to a good society could still be punishable.

6

The Instructional Program

What the courts have enunciated in regard to instruction is important information for all involved in public schools. The various laws and decisions have given shape to instructional programs, teachers' and students' freedoms, and parental concerns.

CATEGORIES OF INSTRUCTIONAL LAW

The court cases that fall under the classification of instruction can be synthesized under nine categories. Although the divisions are not always clear and several issues can be revealed within each case, the legal aspects are most clearly organized under the following headings:

1. Marketplace of ideas
2. Right to teach and learn
3. Reasonableness of academic requirements
4. Student testing and promotion
5. Bilingual education
6. Substantive due process and instruction
7. Libraries
8. Evolution vs. creationism, and
9. Obscenity and sex

The current status of the law in regard to instructional programs has been influenced in several ways. Constitutional issues such as free speech, expression, and religion under the First Amendment, liberty and property interests under the Fourteenth Amendment, and the Civil Rights Act of 1964 have been addressed in the courts. At the same time, principles such as police power, academic freedom, property interest, and instructional validity have shaped today's laws regarding instruction. Rationales and judicial opinions have given meaning to terms such as the "pall of orthodoxy," balanced treatment statute," and "institutional intent."

Generally, the rulings of the courts have promoted openness and expansiveness of knowledge and have leaned heavily toward an "unlimited" exchange of ideas," a "marketplace of ideas," and a "robust exchange of ideas," while oppositional attempts, efforts to reduce the knowledge base, and restraints to access of information have been viewed critically and been prevented from continuation. The concept that public schools are "a marketplace of ideas" is clearly evident in the Supreme Court case *Board of Education v. Pico* (1982). In this case the Court addressed the constitutional rights of students, limitations on school boards' discretionary power, and gave strength to the term "pall of orthodoxy." When the School Board of Island Trees Union Free School District pulled books off library shelves with disregard to the district policy, the board's actions were viewed as irregular and suspicious, limiting students from certain knowledge and perspectives. The Court found that the board denied students' rights when they tried to contract a flow of ideas and made it very clear that it would not tolerate such limitations.

Judicial intervention has not only recognized that students have a right to learn but that teachers also have a right to teach. *Meyer v. Nebraska* (1923) is an extremely important case in education law because it voiced a "substantive" constitutional interest in teaching and learning. In this decision the U.S. Supreme Court held that dismissing a teacher for teaching a foreign language violated the teacher's due process and liberty rights under the Fourteenth Amendment. By prohibiting the teaching of a language other than English, the teacher and the parents were deprived of liberty without due process of law. Rights of teaching and learning merge with the understanding that the learning of languages is a marketplace of ideas, and as such, the teacher's knowledge cannot be considered harmful.

Reasonableness of academic requirements has been established through several Court decisions. *State v. Webber* (1886), in one sense, determined that it is within the state's power to require students to take music instruction. In another sense, this ruling set the precedent that makes it legal for a school to prescribe its own curriculum and without question is significant to the way instructional design is written today. *Steier v. Bethlehem Area School District* (1993) set the precedent that is legal to have students do community service as a school requirement for graduation. Prior to this ruling, it was argued that community service was involuntary servitude, but this case established that such a school assignment is a reasonable academic requirement and does not violate the First Amendment of free speech or the Thirteenth Amendment as involuntary servitude.

Another significant case for education programming is *Lau v. Nichols* (1974) because it helped establish specific guidelines for bilingual education programs. In this case, Chinese-speaking students were required to master the speaking of English in order to graduate, but the district denied them the opportunity to take classes in the English language. The Supreme Court held that the school district was in violation of the Civil Rights Act and brought action under the California Educational Code.

The courts have primarily given the states the authority to determine curriculum and methodology. The U.S. Court of Appeals in *Mozart v. Hawkins County Board of Education* (1987) ruled that basic reader series do not create an unconstitutional denial of free exercise on parents and children and established precedent for schools districts to adopt reading series for instruction. *Brown v. Woodland Joint Unified School District* (1994), another case involving a reading series, determined that readings in the Impressions series and the practice of students chanting poetry as a reading procedure did not constitute the practice of witchcraft and was not in violation of the establishment clause.

When considering the current state of affairs in testing, a key case is *Debra P. v. Turlington* (1983). In this case the federal district court in Florida, for the first time, required a check for curricular validity and asked if schools were testing what they were teaching. The court established that when schools give tests related to graduation requirements, they must give students adequate notice about the test and the test must be valid to the curriculum taught. The court also determined that a state-sanctioned exit-level exam did not violate the due process or equal protection clauses nor did it discriminate against African Americans. In *Sandlin v. Johnson* (1981), the Federal Court of Appeals for the Fourth Circuit held that decisions made by educators based on students' academic performance are within the expertise of the educators. In this case second-graders failed a reading test and were denied promotion to the third grade. The courts ruled that schools are not completely liable for the failure of students. There is a partnership in education; the school has a responsibility, but the student has a responsibility, too.

The courts have tended to be reluctant to intervene when issues of grading and student evaluations have been on trial. In *Campbell v. Board of Education of Town of New Milford* (1984), the Supreme Court of Connecticut held that a local school board policy of denying credit for excessive absences and reducing grades because of absences was not ultra vires and did not violate either the due process or equal protection clauses of the Fourteenth Amendment. The courts have also ruled that schools may not place academic penalties on a student that are irrational or unrelated to educational objectives. The courts have mandated that a diploma must be issued once a student has successfully completed all course requirements. Denial of a diploma for reasons that are not academic is impermissible.

School libraries have always had a special relationship with the law and the First Amendment because they are centers for inquiry and the dissemination of ideas and information. In *Board of Education v. Pico* (1982), the Supreme Court emphasized its respect for the school library as a place of voluntary inquiry and designated that as such an environment, it has special characteristics that make it especially appropriate for recognition of rights to freedom of speech and freedom of press. This case established that school boards have discretion when it comes to determining the content of their school libraries but the power to exercise choice of literary tastes may not be narrowly partisan or political.

Evolution versus creationism never ceases to be an interesting issue for schools and courts. The First Amendment ruling under *Epperson v. Arkansas* (1968) established that it is a violation to dismiss teachers who teach evolution theory and established that evolution theory is a reasonable academic topic because it is a science. The Court also reaffirmed that the state, although it can specify curriculum, may not tailor curriculum to the tenets and dogma of a particular religious sect. Creationism, the other side of this hot debate, was the question up for decision in *Edwards v. Aguillard* (1987). In this case, the U.S. Supreme Court held that the "balanced treatment statute," which stated that the teaching of evolution was not permissible unless accompanied by instruction in creationism, violated the establishment clause of the First Amendment. Creationism is not a science; it is a faith and as a faith it cannot be taught in public schools.

The courts have worked to define obscenity for schools over the years. In *Keefe v. Geanakos* (1969) the Federal Court of Appeals for the First Circuit helped determine obscenity standards and at the same time held that termination for a high school teacher for using a dirty word violated the teacher's academic freedom. The age of the children in the classroom and whether the words have a relationship to the instruction determine the offensiveness and inappropriateness of the language a teacher may use when teaching. The Fourth Circuit for the Federal Court of Appeals case *Cornwell v. State Board* (1969) held that the state's interest in the health of its children overruled parental controls and freedom of religion when it found that the teaching of sex education in elementary and secondary schools did not constitute a violation of either the due process or the free exercise clause.

There are a great number of laws that have bearing on the way schools operate today. The laws were established as a result of the many cases involving instructional dilemmas and educational issues that naturally arise as people interact and go about the day-to-day work of doing schooling, but whether or not the courts have given the final word in regard to instructional programs can only be determined in future cases.

EVOLUTION VERSUS CREATIONISM

The classroom battle between evolution and creationism has been, and continues to be, a bone of contention in public schools. The controversy started in Dayton, Tennessee, in 1925. The *Memphis Flyer* retold the story on February 3, 2000.

MONKEY BUSINESS

Seventy-five years later, the Dayton, Tennessee, Scopes trial still rivets the nation.

By George Shadroui

It would be hard to imagine a more moral town than Dayton. If it has any bootleggers, no visitor has heard of them. Ten minutes after I arrived, a leading citizen offered me a drink made up half of white mule and half of Coca-Cola, but he seems to have been simply indulging himself in a naughty gesture. No fancy woman has been seen in town since the end of the McKinley administration. There is no gambling. There is no place to dance. The relatively wicked, when they would indulge themselves, go to Robinson's drug store and debate theology.

—H. L. Mencken, July 13, 1925

It would be called the trial of the century.

It would pit the greatest courtroom lawyer of the day against the greatest populist in American history, and it would bring one of the most legendary journalists in modern times to Dayton, Tennessee, just to write about it.

That journalist, H. L. Mencken, would call it "the monkey trial."

The name stuck.

Within a week of the trial's end, William Jennings Bryan would be dead, Clarence Darrow would be hated, and Mencken would be disgusted, again, by all the "yokels," "ignoramuses," "bumpkins," and "buffoons" he was forced to encounter on his journey to Dayton, a small town just north of Chattanooga.

During the trial, more than 200 reporters wrote more than two million words for more than 2,000 newspapers across the nation. It has generated thousands of books, articles, and monographs, not to mention plays, three television movies, and a motion picture called *Inherit the Wind* that in 1960 rekindled much of the trial's controversy.

Bryan College was established in Dayton shortly after the trial, where, to this day, staff and townspeople wage a daily campaign to salvage the reputation of the man who gave the college its name.

The trial would so sear the consciousness of the nation that almost 75 years later, *George* magazine (October 1999) would call it the fourth-most significant event of the 20th century.

For all of this, noted historian Garry Wills has called the Scopes case "a comedy of errors" that was "in many respects, a nontrial over a nonlaw, with a nondefendant backed by nonsupporters. Its most profound moment involved non-testimony by a non-expert, which was followed by a non-defeat."

Why the trial continues to fascinate us is not hard to understand. Evolution, the core issue around which the trial revolved, is still hotly debated by those, on the one hand, who call it an undeniable scientific truth, and those, on the other, who consider it theological blasphemy. It is the science-versus-faith issue at its core, an issue that has been around as long as time. And it isn't going to go away.

As recently as last summer, the Kansas board of education decided to remove evolution as a topic from its standardized tests, thereby sparking protests from many quarters, including the American Civil Liberties Union and this newspaper.

Bryan College professor Richard Cornelius, who has authored 18 articles about the Scopes trial, says with some understatement: "It was more a trial of ideas than most other trials have been or could be. It is the ideas that have made the trial so significant."

Hard to believe, then, that the whole episode began as a public relations stunt concocted by a group of men gathered in a small-town drugstore. They succeeded—beyond their wildest expectations, but that success would prove bittersweet.

Many townspeople would rue the day they ever approached the young football coach named John Scopes and asked him to go to court. And the people of Dayton for much of the century would wrestle with the legacy of that hot July of 1925, for it visited upon the town not only fame, but embarrassment, tragedy, anger, and, for some, even doubt.

The Trial

John Scopes in his autobiography, *Center of the Storm*, published 40 years after the trial, stated without exaggeration: "I did little more than sit, proxy-like, in freedom's chair that hot, unforgettable summer—no great feat, despite the notoriety it has brought me. My role was a passive one that developed out of my willingness to test what I considered a bad law."

The law in question had been passed by the Tennessee legislature earlier that year. It read simply: "that it shall be unlawful for any teacher in any of the Universities, Normals, and all other public schools of the State which are supported in whole or in part by the public school funds of the State, to teach any theory that denies the story of Divine Creation of man as taught in the Bible, and to teach instead that man has descended from a lower order of animals."

Anyone found guilty of such an act, the statute goes on, would be fined a minimum of $100 and not more than $500 for the offense.

Scopes considered the law wrong, but he had no intention of making an issue of it until a group of Dayton townsmen called him off the tennis court one day and asked if he would be willing to test the law in court. He agreed, little expecting what followed.

Whatever the merits of the legal issue, it became secondary to the larger drama—a contest of wills between two of the most notable men in America.

That William Jennings Bryan agreed to prosecute the case transformed the Scopes trial into a national event, for Bryan had been a three-time presidential candidate who only a decade before had served as Secretary of State under President Woodrow Wilson. After Teddy Roosevelt, he was arguably the most famous politician of his time.

He was also a political lightning rod, the kind of man about whom it was difficult to be neutral. His remarkable oratory skills ("you shall not crucify mankind on a cross of gold") had won him a massive following for almost three decades, particularly among rural and small-town people who shared his populist ideas and traditional religious convictions. He was at once a progressive and a throwback, a man before his time who championed a woman's right to vote and fair labor practices, but who also embraced what many considered "reactionary ideas" that frightened and angered people of all political stripes.

"Of all public figures, Bryan best represented rural piety," says Kevin Tierney, biographer of opposing attorney Clarence Darrow. "He was its spokesman and even its personification. As such he was Darrow's pet aversion, and the Scopes trial was a dream-come-true for Darrow. In a sense, he had been preparing for it all his life."

Clarence Darrow, for the first time in his storied legal career, which included his defense of Leopold and Loeb, agreed to serve without payment just so he could be in the courtroom to oppose Bryan. He was as anxious to undercut Bryan's credibility as Bryan was to put the "enemies of faith" on trial.

Not surprisingly, the media descended on Dayton. The *Baltimore Sun* alone sent four reporters and a cartoonist, among them Mencken, who spent a great deal of his energy chastising Bryan and his creationist followers.

Eloise Reed was 12 years old that summer. She has become something of a folk hero in Dayton, if only because, as she puts it humbly, "I'm one of the older people here and I happened to be there."

Ms. Reed's older brother Crawford played football for John Scopes, who, amazingly enough, was not even a biology teacher. It was her brother who was playing tennis with Scopes the day he was called to Robinson's drugstore to discuss his willingness to test the Tennessee law.

Scopes, Reed remembers, was a "serious" young man, but a pleasant person who spent a lot of time hanging out with members of the high school football team he coached. He was only 24, but he was chosen to test the Tennessee law because he had substituted for the full-time biology teacher and he happened to be single (no risk for his family) and cooperative.

The men who approached Scopes hoped to bring favorable publicity to Dayton, which was suffering hard economic times. It worked, for a while at least. A carnival atmosphere descended upon Dayton that summer. Hucksters sold souvenirs. Live monkeys were paraded up and down the streets, to the delight of Reed and other Dayton children. Street-corner preachers competed with entrepreneurs who sold cold drinks chilled in ice-filled washtubs. Someone even brought a gorilla into town.

You could see him for 10 cents, Reed recalls. "I guess I saw him two or three times," she adds without apology.

Most vivid in her memory is the confrontation between Darrow and Bryan, which, because of the heat, occurred not in the Rhea County Courthouse, but outside on the lawn. With well over a thousand people watching, Darrow cross-examined Bryan about the Bible. Reed sat in the front row.

That this exchange ever occurred is a reminder of how unorthodox the case was. The scientific experts for Darrow and the defense were prohibited from testifying by the judge, who ruled it was not relevant to the legal issue, which simply dealt with whether or not Scopes taught evolution, not the truth of the theory. Still, the judge relented when Darrow asked if he could call an expert on the Bible, that expert being Bryan. Bryan, not one to shy away from center stage, quickly assented to take the stand.

Bryan, Reed remembers, fanned himself constantly and began to get "a little edgy" as Darrow questioned him. "You could tell there was fatigue there. I know he was surprised by the way Darrow came after him."

The crowd grew restless, too, as Darrow, in white shirt and no tie, grilled Bryan.

"He had on red suspenders and he would hunch over when he talked to Bryan," Reed recalls. "He snapped the suspenders, gestured with his finger and said, 'Do you really believe that whale swallowed Jonah?' Darrow liked to put on his antics."

Darrow would ask Bryan a long series of questions about the age of the Earth, the length of a day as described in Genesis, and whether he believed the Earth actually stood still as described in the Bible. Bryan gradually began to slip, admitting that some interpretation of the Bible might be appropriate.

Just how badly Darrow "humiliated" Bryan, however, has been an issue of contention since the trial. Mencken, who ironically was not even there for the historic confrontation, would later declare that Darrow had won a victory for enlightenment ideas against the dark and backward views of a Neanderthal like Bryan.

Others were not convinced by Mencken's clearly one-sided reporting. Scopes himself in his memoirs described Mencken as a "sensationalist" and remembered Bryan as defiant after the exchange with Darrow—already planning a counterattack.

Bryan's death a few days later created the popular and perhaps understandable perception that the pressure of the trial had brought about "the great commoner's" demise. One person even charged that Darrow had broken Bryan's heart. Darrow, not known for his sentimentality where Bryan was concerned, retorted "he died of a busted belly," a reference to Bryan's large appetite.

There were mixed feelings in Dayton about the trial and the law itself, but almost everyone was deeply saddened that Bryan had died in their town, Reed says. As she recalls it: "He led the prayer at a local church that day and went home, fell asleep, and never woke up."

The Aftermath

The immediate reaction in Dayton to all of the events that occurred that week in July was both a sense of embarrassment and shock, brought on by the kind of attention Mencken and others focused on the town. To this day, Reed and other Dayton citizens contend that it was not the town that turned the event into a circus but the media and opportunists from out of town who hoped to somehow profit from the trial.

Mencken, "that awful man" as Reed calls him, even complained about the water, according to stories handed down from decade to decade.

"What did he care?" Reed says. "People told me that the only thing he drank here was moonshine liquor."

Such were the hard feelings of the small-town people subjected to the glare of national and international publicity.

There is no question, however, that the result of the trial was hardly a clear-cut victory for Darrow, Mencken, and other proponents of evolution. They lost the case in Dayton, which was Darrow's intent in any case because he wanted to appeal to a higher court. The appeal, however, proved anti-climactic. After much infighting with the American Civil Liberties Union, which sponsored the case, Darrow, who was now seen as highly controversial because of his alleged animosity toward religion, remained part of the legal team. But the court dismissed the issue with a subtle maneuver. They overturned Scopes' conviction on the technicality that the jury, not the judge, should have imposed the fine, but refused to overturn the state law. The statute would stand another four decades, and those called "fundamentalists" would mobilize to disprove evolution and to demand, at the very least, equal time for creationism.

It was not until 1967 that the Tennessee legislature, after rancorous debate, repealed the law. A year later, in *Epperson vs. Arkansas*, the United States Supreme Court ruled that laws prohibiting the teaching of theories that contradict the biblical account of creation amounted to establishing a religious perspective. This violated separation of church and state, or so U.S. Supreme Court Justice Abe Fortas argued in 1968 in writing the majority opinion.

Fortas' view was strident even among those on the court who sought to strike down the Arkansas law, and it contained echoes of the Scopes trial, not surprisingly. Fortas grew up in Memphis in the 1920s and had followed the Scopes trial with a mixture of fascination and concern as a high school student.

Dayton Afterwards

Dayton experienced ups and downs over the next few decades, but basically it stayed a simple country town of a few thousand people. Folks wanted to forget the shock of Bryan's death, and the circus atmosphere for which Dayton was labeled "monkey town."

The motion picture, *Inherit the Wind*, changed that for a time. The townspeople at first hoped the film would clear up lingering misunderstandings about the trial, but they were sorely disappointed when the film premiered in Dayton in 1960. Reed, by then running a clothing store, was invited to a reception after the film was shown. She found herself next to the director, Stanley Kramer, who asked her opinion. "I told him it was awful. There was nothing about it like the trial. And he just laughed at me."

The film essentially embraced the Mencken point of view, portraying Bryan (played by Frederic March) for the most part as a buffoon and

Darrow (played by Spencer Tracy) as a hero. While one scene did show
Bryan trying to temper the emotions of a rowdy crowd, that positive depic-
tion changed by the end of the film. The town fared even worse than Bryan,
however. There were dark, sinister forces at work in Dayton, the film implied, and a fictional local minister was introduced to symbolize the harsh,
unrelenting fundamentalist community.

"The community felt burned by Mencken during the original trial and
they felt burned after 1960 and *Inherit the Wind*," says Rick Dye, a relatively new resident of Dayton who has worked with the Chamber of Commerce in recent years to highlight the Scopes trial.

Dayton again tried to downplay the trial as a part of its cultural backdrop.
While Scopes was brought to Dayton to discuss the trial in 1960, Dye, general manager of WDNT Radio in Dayton, said it was not until the mid- or
late 1980s that community leaders began to organize annual events to commemorate the historic event.

Today there is a festival that includes tours, a reenactment of the trial,
and other cultural and economic activities. Sites on the tour include the
courthouse, which now has a small museum in the basement; Bailey
Boarding House where Scopes lived; the old Robinson drugstore site,
where Scopes was first asked to test the Tennessee statute; the Bailey
Hardware Store, the upstairs loft of which was converted to a media room
for reporters; and the Rogers home where Bryan stayed. Media attention
in anticipation of the 75th anniversary has already generated several television appearances by local residents, not to mention a number of interviews with journalists.

While it might be a stretch to say that the Scopes trial is big business
in Dayton, it certainly is no longer the embarrassment it once was. Tom
Davis, director of public information at Bryan College, says: "Most of
the people who had firsthand recollections are gone now. It is looked at
as a major event in America [by townspeople], not something to be
ashamed of."

Another goal is to correct stereotypes and inaccuracies that town residents contend have become a part of the trial's legacy because of one-sided
depictions. "We were not a backward, close-minded, or solely fundamentalist community," Dye explains.

Davis agrees. "Most people accept *Inherit the Wind* as the historical
record," Davis says. "And it's not quite accurate. Just because something
has creationism in it, doesn't mean we accept it. Just because it has evolution in it, does not mean we will reject it out of hand."

Cornelius believes the trial's continued prominence on the cultural and political landscape is rooted in the important issues that underlie the case: science versus faith, academic freedom, media ethics (the first "media" trial), separation of church and state, and parental and community control over curriculum, to name a few.

Bryan College today takes what it considers a reasonable view on the issue: Evolution can be taught as a theory of the origins of man, but other theories also should be allowed in the classroom. That was Bryan's view, though this is forgotten in many popular portrayals that depict him as a close-minded fundamentalist who sought to ban the teaching of evolution completely, Cornelius says.

The ACLU, however, continues to take a hostile view toward any effort to include creationism in science classrooms. When the board of education in Kansas announced recently that it would remove evolution as a topic on standardized tests, the ACLU responded with a statewide mailing and released a statement denouncing the decision: "Having failed to succeed at forcing their so-called 'creation-science' on public school students, proponents of creationism are now resorting to the tactic of removing essential scientific instruction," said Jay Barrish, president of the ACLU's affiliate board. "We think the courts will ultimately see this tactic for what it is—a blatantly unconstitutional attempt to introduce a specific religious viewpoint into the classroom."

Seventy-five years later, the debate goes on.

INSTRUCTIONAL CASE SUMMARIES

State ex. rel. Andrews v. Webber
Supreme Court of Indiana, 1886
108 Ind. 31, 8 N. E. 708

Argued November 19, 1885 **Decided October 16,1886**

Topic: Curriculum.

Issues: Do the parents or the school authorities have discretionary power to enforce reasonable rules prescribing specific curriculum (music)?

Facts:

1. Bram Andrews (appellant's father, guardian, and relator), a bona fide resident of La Porte, Indiana, whose child attends the public schools in La Porte, Indiana.

2. Leroy D. Webber, Edward J. Church, and Ellis Michael were school trustees, and were in charge of public schools of La Porte. William N. Hailman was superintendent of public schools of La Porte, who had, under the board of trustees, the duties of general management, oversight, and supervision of the La Porte public schools.

3. Andrews's son had attended public high school in the fall of 1885 and had been an "obedient and diligent pupil, and had faithfully complied with all of the rules and regulations prescribed by such board of school trustees and superintendent for the government of such schools."

4. One of the areas that was mandated by the superintendent with the sanction of the school trustees was a requirement of studying and practicing of music. Andrews asked the superintendent that his son be excused from the study and practice of music, and directed his son not to participate. Andrews didn't want to break any laws, except that he might legally control and direct the education of his son.

5. On October 14, 1885, the superintendent told Andrews's son that he must participate in the study and practice of music, and suspended Andrews's son from school because of his refusal to participate in music. The school trustees approved the suspension.

6. Andrews wanted the school trustees to revoke their suspension. Andrews said that his son was deprived the right to attend and receive instruction without any reasonable or justifiable cause.

7. Andrews lost in lower court and appellate court, and was ordered to pay court costs for the school trustees.

Rationale: The question may be stated as: Is the rule or regulation of the trustees of La Porte High School requiring the study and practice of music a valid and reasonable exercise of discretionary power?

In Section 4497, Rev. St. 1881, in effect since August 16, 1869, stated that, "The common schools of the state shall be taught in the English language, and the trustees shall provide to have taught in them orthography, reading, writing, arithmetic, geography, English grammar, physiology, history of the United States, and good behavior, and such other branches of learning, and other languages, as the advancement of pupils may require and the trustees from time to time direct."

Also, in section 4497, Rev. St. 1881, in force since March 1873, the trustees were to "'take charge of the educational affairs" of La Porte schools and "may establish graded schools."

The power to establish graded schools carries with it the power to establish and enforce such reasonable rules as may seem necessary to the trustees, in their discretion, for the government and discipline of such schools, and prescribing the course of instruction therein.

The two questions the justices had to answer for the case at hand were:

1. Has the appellant's relator shown that the rules or regulations were an unreasonable exercise of discretionary power conferred by law upon the trustees and superintendent of the school?
2. Assuming the rule to be reasonable and valid, has the relator shown any sufficient or satisfactory excuse for the noncompliance?

In response to the first question, the court held that the relator did not attempt to show that the rule or regulation requiring that each high school student study and practice music was not a reasonable or valid exercise of discretionary power to direct what branches of learning, in addition to those specified in the statute, shall be taught in the public schools. There was absence of sufficient excuse and the relator's complaint was filled with vagueness and uncertainty.

For the second question, the court stated the school trustees used their discretionary power conferred on them by law to adopt the music instruction. The only reason given by the relator for requiring his son to disobey the music instruction was that he did not believe it was in the best interest of his son to participate. "The arbitrary wishes of the relator must yield and be subordinated to the governing authorities of the school . . . and their reasonable rules and regulations for its pupils."

Findings: The court affirmed judgment with costs. (School trustees won, and Andrews had to pay their court costs.)

Sandlin v. Johnson

**Michelle Sandlin, by her parents, Mr. and Mrs.Glenn Sandlin; Gary
Stacy, by his parents, Mr. and Mrs. David E. Stacy; Revonda
Ferrell, by her mother, Mrs. Mozetta Ferrell; Tina Wood,
by her parents, Mr. and Mrs. James Ray Wood**

v.

**Earl Johnson, superintendent, Pittsylvania County Schools; Richard
Huffin, principal, Whitmell Elementary School; E. B. Fjtzgerald,
chairman, Pittsylvania School Board; Dr. D. E. Burnette, vice
chairman, Pittsylvania County School Board; Obie G. Adams,
member, Pittsylvania County School Board; Koyeton H. Beavers Jr.,
member; W. S. Eastly Jr., member; Carter G. Layne, member;
George A. Martin, member; Calvin C. Oakes, member; Carl A.
Obuchowski, member; Edith W. Smith, member; Harold E. Terry,
Member; and William K. Pearson, member**

U.S. Court of Appeals
Fourth Circuit
643 F.2d 1027 (4th Cir. 1980)
No. 80-1213

Argued November 14, 1980   **Decided March 11, 1981**

Topic: Denial of equal protection of the law in regard to being provided
educational opportunities.

Issue: Is a teacher or school district responsible when a student does not
meet the desired level of mastery? Should a student who does not demonstrate required level of mastery be promoted to the next grade?

Prior History: Prior to the hearing, the district court issued an order dismissing the suit on the ground that federal courts should abstain from resolving controversies that involve the administration by a state or subdivision of its own affairs. The district court wanted to keep the suit in the
state courts. Plaintiffs appealed this order.

Facts: During the school year of 1977–1978 at Whitmell Elementary
School, in Pittsylvania, Virginia, only one member of the second-grade
class was promoted to third grade. Four second-graders from the class felt
that they were capable of reading at a third-grade level and should have
been promoted. They did not deny that they failed to complete the re-

quired work, but argued they were denied equal protection of the law. Michelle Sandlin, Gary Stacy, Revonda Ferrell, and Tina Wood, each represented by their parents, filed the case as a class action suit on behalf of themselves and eighteen other second-graders. They argued that their equal protection was denied by either the defendants' negligent and careless supervision of the instruction of plaintiffs, or by their arbitrary and negligent grading and classification of these plaintiffs. The plaintiffs felt second-grade students with similar abilities at other Pittsylvania County Schools that were comparable to Whitmell were not denied their educational opportunities.

Arguments: Plaintiffs argued that the defendants' actions damaged them by delaying the completion of their education and their obtaining employment, by foreclosing "certain lucrative employments . . . because of a lack of education provided them commensurate with their abilities," and by burdening them with the stigma of failure. The plaintiffs sought $25,000.00 each in damages. They also requested that school authorities provide the plaintiffs with third-grade educational opportunities that they had been denied the previous year. The plaintiffs wanted a curriculum of classes designed to prepare them and other similarly situated students for admission to the fourth grade for the 1979–1980 school year.

Defendants responded that they had provided equal opportunities to plaintiffs. They acknowledged that the plaintiffs' intelligence was such that they were capable of reading at the third-grade level, but they had unfortunately failed to progress to that level of mastery. The defendants felt promoting the plaintiffs before they had reached mastery level would increase plaintiffs' reading deficiencies and be counterproductive.

Defendants moved to dismiss and the motion was denied. Keep in mind that, prior to the trial, the district court issued an order dismissing the suit on the ground that federal courts should abstain from resolving controversies that involve the administration by a state or subdivision of its own affairs. The plaintiffs appealed this order.

The court felt that there was no need for heightened scrutiny; the students were not separated into illegal classifications such as religious affiliations, race, gender, wealth, and so forth. The only question that was recognized by all parties was whether the classification by the governmental entity, which was at issue, was rationally related to a permissible governmental end.

Defendants had classified plaintiffs according to their attained reading level. The purpose of classifying the students was to enable the school to provide students with instruction at their appropriate level. This would enable the teacher to better enhance and advance the education of the students.

The court recognized this as the governmental end being a permissible one. Defendants, therefore, had not implicated any constitutional right of the plaintiffs by classifying them according to their reading level.

Plaintiffs lastly claimed that defendants or the teachers under their supervision negligently and carelessly failed to ensure that plaintiffs were properly and appropriately taught. The court explained that the defendants are claiming denial of equal educational opportunity and through that statement it seems the plaintiffs are stating that teachers and school boards have some sort of owed duty to give their pupils an education. This, of course, is not the case and does not rise to the level of a constitutional claim. It is not cognizable in an action pursuant to the equal rights act, reminding them that 42 U.S.C.s 1983 is not a federal remedy for ordinary state tort claims.

The court also stated that "an official may not be held liable on a respondent superior theory in suits filed pursuant to, 42 U.S.C.s 1983, *Vinnedge v. Gibbs*, 550 F.2d 926, 928 (4th Cir. 1977), unless he actually participates or acquiesces in the subordinate's actions." This statement was made reminding the plaintiffs that the defendants were not directly involved with the education of the children in the classroom. It had not been argued that the teacher was purely responsible, so it is possible that the defendants were not aware of what was happening in that second-grade classroom during the 1977–1978 school years.

Findings: The U.S. Court of Appeals Fourth Circuit ruled that the district court was correct in their ruling for the defendants.

Rationale: The U.S. Fourth Circuit Court of Appeals upheld the district court's ruling, stating that evaluation of academic performance of a student, and as it related to promotion, are within the expertise of educators and are particularly inappropriate for review in a judicial context. They did not want to enlarge the judicial presence in the academic community. The court felt that this involvement would put many beneficial aspects of the faculty-student relationship at risk.

Robert Meyer v. State of Nebraska
U.S. Supreme Court, No. 325
262 U.S. 390

Argued 23 February 1923   **Decided 4 June 1923**

Topic: Educational freedom.

Issue: Was a Nebraska school teacher who was tried and convicted for teaching a Bible story in German to a ten-year-old child denied his right to the Fourteenth Amendment?

Facts: Robert Meyer, a parochial school teacher of Hamilton County, Nebraska, was found guilty of violating a 1919 statute mandating English-only instruction in all public and private schools and allowed foreign-language instruction "only after a pupil shall have attained and successfully passed the eighth grade."

On May 25, 1920, while an instructor at Zion Parochial School, he unlawfully taught Raymond Parpart, a ten-year-old child, a Bible story in German.

The Statute (Approved April 9, 1919) in Question:

Section 1. No person, individually or as a teacher, shall, in any private, denominational, parochial or public school, teach any subject to any person in any language but the English language.

Section 2. Languages, other than the English language, may be taught as languages only after a pupil shall have attained and successfully passed the eighth grade as evidenced by a certificate of graduation issued by the county superintendent of the county in which the child resides.

Section 3. Any person who violates any of the provisions of this act shall be deemed guilty of a misdemeanor and upon conviction, shall be subject to a fine of not less than twenty-five dollars ($25), nor more than one hundred dollars ($100), or be confined in the county jail for any period not exceeding thirty days for each offense.

Section 4. Whereas, an emergency exists, this act shall be in force from and after its passage and approval.

The salutary (beneficial) purpose of the statute is clear. The legislature had seen the harmful effects of permitting foreigners, who had taken residence in this country, to rear and educate their children in the language of their native land. The result of this was found to be detrimental to our own safety. To allow the children of foreigners to be taught in their own native language from early childhood was to bring them up with that language as their mother tongue. It was to educate them so that they would always think in that language and, consequentially, naturally instill in them the ideas and thoughts foreign to the best interest of the United States. The statute's intention, therefore, was to ensure that the education of all children was to be in English. Furthermore, until all children had acquired the English language and it had fully become part of them, they should not be taught any other language in the schools. In other words, the most obvious purpose of the statute was to ensure that the English language should be the mother tongue of all children reared in this state. Since the foreign-born population was very large, certain communities commonly used foreign words, followed foreign leaders, and moved in a foreign atmosphere. This was thought to hinder the children from becoming citizens of the most useful type.

The legislature wanted to foster a homogeneous group of people with all the same ideals. However, the state did not have the power to "standardize its children" or "foster a homogenous people" by denying people the chance to choose an educational program. Some thought this restriction was unnecessary because it applied to all citizens of the state and illogically interfered with the rights of citizens who were not of foreign ancestry. It also prevented them, for no reason, from allowing their children the chance to learn a foreign language at school. This argument was not well received, though, because it suggested that every citizen found himself affected by the statute. However, in actuality, the law affected few citizens except those of foreign descent. But in the minds of legislators, the beneficial effect of the statute easily outweighed the restriction placed upon the citizens. It appeared to be a "restriction of no real consequence."

The real question was whether the statute infringed upon the liberty guaranteed to Meyer by the Fourteenth Amendment. "No State shall . . . deprive any person of life, liberty, or property, without due process of law." The American people have always regarded education and acquirement of knowledge as matters of utmost importance that should be conscientiously promoted.

The challenged statute forbad teaching any subject other than English in schools. It also prohibited the teaching of any other language until the pupil had gotten to and successfully passed the eighth grade. Simply knowing German could not reasonably be construed as being harmful. In fact, some found it to be helpful and desirable. Meyer's right to teach this and the right of Raymond Parpart's parents to engage him so to instruct their child were thought to be within the liberty of the amendment.

The state's purpose of the statute was to improve the quality of its citizens in all ways: morally, physically, and mentally. However, the individual has rights that must be protected. "No emergency has arisen which renders knowledge by a child of some language other than English so clearly harmful as to justify its inhibition with the consequent infringement of rights long freely enjoyed."

The statute only interfered with the teaching of modern languages and left absolute freedom for other matters. For this reason, there seemed to be no proper reason for the suggestion that the purpose of the statute was to protect the child's health by limiting his mental abilities.

Decision: The Supreme Court of Nebraska had affirmed the judgment of conviction. It held that the statute forbidding this did not conflict with the Fourteenth Amendment, but was indeed a valid exercise of the police power.

The judgment of the state court was reversed by the U.S. Supreme Court. There was much consideration given to what, exactly, the Fourteenth Amendment included. Without doubt, it included not only "freedom from bodily restraint but also the right of the individual to contract, to engage in any of the common occupations of life, to acquire useful knowledge, to marry, establish a home and bring up children, to worship God according to the dictates of his own conscience, and generally to enjoy those privileges long recognized at common law as essential to the orderly pursuit of happiness by free men." This doctrine has established that one's liberty may not be interfered with, under the premise of protecting the public interest, by legislative action, which is arbitrary or without reasonable relation to some purpose within the competency of the state to effect. To decide what makes up proper exercise of police power is not final or conclusive but rather it is subject to supervision by the courts.

Therefore, the decision was reversed.

Justice Holmes and Justice Sutherland dissented. Due to Holmes' frequent dissents from the majority's opinions, Holmes earned the label "the Great Dissenter." Many of his dissenting opinions formed the basis of later majority rulings.

Debra P. v. Turlington
474 F. Supp. 244 (M.D. FL 1979)
U.S. District Court, M.D. Florida, Tampa Division

Topic: The case *Debra P. v. Turlington* addresses a Fourteenth Amendment challenge to Florida's statewide proficiency testing program. A functional literacy test may be required as a prerequisite for a high school diploma, but the test must be a valid measure of instruction.

Facts: There were three classes of Plaintiffs represented in this case:

- All present and future twelfth-grade public school students in the state of Florida who have failed or who hereafter fail the SSAT II.
- All present and future twelfth-grade black public school students in the state of Florida who have failed or who hereafter fail the SSAT II.
- All present and future twelfth-grade black public school students in Hillsborough County, Florida who have failed or hereafter fail the SSAT II.

The plaintiffs' claims include:

- The defendants have either designed or implemented a test or testing program (SSAT II) that is racially biased and /or violates the equal protection clause of the Fourteenth Amendment.
- The defendants have instituted a program of awarding diplomas without providing the plaintiffs with adequate notice of the requirements (i.e., passage of the SSAT II) or adequate time to prepare for the required examination in violation of the Fourteenth Amendment.
- Defendants have used the SSAT II as a mechanism for resegregating the Florida public schools through the use of remedial classes for those students failing the examination in violation of the Fourteenth Amendment.

The Test: In 1976, the Florida legislature enacted a comprehensive piece of legislation known as the "Educational Accountability Act of 1976." In a subsection of this act entitled "Pupil Progression," the legislature established three standards for graduation from Florida public high schools.

1. Students must complete a minimum number of credits for graduation determined by their school board.
2. The second requirement made compulsory the mastery of basic skills.
3. Required satisfactory performance in functional literacy as determined by the Florida State Board of Education.

This subsection provided that each school district must develop procedures for remediation of students who were unable to meet the required standards.

Also, the legislation provided for a comprehensive testing program to evaluate basic skill development at periodic intervals. In 1978, the act was amended by the Florida legislature to require passage of a functional literacy examination prior to receipt of a state graduation diploma. Those students who completed the minimum number of required high school credits but failed the functional literacy examination would receive a certificate of completion.

The Test Results: In a review of the results (1977), administration of the SSAT indicates that there were substantial numbers who failed the test.

The first administration results: Of the 115,901 students taking the test, 36 percent failed one or both sections; 78 percent of the black students failed one or both sections compared to 25 percent of the white students.

The second administration results: 74 percent of black students taking the test for the second time failed one or both sections as compared to 25 percent of white students.

The third administration results: 60 percent of black students taking the test for the third time failed as compared to 36 percent of the white students.

Note: The failure rate among black students was approximately ten times that among white students.

Findings: The case established two major requirements for diploma sanction testing: adequate notice and curricular validity. Adequate notice requires that students be told what a graduation test will cover several years before the test is implemented. District Judge Carr found that the test violated both the equal protection and due process clauses of the Constitution and enjoined its use as a diploma sanction until the 1982–1983 school year, thus giving students adequate time to prepare for the test.

Curricular validity means that the schools are teaching what is being tested and the state must collect data to demonstrate curricular validity. Regarding the due process claim, the appeals court affirmed the trial court's conclusion that thirteen months' notice of the test requirement was insufficient for students to prepare for the test used as a diploma sanction.

On appeal, the Fifth Circuit Court of Appeals affirmed many of this court's findings; however, the appellate court remanded the case for further factual findings on two issues—specifically, whether or not the functional literacy test covers material actually taught in Florida's classrooms, and, in addition, the court of appeals requested a reexamination of the role of discrimination of twelfth-grade black students.

After a lengthy trial on remand, the district court ruled that the injunction should be lifted, and the appeals court affirmed this decision in 1984. By presenting substantial evidence, including curriculum guides and survey data, the state convinced the judiciary that the test was instructionally valid in that it covered material taught to Florida's students. Also, the state substantiated that lingering effects of past school segregation did not cause racial differences in pass rates. To the contrary, data showing significant improvement among African American students during the six years the test had been administered convinced the court that the testing program could help remedy the effects of past discrimination.

Lau v. Nichols
Supreme Court of United States, 1974
414 U.S. 563, 94 S.Ct. 786

Argued December 10, 1973   **Decided January 21, 1974**

Topic: School system's failure to provide English language instruction to Chinese-speaking immigrants.

Issue: Whether the failure of the San Francisco School District to provide English instruction or other adequate instructional procedures to 1,800 students of Chinese ancestry violates the Fourteenth Amendment and

Section 601 of the Civil Rights Act of 1964. Section 601 of the Civil Rights Act of 1964 bans discrimination based on race, color, or national origin in any program or activity receiving federal financial assistance.

Facts: The district court found that there were 2,856 students of Chinese ancestry in the school system who did not speak English. Of these students, 1,800 did not receive any supplemental courses in the English language.

These students initiated a class action against the school system alleging violations of the Fourteenth Amendment and Section 601 of the Civil Rights Act of 1964. The district court denied relief. The court of appeals affirmed, stating that there was no violation of the equal protection clause of the Fourteenth Amendment nor of Section 601 of the Civil Rights Act of 1964. The appellate court held that all students had different educational advantages and disadvantages. The students appealed.

Findings of the U.S. Supreme Court: The Supreme Court reversed the decision. Justice Douglas delivered the majority opinion. It was held that the school district, which received federal financial assistance, violated Section 601 of the Civil Rights Act of 1964, which bans discrimination based on race, color, or national origin in any program or activity receiving federal financial assistance, and furthermore, the implementing regulations of the Health, Education, and Welfare (HEW) Department were violated by failing to provide a program to deal with the students.

Justice Stewart gave a concurring opinion, in which Justices Burger and Blackmun joined. Justice Stewart expressed an opinion that Section 601 of the Civil Rights Act of 1964, standing alone, had not been violated but that regulations and guidelines of the HEW had been violated.

Justice Blackmun also gave a concurring opinion, in which Justice Burger also joined. Justice Blackmun emphasized the substantial number of students whose needs were not being met. Therefore, he would not consider the decision conclusive where only a few students were involved.

Rationale: The court stated that "there is no equality of treatment merely by providing students the same facilities, textbooks, teachers, and curriculum; for students who do not understand English are effectively foreclosed from any meaningful education." The Court held that basic English skills are at the core of what public schools teach. Therefore, it cannot be assumed that a child will enter school having already acquired these basic language skills.

Also, by Section 602 of the act, HEW is authorized to issue rules, regulations, and orders to make sure recipients of federal aid conduct any projects consistently with Section 601. In 1970, HEW issued clarifying guidelines. They mandated that "where inability to speak and understand the English language excludes national origin-minority group children from effective participation in the educational program offered by a school district, the district must take affirmative steps to rectify the language deficiency in order to open its instructional program to these students."

Based on the HEW regulations and the core of the Civil Rights Act of 1964, the Supreme Court ruled in favor of the students.

Justice Douglas wrote the unanimous opinion of the Court, which determined that:

1. Even though the California Education Code states that English shall be the basic language of instruction in all schools, the school districts may determine when and under what circumstances instructions may be given bilingually.
2. It is the policy of the state to ensure the mastery of English by all pupils in the schools.
3. Bilingual instruction is authorized to the extent that it does not interfere with the systematic, sequential, and regular instruction of all pupils in the English language.
4. The Education Code requires that no pupil shall receive a diploma of graduation from grade 12 who has not met the standards of proficiency in English, as well as other prescribed subjects.
5. The Education Code requires that children between the ages of six and sixteen years are subject to compulsory full-time education.
6. Merely providing students with the same facilities, textbooks, teachers, and curriculum does not provide equality of treatment for students who do not understand English and they are effectively foreclosed from any meaningful education.
7. Imposition of a requirement that a child acquire basic English skills before he can effectively participate in the educational program is to make a mockery of public education.

8. Those who do not understand English are certain to find their classroom experiences wholly incomprehensible and in no way meaningful.
9. The equal protection clause is not violated, but Section 601 of the Civil Rights Act of 1964 is violated.
10. The school system receives large amounts of federal financial assistance and is therefore subject to the Civil Rights Act of 1964.
11. The Department of Health, Education, and Welfare guidelines require school districts that are federally funded to rectify the language deficiency in order to open the institution to students who had "linguistic deficiencies."
12. Discrimination on the basis of race or national origin is barred, even if no purposeful design is present.
13. The district must take affirmative steps to rectify the language deficiency in order to open its instructional program to students who do not speak or understand the English language.
14. Any ability grouping or tracking system employed by the school system to deal with the special language skill needs of national original minority-group children must be designed to meet such language skill needs as soon as possible and must not operate as an educational dead-end or permanent track.
15. Simple justice requires that public funds, to which all taxpayers of all races contribute, not be spent in any fashion that encourages, entrenches, subsidizes, or results in racial discrimination.

Justice Blackmun wrote a concurring opinion that stated, in part, concerning the 1,800 children of Chinese ancestry who do not speak English, "We can only guess as to why they have had no exposure to English in their preschool years. Earlier generations of American ethnic groups have overcome the language barriers by earnest parental endeavors or by the hard fact of being pushed out of the family or community nest and into the realities of broader experience." He said that if there were only a few students involved here, he would not have concurred with the opinion that the district must provide special English language instruction, but the fact that there are 1,800 students involved

in this case make it significant. He said that numbers were at the heart
of the case.

Keefe v. Geanakos
U.S. Court of Appeals
First Circuit, 1969
418 F.2d 359

History: The District Court of Massachusetts denied the plaintiff's request
for injunctive relief. The injunction was sought by the plaintiff for an alleged wrongful suspension and threatened dismissal from the Ipswich
school system. In order for injunctive relief to be issued, a plaintiff must
satisfy two requirements to show himself entitled. According to Chief
Judge Thomsen, neither of the conditions were met. He cited a case with
similar facts, *Parker v. Board of Ed.*, as precedent as to why there is reasonable probability that he will not prevail in litigation. Furthermore,
Judge Thomsen reasoned that there was no evidence of irreparable harm.

Topic: Academic freedom—the use of a "dirty" word in the classroom as
part of instruction.

Issue: This case involves a question of whether a teacher may, for educational purposes, quote and explore a "dirty" word and does the school
have a right to suspend/dismiss the teacher.

Facts: On the first day of school in September 1969, the plaintiff (Mr. Keefe)
gave a copy of *Atlantic Monthly* magazine (September 1969 issue) and assigned an article for reading. The article, authored by Robert J. Lifton, entitled *The Young and the Old*, referenced the "dirty" word in question several
times. Mr. Keefe discussed the article in class and explained the "dirty"
word, its origin, context, and the reasons the author included it.

The school department supplied the copies of the magazine that Mr.
Keefe had used. In addition, Mr. Keefe did offer an alternative assignment
to anyone who was personally offended by the reading.

The next evening, Mr. Keefe was asked to defend his use of the word
at a meeting of the school committee. Following his explanation, a majority of the committee informally asked Mr. Keefe to agree not to use the
word again in class. He then explained that he could not in good conscience agree. No official action was taken at the meeting. Thereafter, Mr.

Keefe was suspended and it was proposed that he be dismissed. The plaintiff was given a list of five charges on which his grounds for dismissal were being sought, but it was agreed that all charges were contingent upon the outcome of the third charge, which was based on "the use of offensive material in a classroom which undermines public confidence and may react unfavorably on the school system of Ipswich."

Findings of the U. S. Court of Appeals: Opinion delivered by Chief Judge Aldrich.

The court found the Lifton article to be scholarly, thought provoking, and not pornographic. The court also recognized that although the word in question may be offensive to some, it is important to the development and conclusion of the article.

The court agreed with defendants that what is said and/or read to students should be age appropriate, citing *Ginsberg v. New York*. Furthermore, in all other instances, the use of improper language, no matter how offensive, is to be dependent on the circumstances surrounding the use of the word or words.

The court of appeals did not accept the district court opinion that *Parker v. Board of Education* was "strikingly similar on its facts" and reasoned that outside of the issue of academic freedom little else about the case is similar. This is relevant because the district court cited this case as precedent to why the plaintiff would not be successful in future litigation and hence did not fulfill one of the two requirements for injunctive relief.

The court of appeals accepted the district court conclusion that "some measure of public regulation of classroom speech is inherent in every provision of public education," but the facts of this case suggest that this concept does not apply here due to a possible infringement on academic freedom and censorship.

The court believed that it was probable that the plaintiff would prevail on the issue of lack of any notice that a discussion of the article with his class was forbidden conduct. This is because the regulation the defendants rely on, although worthy, is not appropriate due to the fact that there are no fewer than five books in the school library that contain the "dirty" word. Since the students can gain access to the word in the school library, the teacher should not be subject to punishment for discussing the content of those books. The court states, "This inconsistency on part of the school is fatal."

It was also the opinion of the court of appeals that irreparable injury is involved because the plaintiff, if successful, may recover monetary damages. The district court had reasoned that there was no risk of irreparable harm, but academic freedom is not preserved by compulsory retirement, even at full pay.

Finally, the question of whether to grant injunctive relief, the court believed this was a case for action under Local Rule 5. The order of the district court denying an injunction is reversed and the case is remanded for further proceedings.

Board of Education v. Pico
Certiorari to the U.S. Court of Appeals
for the Second Circuit
No. 80-2043

Argued March 2, 1982   **Decided June 25, 1982**

Topic: This case questions whether or not the First Amendment does set limitations on the petitioners, the board of education, in removing library books from the Island Trees High School and Junior High School.

Issue: The petitioner, the board of education, rejected recommendations of a committee of parents and school staff that it had appointed, and ordered that certain books be removed from the library shelves. The board characterized the books that were removed as being "anti-American, anti-Christian, anti-Semitic, and just plain filthy." These books were removed from the high school and junior high school libraries. As a result, the students brought an action against the petitioner board members saying that the board of education had denied the students their rights under the First Amendment. The district court granted summary judgment on the board's behalf. The U.S. Court of Appeals reversed the decision. The board petitioned the U.S. Supreme Court, which granted certiorari.

Facts: The petitioners are the Board of Education of the Island Trees Union Free School District in New York. Richard Ahrens was the president of the board and Frank Martin was the vice president. The students, or the respondents in the case, were Steven Pico, Jacqueline Gold, Glenn Yarns, Russel Rieger, and Paul Sochinski.

In September of 1975, three board members—Ahrens, Martin, and Hughes—attended a conference that was given by the Parents of New York United (PONYU), which is a politically conservative organization that consists of parents concerned about education legislation in the state of New York. At the conference, the board members were given a lists of books that were described as being objectionable for students. Martin said that these books were "improper fare for school students."

After the conference the board discovered that nine of these books were in their high school library and that their junior high school library contained one of these books. The high school library contained the following nine books:

1. *Slaughterhouse Five,* by Kurt Vonnegut
2. *The Naked Ape,* by Desmond Morris
3. *Down These Mean Streets,* by Piri Thomas
4. *Best Short Stories of Negro Writers,* edited by Langston Hughes
5. *Go Ask Alice,* anonymous
6. *Laughing Boy,* by Liver Lafarge
7. *Black Boy,* by Richard Wright
8. *A Hero Ain't Nothin but a Sandwich*, by Alice Childress
9. *Soul on Ice*, by Eldrige Cleaver

The junior high school library contained the novel *A Reader for Writers* by Jerome Archer.

In February of 1976, the board members gave an "unofficial direction" that the books be removed from the library shelves and sent to the board offices, so that the board could read them. The publicity of this spread and the board said that it was their "moral obligation to protect the children in our schools from this moral danger."

Soon after this, the board formed a Book Review Committee, which consisted of four parents and four members of the staff to read the books and recommend to the board whether the books should be retained. The committee said that five of the books above should be retained, including one from the twelfth-grade curriculum. These were *The Fixer, Laughing Boy, Black Boy, Go Ask Alice,* and *Best Short Stories of Negro Writers.* They did ask for two to be removed, *The Naked Ape* and *Down These Mean Streets.* The remaining four books the committee could not agree on and one they didn't have time to read.

The Board rejected the committee's recommendations by saying that all the books should be removed from the library except for *Laughing Boy,* and that *Black Boy* could be read with the parents' approval.

The district court said that they agreed with the motivations of the board's actions and the board did not act on religious principles but on conservative educational philosophy. The court said the students' First Amendment rights had not been infringed upon, because school boards had the power to create educational policy.

A three-judge panel of the U.S. Court of Appeals of the Second Circuit reversed the judgment and remanded the action for trial. The case was appealed and heard by the U.S. Supreme Court.

Decision of the U. S. Supreme Court: With a ruling of 5-4, the Court decided that the local school board may not remove books from school libraries because it dislikes the ideas contained in the books.

Findings: Justice Brennan announced the decision of the Court in which Justice Marshall and Justice Stevens joined and Justice Blackmun joined, except for part IIA. The justices based their decisions on two questions: (1) Does the First Amendment impose any limitations upon the discretion of petitioners to remove the library books? and (2) If so, did the petitioners exceed those limitations?

They recognized that the Court has always given schools boards the broad discretion to the management of schools. They also acknowledged that federal courts do not usually intervene in the conflicts that arise in public school systems based on *Tinker v. Des Moines School District.* And the justices do agree that the board "has the right to establish and apply their curriculum in such a way to as to transmit community values." Yet the Court recognized that local school boards must exercise their powers in a manner that deals with the First Amendment. Here they examined *West Virginia Board of Education v. Barnette,* which held that under the First Amendment a student in a public school did not have to salute the flag. In this case it was reasoned that boards of education have highly discretionary functions that they must maintain within the First Amendment rights.

Yet the justices did believe that the First Amendment rights of students might be directly and sharply affected by the removal of books from the shelves of a school library. They reminded the people that Madison wrote, "people who mean to be their own Governors, must arm themselves with the power which knowledge gives." The justices noted that the board of education might be able to extend their power into the classroom environment but that they could not extend this power into the library where reading the books is a voluntary act. Therefore, they decided that school boards may not remove books from school library shelves because they dislike the ideas in the books because they want to decide what is orthodox in matters of politics, nationalism, religion, or other areas.

The Court also ruled that the board's decision to remove the books was extremely irregular, as it ignored the advice of the Book Review Committee. This procedure sent a message to the Court that the board was trying to impose its ideas on the students and that the decision was not based on the educational suitability of the books.

Justice Blackmun: Justice Blackmun agreed with the ideas of the plurality except in part IIA. Blackmun stated that the school board must be able to show that its action was caused by something more than a mere desire to avoid the conflict occurring when different opinions arise. Yet he did state that school boards must be able to choose one book over another when one book relates better to the curriculum, and that those decisions would not implicate First Amendment values. Here, Justice Blackmun cited *Pierce v. Society of Sisters* in stating that the school board can refuse a book because it contains offensive language or because it is psychologically or intellectually inappropriate for the age group. He also pointed out that the school board could choose a book because they believed that one subject was more important than the other. Blackmun, however, did recognize that the school board cannot take books out of the library simply because the board did not like the ideas contained in them.

Justice White: White agreed with Blackmun and the other justices in the decisions of the case, and agreed a trial was necessary to resolve the factual issues. Yet White did not believe it was necessary to discuss the First Amendment issues in the case in terms of how the board's discretion could be limited based on First Amendment issues.

In review of the case, the Fifth Circuit summarized the U.S. Supreme Court's essential points.

1. The library is a place of voluntary inquiry.
2. Students must be free to inquire and to gain understanding, and the school library is the center of this freedom.
3. The power of the school board in educational decisions diminishes when the challenged decision involves a noncurricular matter.

4. Because the library is a voluntary place for public use and because it is not a part of the school curriculum, it is subject to constitutional limitations.
5. School officials cannot remove books from shelves because they dislike the ideas contained in them, because the students do have a First Amendment right to receive information.
6. If school officials remove books because of their intention to deny students access to ideas, then this is a violation of the Constitution.
7. It is not unconstitutional if the school board removes books because they are "pervasively vulgar" or on the grounds of "educational suitability."

Dissenting: Chief Justice Burger with Justice Powell, Justice Rehnquist, and Justice O'Connor dissented. Their dissents all centered on the idea that it was wrong for the Supreme Court to examine a case that centered on educational issues that are traditionally left to the states. They thought it was a lavish expansion of the First Amendment for the Supreme Court to believe that the books inside a school library needed to be reviewed by a federal court.

Epperson v. Arkansas
Supreme Court of the United States
Argued on October 16, 1968   Decided on November 14, 1968

Topic: Instructional programming.

Issue: Is Arkansas's "anti-evolution" statute constitutional? Specifically, is the statute a violation of the teacher's First Amendment right to free speech? In addition is the statute a violation of the Fourteenth Amendment's protection against the establishment of religion by the state?

Facts:

- In 1968, the state of Arkansas had an "anti-evolution" statute, which had been adopted in 1928. That statute made it unlawful for a teacher in any state-supported school or university to teach or to use a textbook that teaches "that mankind ascended or descended from a lower order of animals."
- In a public high school in Little Rock, the school administration on recommendation of the teachers of biology in the school system

adopted and prescribed a textbook that contained a chapter setting forth "the theory about the origin . . . of man from a lower form of animal."

* The following school year, Susan Epperson, a high school biology teacher within the district, brought this action for declaratory and injunctive relief challenging the constitutionality of the "anti-evolution" statute in an effort to protect her job from the state's statute.
* A parent joined the suit wanting to be sure that his two school-aged sons would "be informed of all scientific theories and hypotheses."
* The first court held the statute to be unconstitutional; however, the Arkansas State Supreme Court reversed the lower court's ruling.

Findings of the United States Supreme Court: Justice Fortas, writing for the majority, said,

* The law must be stricken because of its conflict with the constitutional prohibition of state laws respecting a establishment of religion or prohibiting the free exercise thereof.
* The overriding fact is that Arkansas's law selects from the body of knowledge a particular segment that it deemed to conflict with a particular religious doctrine; that is, with a particular interpretation of the book of Genesis by a particular religious group.
* Government in our democracy, state and national, must be neutral in matters of religious theory, doctrine, and practice. It may not be hostile to any religion or to the advocacy of no religion; and it may not aid, foster, or promote one religion or religious theory against another or even against the militant opposite. The First Amendment mandates governmental neutrality between religion and religion, and between religion and nonreligion.
* In *Everson v. Board of Education*, the U.S. Supreme Court, in upholding a state law to provide free bus service to school children including those attending parochial schools, said, "Neither a state nor the federal government can pass laws which aid one religion, aid all religions, or prefer one religion over another."
* In *McCollum v. Board of Education*, the U.S. Supreme Court held that Illinois could not release pupils from class to attend classes of instruction in the school buildings in the religion of their choice. This

would involve the state using tax-supported property for religious purposes, thereby breaching the wall of separation that the First Amendment was intended to erect between church and state.

- Also in *Engel v. Vitale*, while study of religions and of the Bible from a literary and historic viewpoint, presented objectively as part of a secular program of education, need not collide with the First Amendment's prohibition, the state may not adopt programs or practices in its public school or colleges that "aid or oppose" any religion.

Justice Black, concurring, wrote,

- The case does not present a justifiable controversy for this Court to hear. In the forty years that this statute has been on the books, it has never been acted upon.
- The teacher, claiming that she was fearful of dismissal, is not even a teacher in Arkansas anymore, and there is not one iota of concrete evidence to show that the parent intervener's sons have not been or will not be taught about evolution.
- The U.S. Supreme Court leaped "headlong into the middle of the very broad problems involved in federal intrusion into state powers to decide what subjects and schoolbooks it may wish to use in the teaching of state pupils."
- The Arkansas statute should either be struck down as too vague to enforce, or be remanded to the state supreme court for clarification of its holdings and opinions. It should not be struck down as a violation of the First Amendment.

Justice Harlan, concurring, wrote,

- "I think it deplorable that this case should have come to us with such an opaque opinion by the state's highest court. With all respect, that court's handling of the case savors of a studied effort to avoid coming to grips with this anachronistic statute and to 'pass the buck' to this court."
- He concurred only in that the Arkansas statute constitutes an "establishment of religion" forbidden to the state by the Fourteenth Amendment. There should not be any implications otherwise.

Justice Stewart, concurring, wrote,

- The states are free to choose their own curriculums for their own schools. For example, if a state should decide that Spanish will be the only foreign language taught, then it is within its constitutional rights. However, the state does not have the right to make it a criminal offense for a teacher to mention, objectively, that other languages do also exist. This is a clear violation of the teacher's First Amendment's rights.
- It would be for this reason, along with the vagueness, that this statute should be struck down.

Summary: The Arkansas statute was struck down for a variety of reasons:

1. It violated the First Amendment's guarantee to freedom of speech. Teachers should be allowed to objectively present material so long as they do not encourage or discourage one religion over another or religion to nonreligion.
2. It also violated the Fourteenth Amendment's clause that no state shall "establish a religion."
3. It was too vague to be enforced in any reasonable way.

Follow-up Information: McClean v. Board of Education, 1982: In an attempt to circumvent the Epperson decision, Arkansas passed a statute that required balanced treatment for creation science and evolution in the public schools. The U.S. Supreme Court struck down the law, saying that creationism was not a science, but a religious doctrine.

7

Students' Rights

If one had to sum up this chapter in one sentence, the best descriptor would be, "Students do not shed their constitutional rights at the schoolhouse door." Before the case law that has occurred in the last few decades, school officials sometimes answered students' questions about why they should do something by saying, "Because I said so." That kind of dogmatic response describes a time when school officials performed pupil services as if students did not possess procedural or substantive due process rights. That time is past. The wise school administrator creates administrative policy, and follows board policy, based on the principle that students have constitutional rights, perhaps not equivalent to adults, but still significant.

PROCEDURAL DUE PROCESS

For procedural due process to be properly followed, three procedures must be in place. (See *Goss v. Lopez* at the end of this chapter.)

1. Hearing. Before a student can be suspended or expelled, there must be a hearing where the disciplinary charges against the student are specified and explained. The administrator should make the student and the parent aware of what school policy has been violated. If more than one student was involved in the infraction, each individ-

ual student is entitled to a separate hearing. A student is not entitled to have legal counsel present at a disciplinary hearing. This is a quasi-judicial procedure, not a court of law.

2. Notification. The parent of the student must be notified as to the time and place of the hearing so that it can be reasonably assumed that his attendance is assured. Such notification should be done by registered letter to avoid the question as to proper notification.

3. Impartiality. Since the school administrator is serving as both the executive (person who suspended the student) and the judicial (person who hears the appeal), she should ensure that the student be allowed to speak in her own behalf. If new facts come to light that were not known at the time of the suspension or expulsion decision, the administrator should take that into account. Some school systems have separated the functions of suspending or expelling and conducting the hearing to better ensure impartiality. An administrator other than the principal, such as a director of student services, usually conducts the hearing.

Procedural due process as defined by *Goss v. Lopez* creates a time gap between the administrative act of suspension and the beginning of the serving of the suspension. However, there are times when there would be a serious possibility of disruption if the student or students were not removed from the school environment immediately. If there is a clear and present danger, or chance of disruption to the maintenance of an orderly and peaceful learning environment, the student may be removed pending the hearing.

SUBSTANTIVE DUE PROCESS

For over two centuries, the Supreme Court has debated whether there are implicit natural law protections for citizens beyond the explicit wording of the Constitution. Advocates of natural law claim that there are moral laws beyond the specific wording of the Constitution. Among these natural laws are the substantive protection of the right to liberty, equality, and justice (Lloyd L. Weinreb, *Natural Law and Justice*, Cambridge: Harvard University Press, 1987, pp. 224–65). Accordingly, proponents of natural law have argued that there is an implicit meaning in the Constitution that individual rights are not those merely established within the text of the document itself but also include all those natural and moral rights that pertain to fairness, equity, and the pursuit of happiness (D. D. Raphael, *Problems of Political Philsosophy*, London: MacMillan, 1989, pp. 102–3). Justice therefore requires that the courts look not simply to the explicit content of the Constitution but also to the "substance" of the Constitution that is implicit in human rights of transcending moral consequence (Alexander and Alexander, *American Public School Law, 5th ed.*, Belmont, Calif.: West: Thomson Learning, 2001, p. 346).

Although the concept of substantive due process remains somewhat tentative and ambiguous, Supreme Court interpretations and precedents have advanced certain individual rights to be fundamental. Those rights that have particular relevance to education and student rights are the definitions of liberty and property.

In *Meyer v. Nebraska* (see chapter 6), the Court defined liberty to include the right of individuals to contract, to engage in any of the common occupations of life, to acquire useful knowledge, to marry, establish a home and bring up children, to worship God according to dictates of their conscience, and generally enjoy those privileges long recognized in common law as essential to the orderly pursuit of happiness by free men. Thus, the teachers' right to teach and right of parents to engage them so to instruct their children, we think, are within the liberty of the Constitution.

With the *Meyer* decision, the Supreme Court not only acknowledged the substantive protections of due process covering life, liberty, and property but also extended them to protect a person's right to teach and learn.

In *Goss v. Lopez*, the Court cautioned school officials that suspensions and expulsions could seriously damage the students' standing with fellow students and the teachers as well as interfering with later opportunities for higher education and employment. Thus, schools must be diligent in providing procedural due process to ensure no infringement upon substantive due process rights.

The Court also explained property interest in this way: Property interests are not created by the Constitution. Rather they are created and their dimensions are defined by existing rules or understandings that stem from an independent source such as state law-rules or understandings that secure certain benefits and that support claims of entitlement to those benefits. In this regard, the federal Constitution does not create education as a fundamental right, but rather becomes a "property" interest when state law establishes a public educational system, which all children have a right to attend. Thus, when a state creates a public school system, education is effectively established as a property right or interest for all pupils.

IN LOCO PARENTIS

This Latin term, which means in English "in place of the parent," is meant to define the authority that school personnel are given over students in maintaining the order and discipline of the school environment. The concept does not give school personnel chastisement rights equivalent to that of a parent. The proper use of in loco parentis in governing student behavior must be administered through reasonableness and restraint. Although recent court cases and societal trends have challenged many of the aspects of in loco parentis, the concept is still viable in controlling the health, proper surroundings, necessary discipline, and promotion of morality and other wholesome influences, while parental authority is superseded (*Richardson v. Braham*, 125 Neb. 142, 249 N. W. 557 [1933].

FREEDOM OF SPEECH AND EXPRESSION

Legal conflicts between students/parents and the school over free speech and/or expression are decided by balancing the school's interest in maintaining an orderly learning environment with the student's First Amendment rights to free speech and expression. Clearly, students' First Amendment right to free speech/expression is limited. In fact, First Amendment rights to free speech and expression are limited for all citizens. For example, public exposure is illegal except in nudist colonies. A person cannot engage in behavior that causes a public disturbance. If a person stands up in a public place and calls out "Fire!" as a practical joke, he could be arrested for inciting panic. Therefore, it is legally clear that schools may impose limits upon student speech and expression. However, such rights are not unlimited. The courts have ruled differently in cases involving this controversy depending upon circumstances. From these precedents, school officials and personnel can base their policies and actions upon the following reasonably solid principles:

1. Clear policies regarding speech, clothing, hair care, bodily attachments (such as rings, piercing, tattoos, etc.) must be in place prior to any disciplinary action for violations.
2. Policies must be legally defensible as reasonable if challenged by students and parents.
3. Policies must be administered consistently so as to avoid charges of Fourteenth Amendment equal protection, or civil rights violations.
4. School must be able to show that limiting or prohibiting speech or expression is necessary or desirable in order to maintain an orderly teaching and learning environment.
5. In taking disciplinary action, the school must follow procedural due process.
6. In limiting or prohibiting student speech or expression, be able to show that such action was necessary to prevent a "material and substantial" disruption to the educational process.

Two landmark cases, *Tinker v. Des Moines* and *Guzick v. Drebus*, set legal precedent that form the basis for school policymaking concerning student free speech or expression. By comparing and contrasting these cases, school officials can draw the following conclusions:

1. Clear policy must be in place before restrictions on student free speech or expression are exercised. The mere anticipation that student actions may cause a disturbance is not sufficient to sustain serious disciplinary actions such as suspension or expulsion.
2. Past history of the school with regard to student behavior can be a factor to support school policy restricting student expression.
3. Student speech or expression can be limited when the school can show that such expression will cause a material and substantial disruption.

STUDENT PUBLICATIONS

Freedom of the press has long been a cornerstone of American democracy and has been vigorously defended by the Supreme Court. The Court has been especially diligent in preventing "prior restraint," which means censoring publications before they can reach the public. The First Amendment right to free press is strong when the publication is meant for general use, thus creating a public forum.

However, freedom of the press for school-sponsored publications is governed by a different set of rules. School publications are not necessarily a public forum. If the school wishes, it may keep school student publications a "closed forum" or a "nonpublic forum." If the school is consistent in maintaining a nonpublic or closed forum, then it may maintain editorial rights over the student publications subject to certain restrictions. In the landmark case of *Hazelwood v. Kuhlmeier*, the Supreme Court held that educators do not violate students' First Amendment rights to free press by exercising editorial control over school-sponsored newspapers so long as the educators or school board has a legitimate pedagogical reason to prohibit such expression. It is interesting to note that in dealing with the issue of freedom of the press in schools, the Court does not consider germane the *Tinker* precedent of "material and substantial disruption." It is sufficient for educators to show pedagogical reasons for their decisions.

Underground Publications

The *Hazelwood* precedent is clear for school-sponsored publications. Underground publications, not produced on school facilities but distributed there, must be looked at from a different perspective. If the school does not permit any nonschool material to be distributed at school, it could apply this policy to the underground newspaper, and thus prevent its distribution. However, if the school allows other nonschool-sponsored material to be distributed at school, the same rule would apply for the underground newspaper and the educators could not exercise prior restraint. However, if, after distribution, it was held that the underground publication contained objectionable material that caused a material and substantial disruption at school, the school could take disciplinary action against the perpetrators.

If the distribution of nonschool material at school is permitted, the school may place appropriate time, place, and manner restrictions on access to school grounds, but it cannot control the content, as is permitted in school publications. The school has created a limited public forum and thus must remain content-neutral in relation to its policy of distribution.

In summary, school officials may exercise editorial control over school-sponsored publications so long as they have a legitimate pedagogical reason to do so. If the schools allow nonschool publications to be distributed, they have created a "limited public forum" and thus may only control the time, place, and manner of distribution, but relinquish their editorial rights. If the school has a policy that all nonschool publications, including those submitted by students, must be submitted to the administration before distribution, then strong procedural due process must be in place, or the policy is vulnerable to prior restraint violation.

Internet and Free Speech

Law regarding the Internet is in its infancy. The *Reno* case has clearly indicated that the Internet as a communication medium is clearly protected by the First Amendment and is more closely related to print rather than broadcast. Internet, as it relates to instruction or curriculum, clearly comes under the *Hazelwood* precedent, thus making it subject to school regulations. However, student use of the Internet outside the school's curriculum and instructional program, may well be outside the realm of school jurisdiction.

In recent rulings, the Court has realized that the *Hazelwood* precedent does not answer questions concerning Internet use by students that is objectionable to school authorities. Prior restraint is not applicable because of the immediate nature of the Internet. Neither is policy regarding the time, place, and manner of distribution. Therefore, the Court has resorted to the *Tinker* precedent. To discipline a student for Internet activity, the school must show that such activity creates a "material and substantial" disruption with school discipline. Thus, it seems that, until more definitive legal guidelines are drawn, the school authorities could stop Internet communications that depicted educators, students, parents, or the school in a derogatory manner that would interfere with the school's disciplinary policies and procedures.

SEARCH AND SEIZURE

Search and seizure is the subject of the Fourth Amendment to the Constitution. The founding fathers were thinking of the protection of citizens when it was adopted, but as the public school system arose, its application became relevant to school administrators. Due to students' use of drugs, alcohol, tobacco, and the increasing occurrence of the use of violent weapons in schools, the proper use of policy and procedures by school authorities in search and seizure is very important. In the case *New Jersey v. T.L.O.*, the Supreme Court established the guidelines that determine the constitutionality of searches. For the search of a student's person or property to be deemed constitutional, the search must be reasonable at its inception, and be reasonable in scope.

Search and Seizure (Reasonable at Inception)

School authorities are not held to as high a standard as police officers in relation to investigation. The police must have "probable cause" to pursue search. This is, of course, called a search warrant. School authorities are held to the standard of "reasonable suspicion," which carries a lesser "burden of proof." For example, hearsay evidence such as informant's tips are acceptable reasons for school authorities to pursue the search of a student's person or property. Even suspicious behavior in the mind of the school administrator could be reasonable suspicion. The courts recognize that school authorities must be given latitude in administering the disciplinary procedures in a school setting full of minors. Also, teachers and administrators are not trained detectives. However, reasonableness at inception does contain some restrictions. For example, if a principal stops a student for no apparent reason and demands the student empty her personal belongings, reasonableness at inception is not present. If, on the other hand, a principal is walking down a hallway and a group of students immediately disperses in a disorderly and obviously panicked state upon seeing the principal, the principal has reasonable suspicion to act. If a search is initiated, and challenged, the burden of proof is on the school authority to show that "reasonable suspicion" created the reasonableness at inception.

Search and Seizure (Reasonable in Scope)

Once the search has been initiated, the school authority must determine the breadth of the scope. For example, if the principal is following up on an informant's tip that a certain student is selling cocaine, which is stored in his locker, the reasonableness of the scope is restricted to the student's locker. If the drugs are found in the locker, and further investigation reveals that the student is bringing the drugs to school through the use of his automobile, then the scope of the search can be widened to include his car. There must be a nexus between the information guiding the search and the scope of the search.

Let's look at another example to help clarify the meaning of the reasonableness in scope standard. If money was stolen during a physical education class, and the environment was closed to intrusion by other students, the scope of the search to recover the money would be restricted to the facilities used by the students during the class—classroom (the gym), the locker room (where the students dressed and undressed, and the bathroom facilities)—and the clothing and personal possessions of the students in the class. Reasonableness in scope could not be the entire school building and every student in the school.

Strip Searches

Although they are rarely done, strip searches of students are legal. They are sometimes necessary in order to find the evidence needed to pursue disciplinary action, especially in drug investigations. Strip searches should be done by a school authority of the same gender as the student being searched. There should be witnesses of the same gender. Most importantly, assurances should be established that the search is reasonable at inception and in scope. The *Williams* case is an example of a case that was held proper by the courts.

Random Building Searches including Student Lockers

The foregoing discussion of the reasonableness standards might create the impression that random drug searches, using dogs and other devices to detect the presence of drugs, would not be permitted. However, they are considered proper in instances where the school can show that the sale and use of drugs within the school facilities has occurred on a regular basis on a wide scale. This historical precedent creates reasonableness at inception. In view of the fact that the widespread sale and use of drugs by students is occurring, it is reasonable to assume that the drugs are being held throughout the school facilities; therefore the random search could include the entire facilities, thus meeting the reasonable in scope standard (see *Veronica v. Acton*).

WHEN TO CALL THE POLICE

The first rule for school authorities is, "If a crime has been committed, call the police. If disciplinary action only is called for, skin your own skunk." The police want to handle crimes. They do not want to administer and discipline students for school violations.

The second rule for school authorities is, once you turn the matter over to the police, let them handle it. You are not trained in criminal procedures, so do not interfere. Cooperate with the police in the ways that they request.

CORPORAL PUNISHMENT

Interestingly, corporal punishment does not come under the ambit of the Eighth Amendment to the Constitution (see *Ingraham v. Wright*). The courts have upheld the rights of schools to administer corporal punishment as a means of preserving school discipline. The courts have dealt with the degree and reasonableness of the discipline as opposed to whether corporal punishment should be permitted.

In examining a controversy over the administration of corporal punishment, the courts have advocated two standards.

1. The punishment must be reasonable and exerted within bounds of reason and humanity.
2. The punishment must be done in good faith and without malice and not be inflicted wantonly or excessively.

More and more states have stopped permitting corporal punishment. Others give the local school boards the option of deciding the issue at the community level. It is used less often in schools today than in previous eras. Although the courts seem to give educators the benefit of the doubt in these cases, administering corporal punishment puts the teacher or administrator in a vulnerable position. The inflicting of the discipline does not have the same effect or consequence, physically or psychologically. For some students it leaves no physical evidence; for others, serious bruising occurs. The act also causes different psychological reactions.

Opponents of corporal punishment are quick to point out that striking a student with a board paddle and applying terms such as *humane treatment* and *good faith* is an oxymoron. In view of recent legal developments in child abuse and societal mores, from a legal perspective, it seems wise for schools to avoid this type of punishment.

SEXUAL HARASSMENT

Conflicts and controversies involving sexual harassment among teachers, students, and administrators have surfaced in recent years (see *Gebser et al. v. Lago Vista*). The following is a general overview of this emerging legal concept.

Sexual Harassment of Employees

Sexual harassment is a form of sexual discrimination that involves the unwelcome introduction of sexualized conduct into the workplace. The two general categories of sexual harassment are "quid pro quo" and "hostile environment." Such conduct may violate Title VII of the Civil Rights Act of 1964, the U.S. Constitution, and state law.

1. *Quid Pro Quo* occurs when a supervisor/management-level person conditions the granting of a benefit upon the receipt of sexual favors from a subordinate or punishes the subordinate for rejecting the offers.

2. *Hostile Environment* occurs when one or more management-level individuals or coworkers create an atmosphere that has the purpose

or effect of unreasonably interfering with an individual's work performance or of creating an intimidating, hostile, or offensive work environment. The harassment must be sufficiently severe or pervasive to alter the conditions of the complainant's employment. Isolated incidents generally will not support a claim. Courts look at:

a. whether the conduct was verbal, physical, or both;

b. how frequently the conduct was repeated;

c. whether the conduct was hostile, threatening, and/or humiliating or whether it was merely offensive or annoying;

d. whether the alleged harasser was a co-worker or a supervisor; whether others joined in perpetrating the harassment; and

e. whether the harassment was directed at more than one individual.

Examples of types of sexual conduct that may create a hostile environment.

1. Nonverbal/visual: displaying sexually suggestive magazines, cartoons, pinups, posters, and so forth; obscene gestures; lip or tongue motions; sexually explicit e-mail, letters, writing on desks, books, lockers, etc.; sexual computer screensavers; graffiti of a sexual nature; leering/staring in a sexual nature; looking down someone's blouse or up someone's skirt; exposing sexual or private body parts; manipulating objects or food to create a sexual innuendo.

2. Verbal: sexual innuendos, rumors, suggestive comments; comments on clothing or physical appearance; asking unwanted, personal sexual, intimate questions; whistling, catcalls, patronizing names, offensive language; sucking, mooing, kissing, howling sounds; rating appearance, body parts, sexuality; pestering or pressuring for dates/asking for sex or sexual contact; telling sexual jokes, rape jokes or demeaning gender-based jokes; shouting sexual obscenities; teasing, taunting, insulting remarks about sexuality, body parts or attractiveness; commenting about sexual activities, fantasies, sexual orientation/preferences or interests of others or self.

3. Physical: unwanted sexual touching; pulling up, snapping, pulling down, grabbing clothing; physical interference with movements, cornering, blocking or following, leaning over, impeding movement;

blowing on someone's neck, hair, ear; fondling, stroking; licking someone's skin; coerced sexual intercourse, rape, sexual assault; assault; and intimidating physical conduct directed at someone because of her gender; brushing up against, leaning on someone; back or neck rubs; kissing.

Before acting, *always* ask yourself the following:

• Would I want this behavior to be subject of a news article or to appear on the evening news?
• Would I behave this way if my mother, father, sister, or brother were present?
• Would I want someone to act this way toward a loved one?
• Is there equal power and authority between me and the other person?
• Does this conduct further the goals of the school or the district as a whole?

Most people know in their "gut" what is inappropriate behavior. If you answer no to any of these questions, you should reconsider the conduct before acting.

Supervisor to Employee Harassment

Employers can be held vicariously liable for money damages for certain harassing acts of supervisors. When an employee is harassed by a supervisor, the employer will always be liable for the harassment. The question becomes whether or not the employee is entitled to any money damages, and the first question that must be asked is whether the employee has suffered a tangible job detriment:[1]

1. *Tangible job detriment*: if an employee suffers a tangible job detriment, the employer is strictly liable—end of story. A tangible job detriment refers to significant changes in employment status (e.g., termination, demotion, undesirable reassignments, loss of promotion, or significant change in job benefits).

2. *No tangible job detriment exists*: if an employee does *not* suffer a tangible job detriment, the employer can raise an affirmative defense to avoid monetary liability. The employer must show (1) that it "exercised reasonable care to prevent and correct promptly any sexually harassing behavior"; and (2) that the complaining employee "unreasonably failed to take advantage of any preventive or corrective opportunities provided by the employer."

Coworker to Coworker Harassment

The Supreme Court has not addressed the issue of an employer's liability for coworker harassment. Lower courts have, however, held that employers may be liable for coworker harassment, if the employer knew or should have known of the harassment and failed to take immediate corrective action reasonably calculated to end the harassment. The seminal question in most instances is whether a supervisor *with authority to take corrective action* had knowledge of the alleged harassment. If it is determined that a supervisor with authority to take corrective action failed to do so, an employer can be held directly liable for negligently allowing the harassment.

Same-Sex/Gender Harassment

In *Oncale v. Sundowner Offshore Services, Inc.*, 118 S. Ct. 998 (1998), the Supreme Court ruled that same-sex sexual harassment is actionable under Title VII. In this case, a male who was employed as a roustabout on an eight-man platform crew alleged that he was forcibly subjected to humiliating sex-related actions by several of his male coworkers in the presence of the crew and that a male coworker physically assaulted him in a sexual manner and threatened to rape him. After his supervisor's failure to take any action, he quit the job based on his belief that he would have been raped. The Court emphasized that plaintiffs (male or female) "must always prove that the conduct at issue was not merely tinged with offensive sexual connotations, but actually constituted 'discrimination . . . because of sex.'"

Sexual Harassment of Students

Teacher /Faculty on Student Harassment

In Ge*bser v. Lago Vista Independent School District*, 118 S. Ct. 1989 (1998), the Supreme Court imposed a stringent test that a student must meet to recover damages under Title IX of the Education Amendments of 1972, 20 U.S.C. § 1681 et seq., against a school district for the sexual misconduct of a teacher.[2]

1. *Actual knowledge*: the student must first show that the school system had "actual knowledge" of the harassment—"constructive knowledge" will not suffice. In order to show "actual knowledge," an "appropriate person" employed by the school district must have been aware of the sexual harassment. An "appropriate person" is "an official of the recipient entity with authority to take corrective action to end the discrimination."

2. *Deliberate indifference*: the student must also show that the school system reacted with "deliberate indifference" when faced with actual knowledge of the harassment (e.g., the school system took no appropriate action).

Practical Advice: Administrators and teachers should monitor teachers and other staff members who spend an inordinate amount of time with one particular student, who develop an off-campus relationship with a student, who buy expensive gifts for students, or who appear overly interested in the detection of child abuse (e.g., checks students for signs of abuse).

Peer (Student-on-Student) Sexual Harassment

In *Davis v. Monroe County Board of Education*, 119 S. Ct. 1661 (1999), the Supreme Court broadened its ruling in *Gebser v. Lago Vista* by ruling that school districts can be held liable under Title IX of the Education Amendments of 1972, 20 U.S.C. § 1681 et seq., for peer sexual harassment if the school district had "actual" knowledge of the harassment and acted with deliberate indifference.

STUDENTS' RIGHTS CASE SUMMARIES

Norval Goss et al., Appellants v. Eileen Lopez, et al.
Appeal from the U.S. District Court for the Southern District of Ohio Supreme Court of the United States
419 U.S. 565 (1975)
73-898
Argued October 16, 1974   Decided January 22, 1975

Topic: Due Process, hearing, or notice.

Issue: Did the imposition of the suspensions without preliminary hearings violate students' rights, which is guaranteed by the due process clause of the Fourteenth Amendment?

Facts: Nine students were suspended for ten days from their respective schools in Columbus, Ohio, for school misconduct. The school principals did not hold hearings before issuing the suspensions because they claimed that Ohio statute permits this type of action by school administrators without first conducting hearings or giving oral or written notice.

Dwight Lopez, a student at Central High School in Columbus, Ohio, was suspended in connection with a disturbance in the lunchroom, which involved some physical damage to school property. He testified that at least seventy-five other students were suspended from his school on the same day. (The principal suspended seventy-five students for racial disruptions in the lunchroom and damage to school property.) Lopez also claimed that he was just an innocent bystander and was not part of the destructive conduct. He did not have a hearing and there was no evidence in the record to indicate that Lopez was guilty.

Betty Crome along with other students was arrested and taken to the police station. She was released without being charged. Following this event, Betty was suspended for ten days. Again, no hearing was held and there was no record to indicate on what basis this decision was made.

Carl Smith was suspended without a hearing and school files did not contain any information about any evidence against him.

The principals' actions were challenged with a class action against the appellant school officials seeking a declaration that the Ohio statute permitting such suspensions was unconstitutional and an order enjoining the officials to remove the references to the suspensions from the students' records.

On the basis of these facts, the three-judge federal court declared that the students (plaintiffs) were denied due process because they were "suspended without hearing prior to suspension or within a reasonable time thereafter," and that Ohio Rev. Code Section 3313.66 (1972) and regulations issued were unconstitutional in permitting such suspensions. The court also ordered that all references to the plaintiffs' suspensions be removed from school files. The school disagreed and appealed the decision.

Norval Goss, along with other administrators of the Columbus, Ohio, public school system challenged the judgment of the three-judge federal court. They argued that the Administrative Guide of the Columbus Public Schools provided that pupils may be suspended or expelled from school in accordance with the provisions of Section 3313.66 of the Revised Code.

Finding of the U.S. Supreme Court: The Court in a 5-4 decision stated that students who are suspended for ten days or less are entitled to certain rights before their suspension. These rights include oral or written notice of the charges, an explanation of the evidence against them, and an opportunity for students to present their side of the story. Furthermore, a student could be suspended immediately in case of emergency and a hearing scheduled as soon as possible. They were not granted the right to legal council, nor the right to call or cross-examine witnesses.

Rationale: Students facing temporary suspension from a public school have property interests as well as liberty interests that qualify for protection under the due process clause of the Fourteenth Amendment. The most apparent requirement of the due process clause is that states afford certain procedures before depriving individuals of "life, liberty, or property." This is a guarantee of basic fairness. People will feel that the government has treated them fairly and accurate results will follow the use of fair procedures. In this case, the justices considered the meaning of due process for students who were suspended for allegedly violating school rules.

In *Tinker v. Des Moines School District* (1969) protesting students who wore black armbands to protest the Vietnam War were protected from suspension. The students were free to express opinions at odds with the government and therefore could not be indoctrinated with other beliefs by educators. Justice Abe Fortas wrote: "It can hardly be argued that either students or teachers shed their constitutional rights . . . at the schoolhouse gate. . . . Students in school as well as out of school are 'persons' under our Constitution."

Former Justice Hugo Black, one of the Court's strongest defenders of the First Amendment, dissented and wrote that the *Goss v. Lopez* decision "subjects all the public schools in the country to the whims and caprices of their loudest mouthed, but maybe not their brightest, students."

There were four justices who dissented: Chief Justice Burger, Mr. Justice Rehnquist, Mr. Justice Blackmun, and Mr. Justice Powell.

These justices, in dissenting, wrote that in the Court's action to invalidate an Ohio statute that permits student suspension from school without a hearing, and opens the door for judicial intervention in the operation of public schools that may adversely affect the quality of education. Secondly, it allows for the right of students not to be suspended for even a single day without notice and a due process hearing. Finally, in their opinion, "a student's interest in education is not infringed by a suspension within the limited period prescribed by Ohio law. Moreover, to the extent that there may be some arguable infringement, it is too speculative, transitory, and insubstantial to justify imposition of a constitutional rule."

Justices: William O. Douglas—(majority) associate justice; William J. Brennan Jr.—(majority) associate justice; Potter Stewart—(majority) associate justice; Byron R. White—(majority) associate justice, wrote an opinion; Thurgood Marshall—(majority) associate justice; Warren E. Burger—(dissent) chief justice, agreed with opinion written by Powell; Harry A. Blackmun—(dissent) associate justice, agreed with opinion written by Powell; Lewis F. Powell Jr.—(dissent) associate justice, wrote an opinion; William H. Rehnquist—(dissent) associate justice, agreed with opinion written by Powell.

Reasoning: The *Goss v. Lopez* case and other 5-4 Supreme Court decisions raise the question of how the Court could be so severely divided. The answer is found in the nature of reasoning. Reasoning is explaining or justifying why a justice decided to choose one side over another in a conflict. That reasoning is based upon the legal factors that support one side over another. This could include precedents (previously decided Court decisions that are supposed to guide judges in deciding present similar cases), the law (existing constitutional and statutory laws that apply to the case in question), and other factors (these include political affiliation of the justice, his or her personal ideology, or experience, etc.).

List of Precedents for Goss v. Lopez: *Tinker v. Des Moines* (1969): Students do not shed their constitutional rights at the schoolhouse door. And the Court has repeatedly emphasized the need for affirming the comprehensive authority of the States and of school officials, consistent with fundamental constitutional safeguards to prescribe and control conduct in the schools.

West Virginia Board of Education v. Barnette (1943): The Fourteenth Amendment, as now applied to the states, protects the citizen against the state itself and all of its creatures—boards of education not excepted.

Fuentes v. Shevin (1972): The length and consequent severity of a deprivation is not decisive of the basic right to a hearing of some kind.

Wisconsin v. Constantineau (1971): The due process clause forbids arbitrary deprivations of liberty.

Epperson v. Arkansas (1968): By and large, public education in our nation is committed to the control of state and local authorities.

Grannis v. Ordean (1914:): The fundamental requisite of due process of law is the opportunity to be heard.

San Antonio School District v. Rodriguez (1973): Education is not a right protected by the Constitution.

Tinker v. Des Moines Independent School District
Argued November 12, 1968   Decided February 24, 1969

Facts: In December 1965, a group of adults and students in Des Moines held a meeting at the Eckhardt home. The group, determined to publicize their objections to the Vietnam War and their support for a truce, decided to wear black armbands during the holiday season. John Tinker, fifteen years old, his sister Mary Beth Tinker, thirteen years old, and Christopher Eckhardt, sixteen years old, decided to wear their armbands to school. The principals of the involved schools heard about their plan and along with the school board developed a policy that stated that any student wearing the armbands would be asked to remove them and if they refused they would be suspended. When the Tinker children and Christopher Eckhardt wore the armbands to school, they were asked to remove them. The children refused and were suspended until after New Year's Day. The parents of the students filed suit asking that the children not be disciplined and also asked for nominal damages.

The Lower Court Decision: The district court dismissed the case on the grounds that the regulation was within the school board's power in order to prevent a school disturbance. The court referred to but expressly declined to follow the Fifth Circuit's holding in a similar case that the wearing of symbols like the armbands cannot be prohibited unless it "materially and substantially interferes with the requirements of appropriate discipline in the operation of the school" (*Burnside v. Byars*, 1963). The court of appeals was split and offered no opinion and upheld the lower court's decision.

The question presented to the Supreme Court was: Does a prohibition against the wearing of armbands in public school, as a form of symbolic protest, violate the First Amendment's freedom of speech protections?

The Supreme Court's Decision: The Supreme Court reversed the lower court's decision by a 7-2 majority decision against the school and in favor of the students wearing the armbands, provided their actions or speech do not interfere with school work or the rights of others in the classroom. The wearing of armbands was "closely akin to pure speech" protected by the First Amendment. School environments imply limitations on free expression, but in this case, the principals lacked justification for imposing any such limits. The principals had failed to show that the forbidden conduct would substantially interfere with appropriate school discipline.

First Amendment rights, applied in light of the special characteristics of the school environment, are available to teachers and students. Both students and teachers do not give up their constitutional rights to freedom of speech or expression at the "schoolhouse gate." It also stated that the school did not show that there was any disruption involved—only that the regulation was made to avoid the chance of disruption, and the chance of disruption is not a strong enough reason to take away the right to free speech. It was also relevant that the school did not prohibit the wearing of all symbols of political controversial significance. For example, students wore buttons relating to national political campaigns without penalty. The Court said it is clearly unconstitutional to prohibit one particular opinion.

As for teachers' rights, the Court pointed out that teachers are hired to teach a particular curriculum and may be bound by that.

The Precedents:

Waugh v. Mississippi University (1915): The Court ruled that the states control institutions they established and that the state can prohibit things it believes distracts from the purpose which the state desired to exist.

Meyer v. Nebraska (1923): The Court ruled that laws that interfered with the liberty of teacher, student, and parent were unconstitutional.

Cox v. Louisiana (1965): The Court ruled that the rights to free speech and assembly do not mean that anyone with opinions or beliefs to express may address a group at any public place and at any time.

Hammond v. South Carolina State College (1967): Court ruled that people in public schools are protected by constitutional rights.

Thomas Guzick Jr. v. Donald L. Drebus et al.
U.S. District Court, N.D. Ohio, Eastern Division
305 F. Supp. 472–April 2, 1969

Facts: Thomas Guzick was a seventeen-year-old junior at Shaw High School in East Cleveland, Ohio. Guzick wore a button to school on March 11, 1969, that was promoting an antiwar demonstration. The school principal, Mr. Drebus, ordered the plaintiff to remove the button. Guzick refused to remove the button and was suspended from school until he returned to school without the button. Guzick alleged that his right to wear this button was protected by the First Amendment to the Constitution, and that his suspension deprives him of rights guaranteed by the Constitution; and, further that his suspension was without just cause, without a hearing, and without due process of law. Guzick also alleged that similar buttons were being worn in other high schools in the Cleveland area, and that the acts of the defendants denying the plaintiff his right to wear a similar button deprived him of the equal protection of the law as guaranteed by the Fourteenth Amendment.

The plaintiff sought a temporary restraining order enjoining the defendants from interfering with the plaintiff's right to wear the button while attending school and from refusing to reinstate the plaintiff. He also sought a declaratory judgment that any rule or regulation of the East Cleveland Board of Education proscribing the wearing of such buttons was unconstitutional, and sought damages in the amount of $1,000 per day for every day that the plaintiff was compelled to miss school.

Findings: On February 24, 1969, the U.S. Supreme Court decided *Tinker v. Des Moines* and this landmark case helped formed the basis of this litigation.

The Court found that a rule permitting the wearing of some buttons and not others would lead to disruptions of the educational process at Shaw. Similarly, the rule, which permits the wearing of any button, would occasion the wearing of provocative and inciting buttons and would also disrupt the educational process.

The Court found that if all buttons are permitted or if any buttons are permitted, a serious discipline problem would result, racial tension would occur, and the education process would be significantly disrupted.

The Court stated that the evidence in this case had made it abundantly clear that the school authorities have a factual basis upon which to forecast substantial disruption of school activities if student behavioral conduct regarding the wearing of buttons was not regulated. Therefore, the Court found the issues in this case in favor of the defendants.

Guzick v. Drebus
U.S. Court of Appeals, Sixth Circuit
No. 19681–September 16, 1970

Findings: The court of appeals was persuaded that the factual findings of the district judge were fully supported by the evidence and agreed with the decisions.

Rationale: "Denying Shaw High School the right to enforce this small disciplinary rule (not wearing buttons) could, and most likely would, impair the rights of its students to an education and the rights of its teachers to fulfill their responsibilities" (Weik and O'Sullivan).

Dissenting Opinion: "When a few students noticed the button which the appellant was wearing, and asked him 'what it said' the appellant's explanation resulted only in a casual reaction and there was no indication that the wearing of the button would disrupt the work and discipline on the school. I am of the opinion that the judgment of the district court should be reversed and the case dismissed upon the authority of *Tinker v. Des Moines Independent School District*" (McAllister).

Guzick v. Drebus
Supreme Court of the United States
March 1, 1971

Petition for writ of certiorari to the U.S. Court of Appeals for the Sixth Circuit was denied.

It was noted that Justice Douglas is of the opinion that certiorari should be granted.

Hazelwood School District v. Kuhlmeier
484 U.S. 260 (1988)

Topic: The case concerns the extent to which educators may exercise editorial control over the contents of a high school newspaper produced as part of the school's journalism curriculum.

Issue: Were the First Amendment rights of the students violated?

Facts: Petitioners are the Hazelwood School District in St. Louis County, Missouri; various school officials; Robert Eugene Reynolds, the principal of Hazelwood East High School; and Howard Emerson, a teacher in the school district. Respondents are three former Hazelwood East students who were staff members of *Spectrum*, the school newspaper. They contend that school officials violated their First Amendment rights by deleting two pages of articles from the May 13, 1983, issue of *Spectrum*.

The *Spectrum* was written and edited by the Journalism 2 class at Hazelwood East. The newspaper was published every three weeks or so during the 1982–1983 school year. More than 4,500 copies of the newspaper were distributed during that year to students, school personnel, and members of the community.

The board of education allocated funds from its annual budget for the printing of *Spectrum*. These funds were supplemented by proceeds from sales of the newspaper. The printing expenses during the 1982–1983 school year totaled $4,668.50; revenue from sales was $1,166.84. The other costs associated with the newspaper, such as supplies, textbook, and a portion of the journalism teacher's salary, were paid entirely by the board.

The Journalism 2 course was taught by Robert Stergos for most of the 1982–1983 academic year. Stergos left Hazelwood East to take a job in private industry on April 29, 1983, when the May 13 edition of the *Spec-*

trum was nearing completion, and petitioner Emerson took his place as newspaper adviser for the remaining weeks of the term.

The practice at Hazelwood East during the spring 1983 semester was for the journalism teacher to submit page proofs of each *Spectrum* issue to Principal Reynolds for his review prior to publication. On May 10, Emerson delivered the proofs of the May 13 edition to Reynolds, who objected to two of the articles scheduled to appear in that edition. One of the stories described three Hazelwood East students' experiences with pregnancy; the other discussed the impact of divorce on students at the school.

Reynolds was concerned that, although the pregnancy story used false names "to keep the identity of these girls a secret," the pregnant students still might be identifiable from the text. He also believed that the article's references to sexual activity and birth control were inappropriate for some of the younger students at the school. In addition, Reynolds was concerned that a student identified by name in the divorce story had complained that her father wasn't spending enough time with her mom, her sister, and her prior to the divorce, was always out of town on business or out late playing cards with the guys, and "always argued about everything" with her mother. Reynolds believed that the student's parents should have been given an opportunity to respond to these remarks or to consent to their publication. He was unaware that Emerson had deleted the student's name from the final version of the article.

Reynolds believed that there was no time to make the necessary changes in the stories before the scheduled press run and that the newspaper would not appear before the end of the school year if printing was delayed to any significant extent. He concluded that his only options under the circumstances were to publish a four-page newspaper instead of the planned six-page newspaper, eliminating the two pages on which the offending stories appeared, or to publish no newspaper at all.

Findings: The U.S. District Court for the Eastern District of Missouri: No First Amendment rights had been violated. School officials may impose restraints on students' speech in activities that are "an integral part of the school's educational function," including the publication of a school-sponsored newspaper by a Journalism class—so long as their decision has "a substantial and reasonable basis."

The Court of Appeals for the Eighth Circuit reversed: Officials had violated respondents' First Amendment rights by deleting the two pages of the newspaper. The court held at the outset that *Spectrum* was not only "a part of the school adopted curriculum," but also a public forum, because the newspaper was "intended to be an operated as a conduit for student viewpoint."

The U.S. Supreme Court, granted certiorari, and reversed: No violation of First Amendment rights occurred. The Court agreed with the district court, that school officials may impose restraints.

Rationale: Majority Opinion, Justice White (White delivered the opinion of the Court in which Rehnquist, Stevens, O'Connor, and Scalia joined).

A) First Amendment rights of students in the public schools are not automatically coextensive with the rights of adults in other settings, and must be applied in light of the special characteristics of the school environment. A school need not tolerate student speech that is inconsistent with its basic educational mission, even thought the government could not censor similar speech outside the school.

B) The school newspaper here cannot be characterized as a forum for public expression. School facilities may be deemed to be public forums only if school authorities have by policy or by practice opened the facilities for indiscriminate use by the general public, or by some segment of the public, such as student organizations. If the facilities have instead been reserved for other intended purposes, communicative or otherwise, then no public forum has been created and school officials may impose reasonable restrictions on the speech of students, teachers, and other members of the school community. The school officials in this case did not deviate from their policy that the newspaper's production was to be part of the educational curriculum and a regular classroom activity under the journalism teacher's control as to almost every aspect of publication. The officials did not evince any intent to open the paper's pages to indiscriminate use by its student reporters and editors, or by the student body general; accordingly, school officials were entitled to regulate the paper's contents in any reasonable manner.

C) The standard for determining when a school may punish student expression that happens to occur on school premises is not the standard for determining when a school may refuse to lend its name and resources to the dissemination of student expression. *Tinker v. Des*

Moines Independent Community School District, 393 U.S. 503, distinguished that educators do not offend the First Amendment by exercising editorial control over the style and content of student speech in school-sponsored expressive activities so long as their actions are reasonably related to legitimate pedagogical concerns.

D) The school principal acted reasonably in this case in requiring the deletion of the pregnancy article, the divorce article, and the other articles that were to appear on the same pages of the newspaper.

Students in the public schools do not "shed their constitutional rights to freedom of speech or expression at the schoolhouse gate according to *Tinker v Des Moines*." They cannot be punished merely for expressing their personal views on the school premises—whether "in the cafeteria, or on the playing field, or on the campus during the authorized hours"—unless school authorities have reason to believe that such expression will "substantially interfere with the work of the school or impinge upon the rights of other students."

A school need not tolerate student speech that is inconsistent with its "basic educational mission," even though, the government could not censor similar speech outside the school. Accordingly, we held in *Fraser v. Bethel* that a student could be disciplined for having delivered a speech that was "sexually explicit" but not legally obscene at an official school assembly, because the school was entitled to "disassociate itself" from the speech in a manner that would demonstrate to others that such vulgarity is "wholly inconsistent with the fundamental values of public school education."

We deal first with the question whether *Spectrum* may appropriately be characterized as a forum for public expression. The public schools do not possess all of the attributes of streets, parks, and other traditional public forums that have been used for purposes of assembly, communicating thoughts between citizens, and discussing public questions. Hence, school facilities may be deemed to be public forums only if school authorities have a "by policy or by practice" opened those facilities "for indiscriminate use by the general public." "The government does not create a public forum by inaction or by permitting limited discourse, but only by intentionally opening a nontraditional forum of public discourse."

The policy of school officials toward *Spectrum* was reflected in Hazelwood School Board Policy 348.51 and the Hazelwood East Curriculum Guide. Board Policy 348.51 provided that "school sponsored publications are developed within the adopted curriculum and its educational implications in regular classrooms activities." The Hazelwood East Curriculum Guide described the Journalism 2 course as a "laboratory situation in which the students publish the school newspaper applying skills they have learned in Journalism 1." School officials did not deviate in practice from their policy that production of *Spectrum* was to be part of the educational curriculum and a "regular classroom activity." Respondents' assertion that they had believed that they could publish "practically anything" in *Spectrum* was therefore dismissed as simply "not credible."

We conclude that the standard articulated in *Tinker* for determining when a school may punish student expression need not also be the standard for determining when a school may refuse to lend its name and resources to the dissemination of student expression. Instead, we hold that educators do not offend the First Amendment by exercising editorial control over the style and content of student speech in school-sponsored expressive activities so long as their actions are reasonably related to legitimate pedagogical concerns. It is only when the decision to censor a school-sponsored publication, theatrical production, or other vehicle of student expression has no valid educational purpose that the First Amendment is so "directly and sharply implicated, as to require judicial intervention to protect students' constitutional rights."

The courts have always been particularly suspicious of prior restraint; that is, when a publication is censored before it can reach the street. School determinations should be based on a school rule that advances an educational purpose and is uniformly enforced. The Supreme Court has identified two evils of prior restraint. First, unbridled discretion in the hands of a government official constitutes a prior restraint and may result in censorship. Officials should be content-neutral. And second, officials must decide in an expeditious manner and not restrain by inaction.

Rationale for the Dissenting Opinion: Brennan filed a dissenting opinion, in which Marshall and Blackmun joined.

Only speech that materially and substantially interferes with the requirements of appropriate discipline can be found unacceptable and therefore prohibited (*Tinker*).

In my view the principal violated the First Amendment's prohibitions against censorship of any student expression that neither disrupts class work nor invades the rights of other, and against any censorship that is not narrowly tailored to serve its purpose.

If mere incompatibility with the school's pedagogical message were a constitutionally sufficient justification for the suppression of student speech, school officials could censor most students or student organizations, converting our public schools into "enclaves of totalitarianism," that "strangle the free mind at its source."

The young men and women of Hazelwood East expected a civics lesson, but not the one the Court teaches today. I dissent.

New Jersey v. T.L.O.
469 U.S. 325 (1985)
U.S. Supreme Court
No. 83-712

Argued March 28, 1984   **Decided January 15, 1985**

Topic: Student rights: Search and seizure conducted at public schools.

Issues: The case concerns the extent to which a school official can conduct a search of a student without infringing on his privacy and Fourth Amendment rights.

Facts: In March 1980, a teacher in a New Jersey high school discovered two girls smoking in the school lavatory. One was T.L.O., a fourteen-year-old freshman. Since this act was in violation of school rules, the two were taken to the principal's office. The assistant vice principal questioned T.L.O., who denied smoking in the lavatory and even denied that she smoked at all. He demanded to see her purse. He opened it and found a package of cigarettes and a package of cigarette rolling papers. In his experiences, possession of the papers were usually associated with the use of marijuana. His further search revealed "a small amount of marijuana, a pipe, a number of empty plastic bags, a substantial quantity of money in one-dollar bills, an index card that appeared to be a list of students who owed T.L.O. money, and two letters that implicated in marijuana dealing."

She received a three-day suspension from school for smoking on campus and a seven-day suspension for possession marijuana. The evidence was turned over to the police, who proceeded against her on a delinquency charge.

Juvenile Court (1980): T.L.O. contended that the search of her purse violated her Fourth Amendment right and that the evidence and her confession were to be suppressed on the ground of an unlawful search. The Fourth Amendment states, "The right of people to be secure in their persons, houses, papers and effects against unreasonable search and seizures shall not be violated, and no warrants shall issue, but upon probable cause." The juvenile court ruled that no violation of Fourth Amendment occurred and not to suppress evidence. The court stated that "a school official may properly conduct a search of a student's person if the official has a reasonable suspicion that a crime has been or is in the process of being committed, of reasonable cause to believe that the search is necessary to maintain school discipline and enforce school policies." T.L.O. appealed to the state appellate division where they affirmed the trial court's finding.

T.L.O. appealed the lower court ruling to the State Supreme Court of New Jersey. The court agreed with the lower courts that the Fourth Amendment applied to searches conducted by school officials. But the search of the purse was unreasonable and had no bearing on the accusation against T.L.O. The court established that, "if an official's search violated constitutional rights the evidence is not admissible in criminal proceedings." The court held that the evidence within the purse had no bearing on the charge of smoking in the lavatory and possession of cigarettes was not a violation of school rules.

The state supreme court granted certiorari to the U.S. Supreme Court to examine the appropriateness of the exclusionary rule (illegally seized material/evidence be admissible in a criminal proceeding). The Court reversed the ruling of the State Supreme Court of New Jersey, stating that the facts surrounding the search were reasonably related in scope to the circumstances that justified the interference in the first place. The decision for the assistant vice principal to open T.L.O.'s purse was reasonable under the exclusionary of the Fourth Amendment.

Findings: Justice White delivered the opinion of the U.S. Supreme Court (1985). The Court concluded that the search of T.L.O.'s purse did not violate the Fourth Amendment. The Court was now to question the proper standard for assessing the legality of searches conducted by public school officials.

The U.S. Supreme Court upheld that the Fourth Amendment applies to searches conducted by school authorities, but the special needs of the school environment require assessment of the legality of such searches against a standard less exacting than that of "probable cause." These courts have, by and large, upheld unwarranted searches by school authorities provided that they are supported by reasonable suspicion that the search will uncover evidence of an infraction of school disciplinary roles of a violation of the law.

Do schoolchildren have legitimate expectations of privacy? Schools are faced with striking a balance between the legitimate expectations of privacy and the equally legitimate need to maintain an environment in which learning can take place. Thus, a school official does not need to obtain a warrant before searching a student who is under his or her authority. Obtaining a warrant would interfere with the maintenance of the swift and informal disciplinary procedures needed in the school. Searches will be based not on probable cause as stated in the Fourth Amendment but will be based simply on reasonableness. Determining the reasonableness of any search involves a twofold inquiry: first, one must consider "whether the . . . action was justified at its inception" and second, one must determine whether the search as actually conducted "reasonably related in scope to the circumstances which justified the interference in the first place," and that the search is not excessively intrusive in light of the age and sex of the student and the nature of the infraction.

Side note: Many court cases have avoided the constraints of the Fourth Amendment by dealing with school officials conducting in-school searches of students as private parties acting in loco parentis (in place of the parents; charged with some of the parent's rights, duties, and responsibilities).

The U.S. Supreme Court reversed the ruling of the Supreme Court of New Jersey stating that the facts surrounding the search are reasonably related in scope to the circumstances, which justified the interference in the first place. The decision for the assistant vice principal to open T.L.O.'s purse was reasonable. The discovery of the rolling papers provided reasonable suspicion to justify the further exploration of the purse and the seizure of the names of people who owe T.L.O. money and the letters of interference of involvement in marijuana trafficking.

Dissenting: Justice Brennan, with whom Justice Marshall joined, concurring in part and dissenting in part. They agree with the courts that school officials must confirm their conduct to the Fourth Amendment's protections of personal privacy and personal security. The dissenting opinion in the decision to allow a school official to conduct a in-school search on "reasonableness" is not the same as "probable cause" found in the text of the Fourth Amendment. Schools must use the test for probable cause.

Justice Stevens, with Justice Marshall and Justice Brennan joined, concurring in part and dissenting in part. Dissented is the argument that the exclusionary rule shouldn't apply to searches conducted by school officials. Evidence collected illegally is inadmissible in a criminal proceeding.

Additional Search and Seizure Case Laws: In the case of Angela Lee Williams, a minor, by her father and next friend, *William Hardy Williams v. Jerald M. Ellington et al.*, U.S. Court of Appeals for the Sixth Circuit, Case No. 90-5993, decided June 24, 1991. Plaintiff Williams sought monetary damages and injunctive and declaratory relief for an alleged warrantless strip search of her performed by officials of the Graves County High School, Mayfield, Kentucky.

On January 19, 1988, the principal of Graves County High School, Jerald Ellington, received a telephone call from a student's mother who expressed concern over a situation in which her daughter, Ginger, was confronted with drugs. Although no names were disclosed, the mother reported that a student had offered drugs to her daughter. Later that day, Ellington called Ginger into his office to learn more about the incident. Ginger reported that during typing class on the day before, she had seen Williams and another girl, Michelle, with a clear glass vial containing a white powder. Ginger also stated that the two girls placed the powder on the tips of their fingers and sniffed it. One of the girls then offered the powder to Ginger, but she refused it. Ellington asked Ginger if she had any problems with the girls, and was satisfied there was no animosity between them to provide Ginger with an ulterior motive for reporting the incident.

Ellington then spoke with Williams' typing instructor, Brenda Cobb, in whose class the alleged drug use occurred. When asked if she had noticed anything peculiar during class on the day of the purported drug use, Cobb indicated that Michelle's behavior was strange. Cobb approached Michelle, who told the teacher she had the flu. Ellington then relayed Ginger's report to Cobb, prompting her to remember an incident involving Williams the previous semester. During the first semester, Cobb found a typed note under Williams' desk in which she had referred to parties involving her friends and the use of the "rich man's drug." When Cobb questioned Williams about the letter, she passed it off as a joke.

During the next few days, Ellington also spoke with Mary Jean Young, Williams' aunt and school guidance counselor, and Michelle's father, so that both families would be apprised of the situation. Michelle's father expressed concern that Michelle might be using drugs and disclosed that Michelle had recently stolen $200.00 from his bureau drawer.

Also during this same week, Michelle came to Ellington and reported that another student, Kim, and Kim's boyfriend Steve were inhaling a substance called "rush." "Rush" is a volatile substance that can be purchased over the counter, and while possession of "rush" is legal, inhalation of it is illegal under Kentucky law. Coincidentally, Kim and Steve also came to Ellington and insisted that it was not they, but other students, who were using the substance. Following these reports, Ellington questioned the motives of these students in coming forward and the validity of the information.

On January 22, Ginger stopped in to see Ellington during her fifth-period geometry class to report "those girls are at it again," or words to that effect, and indicated she had observed the two girls with the white powdery substance again. Ellington sent Ginger back to class and decided to act on the information before the end of the fifth period. Ellington contacted assistant principal Maxine Easley and apprised her of the week's events. Ellington and Easley then went to the geometry class and called Williams and Michelle out into the hall. Although Ellington observed that neither student appeared disoriented or intoxicated, the two girls were taken to the administrative offices. After escorting the girls into his office and confronting them with his suspicions, Michelle produced a small brown vial from her purse that contained "rush." Michelle claimed the vial belonged to Kim, and although both girls denied possession of any drugs, Ellington wanted to search the girls' lockers because the brown vial did not match the description given by Ginger.

At that time, Assistant Principal Donald Jones, who was also aware of the week's events, went to search Williams' assigned locker. No drugs were found in this locker, nor in the locker Williams had been using to store her personal items. Likewise, a search of Williams' books and purse conducted by Assistant Principal Easley produced no evidence of drugs. Finally, Ellington asked Easley to take Williams into her office and search her person in the presence of a female secretary. It should be noted at this point that the search and seizure policy in effect at the time Williams was searched was instituted by the board in 1985 and stated the following: "A pupil's person will not be searched unless there is a reasonable suspicion that the pupil is concealing evidence of an illegal act. . . . When a pupil's person is searched, the person conducting the search shall be the same sex as the pupil; and a witness of the same sex shall be present during the search."

Inside Easley's office, Williams was asked to empty her pockets, which she did. Easley then asked her to remove her T-shirt. After some hesitation, Williams complied, and was then asked to lower her blue jeans to her knees. Easley found no evidence of drugs as a result of this search.

In the present case, the search and seizure policy promulgated by the Graves County School Board is a facially valid districtwide policy, allowing for the search of a pupil's person if there is a reasonable suspicion that the student is concealing evidence of an illegal activity. Moreover, the exact language of its policy reiterates the criteria set forth by the U.S. Supreme Court in the case of *New Jersey v. T.L.O.* (1985) that "in balancing a student's privacy interests under the Fourth Amendment against the need for order and safety in schools, the legality of a search of a student should depend upon the reasonableness of the search, under all circumstances."

It is well established that students do not "shed their constitutional rights at the schoolhouse gate." In *New Jersey v. T.L.O.*, the Court, in discussing Fourth Amendment rights of school students within the confines of the educational environment, stated, "The accommodation of the privacy interests of schoolchildren with the substantial need of teachers and administrators for freedom to maintain order in the schools does not require strict adherence to the requirement that searches be based on probable cause to believe that the subject of the search has violated or is violating the law."

In such cases, courts apply a twofold inquiry to determine what constitutes "reasonableness, under all the circumstances." First, the search must be "justified at its inception and a search will meet this requirement "when there are reasonable grounds for suspecting that the search will turn up evidence that the student has violated or is violating either the law or the rules of the school. Second, the search must be reasonable in its scope, and the search will be permissible when the measures adopted are reasonably related to the objectives of the search and not excessively intrusive in light of the age and sex of the student and the nature of the infraction."

In this case, the Court found that in light of the established acts at the time of the search, it was not unreasonable for Principal Ellington to believe that the ordered searches were not a violation of Williams' constitutional rights.

In *Williams*, the court of appeals also made note of the Supreme Court's ruling with regard to an "informant's tip." In determining the threshold of reasonable suspicion, the court held that there must be an independent indicia of reliability to warrant a search. Principal Ellington's actions were based in part on the information given to him by Ginger. Ellington felt that there was not an ulterior motive to Ginger reporting the incidents to him and felt that she was not motivated by malice. The court of appeals agreed with Ellington and stated that the informant's tip, although unverified, was extremely helpful in establishing reasonable suspicion. Ellington carefully questioned Ginger about any improper motive for making the allegations, and was satisfied none existed. Moreover, in addition to Ginger's "tip," other evidence was presented to Ellington during the course of the week. There was the discovery of Williams's letter found in the typing class, the suspicions of Michelle's father that his daughter was using drugs, and Michelle's production of the vial containing "rush." Based on the totality of the circumstances, there existed both the quality and quantity of information for Ellington to reasonably suspect Williams was concealing evidence of illegal activity on her person.

Ingraham v. Wright
Supreme Court of the U.S. 1977
430 U.S. 651
97 S. CT. 1401

Topic: Compensation and punitive damages for injuries caused by corporal punishment.

Issue: Is corporal punishment cruel and unusual? Does the "paddlee" have the right to seek restitution for personal injuries caused by corporal punishment?

Facts: Lemmie Deliford and Solomon Barnes were assistant principals at Drew Junior High School in 1970–1971. Deliford policed the halls wearing brass knuckles. Barnes wore the brass knuckles as well, but was usually seen carrying a large wooden paddle.

One day a fourteen-year-old boy by the name of James Ingraham was moving off of a stage a bit slower than what the principals had in mind, so the two assistant principals held him face down over a table while the principal, Willie Wright, struck him on the buttocks at least twenty times with a paddle. This beating required immediate medical attention. The physician noted that the boy's backside sustained severe hematomas, which required one weeks' worth of bed rest, along with an assortment of pain managers and laxatives for James. When he returned for his followup visit, the physician found that there was still bruising as well as oozing fluid. The doctor recommended an additional seventy-two hours of bed rest.

Another student, Roosevelt Adams, was paddled on at least ten different occasions during the school year. During one episode he was struck on the arm, leg, neck, and back. On another occasion he was hit across the wrist, which prevented him from being able to use his arm for one week.

Daniel Lee was a bystander who was told to bend down and "get a little piece of the board." Barnes hit Lee on the hand four or five times, which fractured, enlarged, and disfigured his hand.

Rodney Williams was in class and stood up to wipe particles off his chair, which bought him a beating of his head and back with a paddle, and an additional whipping with a belt. Williams required surgery to remove the lump on the side of his head, resulting from paddling. As a result of another beating, Williams reportedly coughed up blood.

Findings of the U.S. District Court: Mr. Justice Powell delivered the opinion of the Court.

> The Supreme Court of the United States reiterates that the 8th Amendment provides, "excessive bail shall not be required, nor excessive fines imposed, nor cruel and unusual punishment inflicted." It is the Court's belief that those tenets have been traditionally interpreted to protect the right of the criminals. Further, the school child has little need for the protection of the 8th Amendment. They stated that the openness of the public school creates natural safeguards for the students.

The Constitutional question is whether the imposition abides by the requirements of due process according to the 14th Amendment. Three factors to be considered:

- The private interest being affected
- The risk of an erroneous deprivation of such interest and the questioning of whether more procedural safeguards are necessary
- The state's financial interest in the changing of procedure

Because there are few reports of abuse at the hands of the school, the Court believes that the state statute is working as intended. Imposing further safeguards for the child would be of little, if any, benefit. The Due Process Clause does not require advance notice of disciplinary action of the student. Corporal Punishment is authorized and limited by common law, and in some instances by state statute.

Gebser et al. v. Lago Vista Independent School District
524 U. S. 274 (1998)
No. 96-1866

Argued March 25, 1998   **Decided June 22, 1998**

Topic: The liability of the school district under Title IX for a teacher's sexual harassment of a student.

Issue: What standard of liability applies to a school district under Title IX for a teacher's sexual harassment of a student?

Fact: Frank Waldrop was a teacher at Lago Vista High School. In Jane Doe's ninth-grade year she was assigned to Mr. Waldrop's advanced social studies class. Mr. Waldrop often flattered the student and would sometimes spend time alone in his room with her.

In the spring of 1992, Waldrop went to Doe's house at a time when her parents weren't home, claiming the need to return a book to the student. Waldrop made sexual advances toward the student by fondling her breasts and unzipping her pants. The summer following this episode, the fifteen-year-old and the teacher frequently engaged in sexual encounters, but never on the school grounds.

The next school year, parents complained to Michael Riggs, the principal, claiming Mr. Waldrop was making sexually inappropriate comments around female students. Riggs responded to the complaints with a cursory investigation, where Waldrop denied the accusation and the investigation ceased. The superintendent was never apprised of the complaints.

In January 1993, the affair ended when a Lago Vista police officer happened upon the teacher and student having sex.

Finding of the U.S. Supreme Court: Justice O'Connor delivered the opinion of the Court.

The Court held that school districts are not liable under Title IX for teacher-student sexual harassment unless an employee with supervisory power over the offending employee actually knew of the abuse, had the power to end it, and failed to do so. They ruled that petitioners could not satisfy that standard.

Judge O'Connor acknowledged that this affirmation of the judgment of the court of appeals did not affect any right of the recovery that any individual may have against a school district or the teacher in his or her capacity under state law.

Vernonia School District 41J v. Wayne Acton
Supreme Court of the United States
515 U.S. 646; 115 S. Ct. 2386
Argued March 28, 1995   **Decided June 26, 1995**

Topic: Random drug testing as a requirement for participation in school athletics.

Issue: Do random urinalysis drug tests of student athletes constitute "unreasonable searches" and an invasion of privacy by public school officials, which are prohibited by the Fourth and Fourteenth Amendments of the U.S. Constitution?

Facts: The school district is located in the logging community of Vernonia, Oregon, and consists of one high school and three grade schools. Like many school districts across the nation, school athletics play a prominent role in the community.

In the mid to late 1980s, district teachers and administrators observed a sharp increase in drug use. Not only were student athletes included among the drug users, but athletes were leaders of the drug culture because, as athletes, they were considered role models. This caused the district's administrators particular concern because drug use has been found to increase the risk of sports related injury. Experts have confirmed that the use of drugs can deteriorate an athlete's motivation, memory, judgment, reaction, coordination, and performance.

District officials began considering a drug-testing program and proposed a Student Athlete Drug Policy. The school board approved the policy for implementation in the fall of 1989 after unanimous approval was given by parents who attended a parent "input night." The policy's express purpose was to prevent student athletes from using drugs, to protect their health and safety, and to provide drug users with assistance programs.

The policy applies to all students participating in interscholastic athletics. Each student who wishes to participate in sports must sign a form consenting to random urinalysis drug testing and must obtain the written copy sent to his or her parents. Athletes are tested at the beginning of the season for their sport. In addition, once a week during the season the names of the athletes are placed in a "pool." A student, with the supervision of two adults, blindly draws the names of 10 percent of the athletes for random testing. Those selected are notified and tested the same day if possible.

To obtain the sample, the student and an adult monitor of the same sex then enter an empty locker room. Each boy produces a sample at a urinal, remaining fully clothed with his back to the monitor, who stands twelve to fifteen feet behind the student. Although they do not always, monitors may watch the student while he produces the sample and they listen for normal sounds of urination. Girls produce samples in an enclosed bathroom stall, so that they can be heard but not observed. The samples are sent to an independent laboratory, which tests them for amphetamines, cocaine, and marijuana.

In the fall of 1991, James Acton, a seventh-grader signed up to play football at one of the district's grade schools. He and his parents refused to sign the drug-testing consent forms and thus, the district would not allow him to participate in the football program. The Actons filed a lawsuit against the district seeking declaratory and injunctive relief from enforcement of the policy on the grounds that it violated the Fourth and Fourteenth Amendments of the U.S. Constitution.

Findings of the Supreme Court: According to the Supreme Court, Vernonia's Student Athlete Drug Policy does not violate the Fourth and Fourteenth Amendments of the U.S. Constitution.

Rationale: The Court concluded that school children are not entitled to full Fourth Amendment protections. The basic premise is that when a child is in school, his or her parents have delegated their "custodial and tutelary" parental powers to the school officials. Such delegated power permits school officials to display a "degree of supervision and control that could not be exercised over free adults."

The Court further concluded that the urinalysis testing and related disclosure statements about current medications constituted only a "negligible" invasion of privacy. Athletes voluntarily subject themselves to regulations that are not imposed on nonathletes. For example, athletes undergo preseason physical examinations, they undress and shower in a "'communal" setting each day in the locker room, they must acquire insurance coverage or sign an insurance waiver, and they must maintain minimum grade point averages. As a result, the Court concluded that "athletes have a reduced expectation of privacy" and thus, if there were any invasion of privacy, it was negligible.

NOTES

1. *See*
   - *Burlington Industries, Inc. v. Ellerth, 524 US 742, 1998.* Plaintiff quit her job as a salesperson after repeated offensive remarks and gestures by a supervisor. Specifically, she alleged that he threatened to deny her tangible job benefits for refusal of his advances. The Supreme Court held that under Title VII of the Civil Rights Act of 1964 an employee who refuses unwelcome and threatening sexual advances of a supervisor, but suffers no adverse, tangible job consequents, may recover damages against an employer without showing the employer is at fault for the supervisor's conduct. The employer, however, may raise an affirmative defense to liability or damages. That is, employers can protect themselves by adopting policies and procedures to prevent harassment, by correcting harassing behavior, and by showing that the employee failed to take advantage of corrective or preventive opportunities provided by the employer.
   - *Faragher v. City of Boca Raton,* 524 US 775 (1998). Plaintiff, a lifeguard for the city, alleged that her supervisors had created a sexually hostile environment by repeatedly subjecting her and other female lifeguards to "uninvited and offensive touching," by making lewd remarks, and by

speaking of women in offensive terms. The Court held, as in *Burlington*, that any employer is subject to vicarious liability for a hostile environment created by a supervisor with immediate (or higher) authority over an employee. When an employee suffers no tangible adverse job consequences, however, an employer may raise an affirmative defense to liability or damages.

2. Ge*bser v. Lago Vista Independent School District*, 118 S. Ct. 1989 (1998). A high school girl was allegedly seduced by a fifty-two-year-old male teacher during the 1992–1993 school year. The teacher and the student allegedly had sexual intercourse numerous times off school grounds. No one employed by the school district knew about the relationship. The teacher had never previously been accused of sexual misconduct. In the fall of 1992, however, two parents complained that the teacher had made numerous sexual remarks to Miss Gebser and other students. The principal talked to the teacher about the alleged sexual comments, but the teacher was not reprimanded, and the incident was not reported to the superintendent. The student argued that the school district should be held liable because teachers have special authority over students that enables them to manipulate their students. The student asked the Court to utilize principles found in Title VII cases. The Court rejected the students' arguments in favor of a standard that requires "actual knowledge" by a school official who, at a minimum, has authority to address the alleged discrimination and to institute "corrective measures" on behalf of the school district. Liability will be imposed if the school official responds with "deliberate indifference" to the harassment. While recognizing that sexual abuse is a major concern, the Court determined that Congress did not intend to impose open-ended liability on schools for misconduct that the schools did not even know about. The Court distinguished Title IX from Title VII, noting differences between the two statutes.

8

Teacher Contracts, Rights, and Freedoms

TEACHERS' CONTRACTS

Elements of a Contract

Offer and Acceptance

For a teacher contract to be legal and binding, there must be an offer from the proper school officials and an acceptance by the employee (teacher). A contract is not binding until both parties have agreed to the terms of the written contract through their authorized signatures.

Valid Consideration

For a contract to be legal, it must contain some reward for the person performing the duties outlined in the contract. In teacher contracts, the valid consideration will be a sum of money. The only times this could become a legal controversy for schools are instances where educators or noneducators volunteer to perform employment tasks for schools, such as coaching athletics, directing a play, and so forth. If a contract is entered into between the school and the volunteer, there must be some valid consideration, even if it is only a dollar.

Legal Subject Matter

In relation to teacher contracts, legal subject matter would be any content area (subject) or school activity in which the teacher signing the contract is licensed or certified. The legal subject matter for the contract is contained within the license or certificate that is held by the teacher, and curriculum and extracurricular activities that have been created and approved by administrative or board of education policy.

Competent Parties

Any individuals signing a teaching contract must be an adult, sound of mind, and in full control of their faculties at the time of the contract signing. For example, someone under the influence of alcohol or drugs, or a person deemed insane by the courts would not be considered a competent party.

The competent party for the school is determined by the statutes of the state. Since only school officials can perform discretionary duties, and discretionary powers can only be granted by the state legislature, one must look to the statutes for guidance. In most states, teacher contracts can only be granted by the board of education. In some rare instances, the statutes have designated some other school authority this discretionary power.

This is often misunderstood by the public and by entry-year teachers. Some boards of education often instruct the superintendent or personnel director to offer contracts to prospective teachers. Sometimes the contracts offered have been signed by the president of the board. However, in states where school administrators are employees and not officials, the board of education would have to approve the contracts at an open board meeting through the passage of a formal motion.

Definite Terms

Teacher contracts specify only that the teacher is employed to teach subjects for which he is licensed and to perform other duties as prescribed by board and administrative policy, usually defined as "and perform other duties assigned by the principal [or appropriate administrator]." The contract does not have to contain the specific subjects to which the teacher will be assigned. The school authorities have the flexibility to assign teachers in any subject for which she is licensed.

Some school districts have negotiated agreements with the teachers' union that restrict the board's flexibility with regard to specific teacher assignments. For example, some negotiated agreements specify a date that the teacher must be notified of his assignment, and that no change can be made thereafter without his approval. If no negotiated agreement on this issue is in place, or if there is no board policy to the contrary, common law concerning contracts would give the school authorities flexibility to assign teachers to subjects in any manner consistent with their teaching license.

Types of Teacher Contracts

Limited Contracts

These contracts usually range from one to five years in duration. Entry-year teachers start with a one-year contract. Many school systems offer only one-year limited contracts and continuing contracts (tenure). Others allow teachers to progress from one- to five-year contracts through graduated steps (such as one-, two-, three-, and five-year contracts) until they achieve tenure or work their entire career on limited contracts. States that do not offer tenure operate solely on limited contracts.

A limited contract is not considered a property right, and therefore the teacher is not in a legal position of the natural anticipation of continued employment. A limited contract can be nonrenewed by following procedural due process as determined by state statute. Nonrenewal can only occur at the end of the contract period. For one-year contracts, nonrenewal could occur at the end of each year. For a teacher on a three-year limited contract, the nonrenewal could only occur at the end of the third year, and so forth.

Continuing Contracts

Teachers obtain continuing contracts (tenure) through graduate degrees and successful experience. Once the continuing contract has been granted, such contract bestows upon the teacher a property right that includes the anticipation of continual employment. Continuing contracts cannot be nonrenewed as limited ones can. They must be terminated for specific reasons. Otherwise, the teacher is under continuing employment status.

Termination of Contracts

Teacher contracts, both limited and continuing, and limited administrator contracts, can be terminated during the contract. Grounds for dismissal of educators under contract are:

Incompetency

The two most common discussed forms of incompetency in teachers are the lack of subject matter knowledge and the lack of classroom management skills, including the ability to maintain student discipline. However, there are other forms of incompetency that are recognized by the courts. They fall under the following categories:

• Poor relationship with other teachers
• Lack of cooperation with administration
• Poor attitude/disruptive influence
• Not in harmony with the philosophy of the school

These categories are affective in nature and indicate the court's acceptance of the fact that teaching is no longer an isolated profession. Instructional schemes and schedules require teachers to work closely with other teachers and the administration. The effectiveness of the instructional program depends on teamwork and the creation of a learning community. If a teacher is preventing this from happening through his attitude and behavior, the courts have deemed this to be a form of incompetency.

Insubordination

Insubordination is defined as the willful and deliberate refusal to follow board policy, administrative policy, or administrative directive. Such blatant behavior can result in the immediate dismissal of a teacher, and is almost indefensible if the charges are accurate.

Immorality

For educators to be dismissed or terminated under a charge of immoral behavior or moral turpitude, there must be a nexus (connection) between the personal behavior that is considered immoral and their effectiveness as professional educators. Said another way, their private or personal actions must have an adverse effect upon the school and the community. This adverse effect would create an environment that would seriously hinder their ability to be effective teachers.

This legal standard precludes any universal definition of immorality. Each charge must be judged by whether or not a nexus between private and professional life has been created. Needless to say, what some communities and boards of education would consider immoral would not be taken seriously in other localities.

Reduction in Force

There are times when a school board may reduce the teaching staff without the presence of incompetence, insubordination, or immorality. For legitimate reasons a board may reduce the teaching staff by dismissing teachers, both tenured and nontenured. Legitimate reasons for reduction in force are:

1. Financial Crises. Most states have a minimum staffing level for teaching, usually determined on a per-pupil basis. For example, schools could be held to a minimum staffing level of forty teachers for every 1,000 students. Most schools operate above that minimum standard. If the district had a financial crisis, it could reduce the staff to the minimum level by reducing the teaching force accordingly.

2. A Pattern of Declining Enrollment. If the school system has experienced a pattern of declining enrollment, they may reduce the staff to accommodate this demographic shift. If should be noted that a one-year aberration in enrollment may not be considered a pattern of declining enrollment. For example, if a school system had 500 seniors, 400 juniors, 488 sophomores, and 490 freshmen, the small junior class would not be considered a pattern of declining enrollment.

3. Elimination of Programs. If a school system eliminates a program, the teaching positions within those programs could be eliminated. An example could be a school system with a comprehensive high school could decide to join or contract with a vocational

district for all career and technical courses. The elimination of a program would have to be done for educational reasons and not solely to rid the school system of the teachers currently employed in the program.

4. School Reorganizations. If school districts are merged or consolidated, the new district may reduce staff if the reorganization has created an excess of teachers in a certain field. For example, if two small districts merged, with each having two advanced science teachers, the new district might only need a total of three for these advanced courses. One science teaching position could be eliminated.

Unless there is a negotiated agreement with the teacher's union to the contrary, reduction in force is based on the type of contract held by the teacher and the years of experience in the school district. The most protected teachers are those on continuing contracts from most experienced to least experienced. The protection then goes to teachers on limited contracts from most experienced to least experienced. Following is a chart that illustrates teacher protection, from most to least:

	Type of Contract	Experience
Teacher A	Continuing	20 years
Teacher B	Continuing	5 years
Teacher C	Limited	12 years
Teacher D	Limited	8 years

The "Bumping" System

If a teacher holds dual licensing and his or her teaching position has been eliminated due to a reduction in force, that teacher may "bump" a teacher with less protection. For example, if a teacher holding dual licensing in English and social studies is a victim of reduction of force in English, but has a higher contract and experience level than a teacher in social studies, the teacher could claim the social studies position and thus "bump" the least protected social studies teacher. The fact that the English teacher has never taught social studies is not a legal consideration.

TEACHERS' RIGHTS AND FREEDOMS

Freedom of Expression

In determining the extent of freedom granted to teachers in relation to free speech and expression, three legal sources must be considered: (1) the constitutional rights of the teacher as a citizen, primarily the First Amendment right to free speech; (2) the statutory rights of the school board to govern the school; and (3) contractual conditions of employment.

Criticism of School Policy or Personnel

In examining the right of a teacher to speak as a citizen on a matter of public concern, the courts use a balance of interest test as referred to in the *Pickering* case (see *Pickering v. Board of Education of Township High School* in the case summaries). The interest of the teacher to speak out as a citizen on a matter of public concern is balanced against the state's interest to have an orderly educational environment. Following are significant points that will affect the balance test:

- Teachers may be forced to relinquish First Amendment rights they would otherwise possess to comment on matters of public interest in connection with the operation of the public schools if such comments (written or spoken) interfere with the school's interest in promoting an efficient educational system. (See *Perry v. Sindermann, Mt. Healthy Board of Education v. Doyle*, and *Board of Regents of State Colleges et al. v. Roth.*)
- As a general rule of thumb, the criticism is more likely to be protected if the teacher is not speaking about immediate superiors or peers. If the teacher criticizes fellow teachers or the principal, there is a greater likelihood that such action will disrupt the educational environment, and will thus be afforded less First Amendment protection.
- Keep in mind that, in order to claim First Amendment protection, the teacher must be speaking as a citizen and on matters of public concern. The controversy usually arises over whether the school situation that has been aired publicly is serious enough that it has become a matter of public concern.

- The school may not declare that any speech by a teacher is inappropriate because by doing so the teacher did not follow the chain of command. If the issue is of vital importance to the community, thus creating a matter of public concern, the teacher may have a right to speak out as a citizen if he thinks the problem is not being properly addressed.

Controversial Teaching Methods

If a teacher uses a controversial teaching method and is challenged, the teacher must show that the methodology is related to a valid instructional objective (see *Keefe v. Geanakos*). In another instance, a teacher showed the film *Pink Floyd, the Wall* without any attempt to tie the content of the film to her instructional objectives. Here, dismissal was upheld by the court (*Fowler v. Board of Education of Lincoln County, Kentucky*, 1987). These two contrasting cases illustrate when controversial methods are legally acceptable and when they are not.

Academic Freedom

Academic freedom includes the right of teachers to speak freely concerning their subjects, to use innovative approaches, to experiment with new ideas, to choose appropriate pedagogical strategies, and to select educational materials. Academic freedom comes under the ambit of the First Amendment. The courts have held that it is fundamental in the promotion of a democratic society. Academic freedom allows the evaluation and criticism of values and practices in order to allow for political, social, economic, and scientific progress. Academic freedom, however, is not absolute. The courts will balance its interest against that of competing educational values. Some areas to which academic freedom does not extend include the following:

1. Teachers cannot preach their religious beliefs in class.
2. Teachers may not disregard texts and syllabi.
3. Teachers cannot discuss topics or distribute material that is not relevant to the curriculum or instruction.

Religious Holidays for Teachers

State statutes and school policies usually permit teachers to be absent for major holidays of recognized religions. School calendars reflect these holidays. Sometimes, teachers request holidays for personal religions that do not match the school calendar. For example, if the school calendar follows the Judeo-Christian holidays, an Islamic person could request days off to worship during Ramadan. Schools can grant such a request; however, schools do not have to pay for such days. Also, teachers cannot take unpaid religious holidays at will. Although the number of days does not have to exactly correspond to the number of paid leave days as specified in board policy and the school calendar, the courts have used this data as a guideline to determine the number of religious holidays a teacher may use. The courts have used as a criterion how much the absenteeism affects the quality of the instructional program.

Teachers' Rights to Wear Religious Clothing in Public Schools

Most public schools, through policy or state statute, prohibit the wearing of religious garb by teachers. The courts have generally upheld the restrictions as a valid interpretation of the establishment clause of the First Amendment. A majority of educators and jurists believe that the wearing of religious garb by educators introduces a sectarian influence that should not be present in a public school. Such religious garb also seems to give the impression that the school supports a particular religion. Although schools may not infringe upon a teacher's religious beliefs, actions based on this religious belief may be limited when a compelling interest of the state is at stake.

Copyright Law

Teachers are permitted, under the fair use doctrine, to use certain copyrighted material, both hard copy and technology, under certain conditions. When examining the fair use standard, the court uses four criteria:

1. The purpose and character of the use, including whether such use is of a commercial nature or is for nonprofit educational purposes;
2. The nature of the copyrighted work;

3. The amount and substantiality of the portion used in relation to the copyrighted work as a whole; and
4. The effect of the use upon the potential market for or value of the copyrighted work.

Specific exceptions for teachers include:
Single copies of:

1. a chapter of a book;
2. an article from a periodical or newspaper;
3. a short story, short essay, or short poem; and
4. a chart, graph, diagram, drawing, cartoon, or picture from a book, newspaper, or periodical.

Teachers can make multiple copies of copyrighted material for classroom use only. The number of copies must not exceed the number of students in the class. Also, the copying must meet tests of brevity, spontaneity, and cumulative effect, and each copy must include a notation of copyright.

Brevity is defined as using excerpts from longer published works, or complete works of short length such as 250-word poems, or articles of less than 2,500 words. Spontaneity is defined as an inspiration of the teacher and the decision to use the works was so close to the time of instruction that it would be unreasonable to expect a timely reply to a request for permission. Cumulative effect means that the material can only be used for one course, and evaluates the number of instances the work was copied without permission.

Teachers should be careful when extending the fair use doctrine to technology, such as DVDs and videos. Although the interpretation of the law concerning technology, including the Internet, is in its infancy, it is reasonable to assume that the fair use doctrine will be applied by the courts.

TEACHER CONTRACTS, RIGHTS, AND
FREEDOMS CASE SUMMARIES

Pickering v. Board of Education of Township High School
District 205, Will County
Appeal from the Supreme Court of Illinois

Argued March 27, 1968   **Decided June 3. 1968**

Topic: Teachers' rights.

Issue: Teachers' right to speak out freely on matters of public concern.

Facts: The appellant, Marvin L. Pickering, was dismissed from his job as a teacher in Township High School District 205, Will County, Illinois, for sending a letter to a local newspaper criticizing the board's allocation of school funds between education and athletic programs, and the board's and superintendent's methods of informing or preventing the informing of the school district's taxpayers the real reasons why tax revenues were being sought for the schools.

In February 1961, the appellee board of education tried to get the voters to approve a bond issue to raise $4,875,000 to build two new schools. The proposal was defeated. The board went back to the voters in December 1961 and a bond issue was passed to raise $5,500,000 to build the schools. The schools were built with the money raised and in May 1964, they proposed a tax increase for educational purposes. It was defeated then and again in September of that year. It was after the second defeat of the proposal that appellant Pickering wrote the letter to the editor. The letter criticized the board for not being honest about where the money was spent when the new schools were built, for not being honest about how money was being allocated, and for misrepresenting teachers' support of the tax proposal. He also charged that the superintendent coerced teachers into supporting it. His real issue was how much money was going into athletics at, what he believed, the expense of other educational needs, particularly teachers' salaries.

Pickering was dismissed for writing and publishing the letter because the board determined that the letter was "detrimental to the efficient operation and administration of the schools of the District" and that "interests of the school required his dismissal." The board held the required full hearing and charged that many of the statements in the letter were false and that the publication of the statements unjustifiably impugned the "motives, honesty, integrity, truthfulness, responsibility, and competence" of both the board and the school administration. The board also charged that the false statements damaged the professional reputation of its members, and of the school administration, would be disruptive of faculty and discipline, and would tend to foment "controversy, conflict and dissension" among teachers, administrator, the board of education, and the residents of the district.

At no time during the proceedings was any evidence introduced as the effect to the publication of the letter on the community as a whole or on the administration of the school system in particular, and no specific findings along these lines were made.

Pickering claimed that his letter was protected by the First Amendment. The Illinois courts reviewed the proceedings solely to determine whether the board's findings were supported by substantial evidence and whether the facts as found supported the board's conclusion that the letter was "detrimental to the best interests of the school." They upheld Pickering's dismissal, rejecting his claim on the grounds that acceptance of a teaching position in the public schools obliged him to refrain from making statements about the operation of the schools "which in the absence of such position he would have an undoubted right to engage in."

Findings of the U.S. Supreme Court: Justice Thurgood Marshall delivered the opinion of the Court, which reversed the lower court's decision for a number of reasons.

1. The premise that teachers may constitutionally be compelled to give up their First Amendment rights they would otherwise enjoy as citizens to comment on matters of public interest in connection with the public schools in which they work has been unequivocally rejected in many prior decisions of the Court. There has to be a balance between the interests of the teacher, as a citizen, in commenting upon matters of public concern, and the interest of the state, as an employer, in promoting the efficiency of the public services it performs through its employees.

2. The board contended that Pickering had a duty to be loyal and supportive of his superiors or at the very least a responsibility to speak factually. The Supreme Court found that in this case the statements appellant made were in no way directed toward any person with whom he would normally be in contact with in the course of his daily duties as a teacher and that his statements did not impact the board's ability to operate the school. They also felt that teachers needed to be able to speak out freely on matters concerning schools without fear of retaliation or dismissal. In addition, no evidence was introduced to support the allegations that the letter damaged the

professional reputations of the board or the superintendent or that it would "foment controversy and conflict among the Board, teachers, administrators, and the residents of the District." The tax issue had already failed so his letter couldn't impact it and all the board had to do was publish a factual statement contradicting Pickering's statement. The board had to make sure that they were not confusing the district's interests with their interests. For the most part, other than the board, people were either disbelieving or apathetic about the whole thing.

3. The board claimed that Pickering's statements were false. The Supreme Court found that there was some truth in what Pickering said and that even the false statements were innocently or negligently made. Even false statements made under these circumstances are protected by the First Amendment.

4. Because of prior rulings, the Court was hesitant to make an across-the-board ruling about dismissal of public employees making libelous statements against employers. In this case they felt that because Pickering's employment "is only tangentially and insubstantially involved in the subject matter of the public communication made by a teacher, we conclude that it is necessary to regard the teacher as the member of the general public he seeks to be."

Dissenting: Justice White concurred in part and dissented in part. The Court held that truthful statements by a teacher critical of the school board are within the scope of the First Amendment. White agreed with this part of the ruling. However, even false statements that are innocently and negligently made are protected. Justice White felt that the Court spent too much time reexamining the effect of Pickering's letter on the school system. He thought this was irrelevant, because even if damage had been done, Pickering would have been protected if he made the statements innocently or negligently. If, on the other hand, he knowingly and recklessly made the false statements, he would not be protected by the First Amendment and could be dismissed regardless of impact on the school system.

Appellant's Letter:
Letters to the Editor
Graphic Newspapers. Inc.
Thursday, September 24, 1964, Page 4

Dear Editor:

I enjoyed reading the back issues of your paper, which you loaned to me. Perhaps others would enjoy reading them in order to see just how far the two new high schools have deviated from the original promises by the Board of Education. First, let me state that I am referring to the February thru November 1961 issues of your paper, so that it can be checked.

One statement in your paper declared that swimming pools, athletic fields, and auditoriums had been left out of the program. They may have been left out but they got put back in very quickly because Lockport West has both an auditorium and athletic field. In fact, Lockport West has a better athletic field than Lockport Central. It has a track that isn't quite regulation distance even [576] though the board spent a few thousand dollars on it. Whose fault is that? Oh, I forgot, it wasn't supposed to be there in the first place. It must have fallen out of the sky. Such responsibility has been touched on in other letters but it seems one just can't help noticing it. I am not saying the school shouldn't have these facilities, because I think they should, but promises are promises, or are they?

Since there seems to be a problem getting all the facts to the voter on the twice defeated bond issue, many letters have been written to this paper and probably more will follow, I feel I must say something about the letters and their writers. Many of these letters did not give the whole story. Letters by your Board and Administration have stated that teachers' salaries total $1,297,746 for one year. Now that must have been the total payroll, otherwise the teachers would be getting $10,000 a year. I teach at the high school and I know this just isn't the case. However, this shows their "stop at nothing" attitude. To illustrate further, do you know that the superintendent told the teachers, and I quote, "Any teacher that opposes the referendum should be prepared for the consequences." I think this gets at the reason we have problems passing bond issues. Threats take something away; these are insults to voters in a free society. We should try to sell a program on its merits, if it has any.

Remember those letters entitled "District 205 Teachers Speak," I think the voters should know that those letters have been written and agreed to by only five or six teachers, not 98% of the teachers in the high school. In fact, many teachers didn't even know who was writing them. Did you know that those letters had to have the approval of the superintendent before they could be put in the paper? That's the kind of totalitarianism teachers live in at the high school, and your children go to school in.

In last week's paper, the letter written by a few uninformed teachers threatened to close the school cafeteria and fire its personnel. This is ridiculous and insults the intelligence of the voter because properly managed school cafeterias do not cost the school district any money. If the cafeteria is losing money, then the board should not be packing free lunches for athletes on days of athletic contests. Whatever the case, the taxpayer's child should only have to pay about 30 cents for his lunch instead of 35 cents to pay for free lunches for the athletes.

In a reply to this letter your Board of Administration will probably state that these lunches are paid for from receipts from the games. But $20,000 in receipts doesn't pay for the $200,000 a year they have been spending on varsity sports while neglecting the wants of teachers.

You see we don't need an increase in the transportation tax unless the voters want to keep paying $50,000 or more a year to transport athletes home after practice and to away games, etc. Rest of the $200,000 is made up in coaches' salaries, athletic directors' salaries, baseball pitching machines, sodded football fields, and thousands of dollars for other sports equipment.

These things are all right, provided we have enough money for them. To sod football fields on borrowed money and then not be able to pay teachers' salaries is getting the cart before the horse.

If these things aren't enough for you look at East High. No doors on many of the classrooms, a plant room without any sunlight, no water in a first aid treatment room, are just a few of many things. The taxpayers were really taken to the cleaners. A part of the sidewalk in front of the building has already collapsed. Maybe Mr. Hess would be interested to know that we need blinds on the windows in that building also.

Once again the board must have forgotten they were going to spend $3,200,000 on the West building and $2,300,000 on the East building.

As I see it, the bond issue is a fight between the Board of Education that is trying to push tax-supported athletics down our throats with education, and a public that has mixed emotions about both of these items because they feel they are already paying enough taxes, and simply don't know whom to trust with any more tax money.

I must sign this letter as a citizen, taxpayer and voter, not as a teacher, since that freedom has been taken from the teachers by the administration. Do you really know what goes on behind those stone walls at the high school?

Respectfully,

Marvin L. Pickering

Perry v. Sindermann
U.S. Supreme Court 1972
408 U.S. 593, 92 S. Ct 2694

Topic: Due process.

Issue: Whether Robert Sindermann's First and Fourteenth Amendment Rights were violated by termination of his employment by the Board of Regents in the State of Texas.

Facts: Robert Sindermann was a teacher in the state college system of the state of Texas from 1959 to 1969. He taught two years at the University of Texas and four years at San Antonio Junior College. He was then employed four successive years under a series of one-year contracts at Odessa Junior College from 1965 to 1969. He became a professor of government and social services in 1965 and was appointed, for a time, the cochairman of his department.

During the 1968–1969 academic year, controversy arose between Sindermann and the administration. He was elected president of the Texas Junior College Teaching Association. In this capacity, he became involved in public disagreements with the board's policies, including aligning himself with a group advocating the elevation of the college to four-year status, a change opposed by the regents.

As a result, his one-year contract was not renewed when it ended in May. Also, he was not allowed an opportunity for a hearing to challenge the basis of the nonrenewal.

Sindermann brought this action in federal district court. He alleged that the regents' decision not to rehire him was based on his public criticism of the policies of the administration and this infringed on his right to freedom of speech. Also, the regents' failure to provide him an opportunity for a hearing violated the Fourteenth Amendment's guarantee of procedural due process.

Federal District Court Findings: The federal district court granted summary judgment for the board of regents (petitioners).

Rationale: The federal district court concluded that the respondent had no cause for action against the petitioner, since his contract of employment terminated May 31, 1969, and Odessa Junior College had not adopted the tenure system.

Court of Appeals Findings: The court of appeals reversed the judgment of the district court 430 F. 2d 939.

The court of appeals granted a writ of certiorari, 403 U.S. 917, 91 S. Ct 2226, 29 L. Ed. 2d 694.

Rationale: First, it held that despite the respondent's lack of tenure, the nonrenewal of his contract would violate the Fourteenth Amendment if it in fact was based on his protected speech. Since the actual reason for the regents' decision was "in total dispute" in the pleadings, the court remanded the case for a full hearing on this contested issue.

Second, despite the respondent's lack of tenure, the failure to allow him an opportunity for a hearing would violate the constitutional guarantee of procedural due process if the respondent could show that he had an "expectancy" of reemployment. The court recommended a full hearing on this issue of fact.

U.S. Supreme Court Findings: "While we do not wholly agree with the opinion of the Court of Appeals, its judgment remanding this case to the District Court is affirmed."

Rationale:

> The first question presented is whether the respondent's lack of a contractual or tenure right to reemployment, taken alone, defeats his claim that a nonrenewal of his contract violated the First and Fourteenth Amendment. We hold it does not.
>
> The District Court foreclosed any opportunity for the respondent to show that the decision not to renew his contract was in fact made in retaliation when it granted summary judgment.

We agree with the Court of Appeals that there is a genuine dispute as to whether the college refused to renew the teaching contract on an impermissible basis.

The respondent's lack of formal contractual or tenure security in continued employment at Odessa Junior College though irrelevant to his free speech claim is highly relevant to his procedural due process claim. But it might not be entirely dispositive.

A teacher, like the respondent, who has held his position for a number of years, might be able to show from the circumstances of his service and from other relevant facts that he has a legitimate claim of entitlement to job tenure.

We disagree with the Court of Appeals insofar as it held that a mere subjective "expectancy" is protected by procedural due process. However, we agree that the respondent must be given an opportunity to prove the legitimacy of his claim of such entitlement in the light of the policies and practices of the institution.

Proof of such a property interest would not, of course, entitle him to reinstatement. But such proof would obligate college officials to grant a hearing at his request, where he could be informed of the grounds for his nonretention and challenge their sufficiency.

Mt. Healthy City Board of Ed. v. Doyle
429 U.S. 274 (1997)

Issue: Evidence must show that a teacher's exercise of constitutional rights was the motivating factor not to rehire before judicial action is justified.

Findings: District Court: Doyle was entitled to reinstatement with back pay. Court of Appeals for the Sixth Circuit: Affirmed the judgment of the District Court. U.S. Supreme Court: The judgment of the court of appeals is vacated, and the case was remanded for further proceedings consistent with this opinion.

Facts: Doyle was a nontenured employee prior to the board not renewing his contract. He was elected president of the Teachers' Association in 1969 for one year and the succeeding year served on its executive committee and there was apparently some tension in relations between the board and the association. Beginning in 1970, he was involved in several incidents.

- An argument with another teacher who slapped him. He refused to accept an apology and they both were suspended, causing a teacher walkout, forcing the board to lift the suspension.
- An argument with employees of the school cafeteria over the amount of spaghetti served him.
- He referred to students, in connection with a disciplinary complaint, as "sons of bitches."
- He made an obscene gesture to two girls in the cafeteria.
- He made a telephone call to a local radio station, WSAI, giving information about a memorandum from the principal regarding teacher dress, which he understood was to be settled by a joint teacher-administration action. He later apologized.

One month later, the superintendent recommended that Doyle not be rehired, along with nine other teachers. He requested a statement of reasons and received a statement saying:

You have shown a notable lack of tact in handling professional matters which leaves much doubt as to your sincerity in establishing good school relationships.

A. You assumed the responsibility to notify WSAI Radio Station in regards to the suggestion of the Board of Education that teachers establish an appropriate dress code for professional people. This raised much concern not only within this community, but also in neighboring communities.

B. You used obscene gestures to correct students in a situation in the cafeteria causing considerable concern among those students present.

Sincerely yours,

Rex Ralph, Superintendent

Board of Regents of State Colleges et al. v. Roth
Certiorari to the United States Court of Appeals
for the Seventh Circuit

Argued January 18, 1972   **Decided June 29, 1972**

Topic: Tenure/teacher's rights.

Issue: Mr. David Roth, an assistant professor at a state university, had no tenure rights to continued employment. He was informed that he would not be rehired after his first academic year, and he alleged that the decision not to rehire him infringed on his Fourteenth Amendment rights.

Facts: In 1968, Mr. Roth was hired for a fixed term of one academic year to teach at his first teaching job as assistant professor of political science at Wisconsin State University-Oshkosh. The notice of his faculty appointment specified that his employment would begin on September 1, 1968, and would end on June 30, 1969. The respondent completed that term. Though Roth was rated by the faculty as an excellent teacher, he had publicly criticized the administration for suspending ninety-four black students without determining individual guilt. He also criticized the university's regime. He was informed, without explanation, that he would not be rehired for the ensuing year.

A statute provided that all state university teachers would be employed initially on probation and that only after four years' continuous service would teachers achieve permanent employment "during efficiency and good behavior" with procedural protection against separation. University rules gave a nontenured teacher dismissed before the end of the year some opportunity for review of the dismissal but provided that no reason need be given for nonretention of a nontenured teacher and no standards were specified for reemployment. Respondent brought this action claiming deprivation of his Fourteenth Amendment right, alleging infringement of free speech right because the true reason for his nonretention was his criticism of the university administration and his procedural due process right because of the university's failure to advise him of the reason for its decision. The U.S. District Court for the Western District of Wisconsin granted summary judgment for Roth on procedure issues, ordering university officials to provide him with reasons and a hearing. The court of appeals affirmed the partial summary judgment, and certiorari was granted.

Findings: The U.S. Supreme Court, with Justice Stewart writing, held that where the state did not make any charge against the assistant professor that might seriously damage his standing and associations in his community and there was no suggestion that state imposed on him a stigma or other disability that foreclosed his freedom to take advantage of other employment opportunities, he was not deprived of "liberty" protected by the Fourteenth Amendment when he simply was not rehired in the job but remained as free as before to seek another. The Court further held that where terms of appointment of assistant professor secured absolutely no interest in reemployment of the next year and there was no state statute or university rule or policy that secured his interest in reemployment or that created any legitimate claim to it, he did not have a property interest protected by the Fourteenth Amendment that was sufficient to require university authorities to give him a hearing when they declined to renew his contract of employment. Judgment of the court of appeals reversed and case remanded.

Justice Stewart delivered the opinion of the Court, in which Justices Burger, White, Blackmun, and Rehnquist joined. Justices Douglas and Marshall filed dissenting opinions. Chief Justice Burger filed a concurring opinion, and Justice Powell took no part in the decision of the case.

Rationale: Justice Stewart delivered the opinion of the Court.

The respondent had no contract of employment. Rather, his formal notice of appointment was the equivalent of an employment contract. The notice of his appointment provided that: "David Roth is hereby appointed to the faculty of the Wisconsin State University." . . . The notice went on to specify that the respondent's appointment basis was for the academic year. And it provided that regulations governing tenure are in accord with Chapter 37.31 Wisconsin Statutes. The employment of any staff member for an academic year shall not be for a term beyond June 30th of the fiscal year in which the appointment was made.

The respondent had no tenure rights to continued employment. Under Wisconsin statutory law, a state can acquire tenure as a "permanent" employee only after four years of year-to-year employment. . . . A relatively new teacher without tenure, however, is under Wisconsin law entitled to nothing beyond his one-year appointment. There are no statutory or administrative standards defining eligibility for re-employment. State law thus clearly leaves the decision whether to rehire a nontenured teacher for another year to the unfettered discretion of university officials.

The procedural protection afforded a Wisconsin State University teacher before he is separated from the University corresponds to his job security. As a matter of statutory law, a tenured teacher cannot be "discharged" except for cause upon written charges and pursuant to certain procedures. A non-tenured teacher, similarly, is protected to some extent during his one-year term. Rules promulgated by the Board of Regents provide that a non-tenured teacher "dismissed" before the end of the year may have some opportunity for review of the 'dismissal'. But the rules provide no real protection for a non-tenured teacher who simply is not re-employed for the next year. He must be informed by February 1 concerning retention or nonretention for the ensuing year. But no reason for non-retention need be given. No review or appeal is provided in such a case.

In conformance with these rules, the President of Wisconsin State University-Oshkosh informed the respondent before February 1, 1969 that he would not be rehired for the 1969–1970 academic year. He gave the respondent no reason for the decision and no opportunity to challenge it at any sort of hearing.

The District Court granted summary judgment of the respondent on the procedural issue, ordering the University officials to provide him with reasons and a hearing. The Court of Appeals, with one judge dissenting, affirmed this partial summary judgment. We granted certiorari. The only question presented to us at this stage in the case is whether the respondent had a constitutional right to a statement of reasons and hearing on the University's decision not to rehire him for another year. We hold that he did not.

The requirements of procedural due process apply only to the deprivation of interests encompassed by the Fourteenth Amendment's protection of liberty and property. When protected interests are implicated, the right to some kind of hearing is paramount. But the range of interests protected by procedural due process is not infinite.

The District Court decided that procedural due process guarantees apply in this case by assessing and balancing the weights of the particular interests involved. Undeniably the respondent's re-employment prospects were of major concern to him—concern that we surely cannot say were insignificant. And a weighing process has long been a part of any determination of the form of hearing required in particular situations by procedural due process. But, to determine whether due process requirements apply in the first place, we must look not to the "weight" but to the nature of the interests at stake. We must look to see if the interest is in the Fourteenth Amendment's protection of liberty and property.

The State, in declining to rehire the respondent, did not make any charge against him that might seriously damage his standing and associations in the community. It did not base the non-renewal of his contract on a charge, for example, that he had been guilty of dishonesty or immorality. . . . The State did not invoke any regulations to bar the respondent from all other public employment in state universities. . . .

To be sure, the respondent has alleged that the non-renewal of his contract was based on his exercise of his right to freedom of speech. But this allegation is not now before us. The District court stayed proceedings on this issue, and the respondent has yet to prove that the decision not to rehire him was, in fact, based on his free speech activities. . . .

Our analysis of the respondent's constitutional rights in this case in no way indicates a view that an opportunity for a hearing or a statement of reasons for non-retention would, or would not, be appropriate or wise in public colleges and universities. . . . We must conclude that the summary judgment for the respondent should not have been granted, since the respondent has not shown that he was deprived of liberty, or property protected by the Fourteenth Amendment. The judgment of the Court of Appeals, accordingly, is reversed and the case is remanded for further proceedings consistent with this opinion. Reversed and remanded.

Mr. Justice Douglas, Dissenting:

Respondent Roth had no tenure under Wisconsin law and he had only one year of teaching at Wisconsin State University-Oshkosh. Though Roth was rated by the faculty as an excellent teacher, he had publicly criticized the administrations for suspending an entire group of 94 black students without determining individual guilt. He also criticized the university's regime as being authoritarian and autocratic. He used his classroom to discuss what was being done in the black episode; and one day, instead of meeting his class, he went to the meeting of the Board of Regents. In this case, an action was started in federal district court claiming in part that the decision of the school authorities not to rehire was in retaliation for his expression of an opinion. The district court, in partially granting Roth's motion for summary judgment, held that the Fourteenth Amendment required the University to give a hearing to teachers whose contracts were not to be renewed and to give reasons for its action. The Court of Appeals affirmed.

There may not be a constitutional right to continued employment if private schools and colleges are involved. The First Amendment, applicable to the states by reason of the Fourteenth Amendment, protects the individual against state action when it comes to freedom of speech and of the press and the related freedoms guaranteed by the first amendment. . . .

No more direct assault on academic freedom can be imagined than for the school authorities to be allowed to discharge a teacher because of his or her philosophical, political, or ideological beliefs. The same way will be true of private schools, if through the device of financing or other umbilical cords they become instrumentalities of the state. . . .

When a violation of the First Amendment rights is alleged, the reason for dismissal or for nonrenewal must be examined to see if the reasons given are only a cloak for activity or attitudes protected by the constitution.

In the case of teachers whose contracts are not renewed, tenure is not the critical issue. . . .

Conditioning renewal of a teacher's contract upon surrender of First Amendment, then Roth was deprived of constitutional rights because his employment was conditioned on surrender of First Amendment rights and, apart from the First Amendment, he was denied due process when he received no notice and hearing of the adverse action contemplated against him. Without a statement of the reasons for the discharge and an opportunity to rebut those reasons—both of which were refused by the petitioners, there is no means short of a lawsuit to safeguard the right not to be discharged for the exercise of First Amendment guarantees.

Accordingly, I would affirm the judgment of the court of appeals.

Robert J. Keefe, Plaintiff, v. George J. Geanakos et al., Defendants Civ. A. No. 69-1093

Topic: In Massachusetts's district court a teacher seeks injunction and money damages for an allegedly wrongful suspension and threatened dismissal. These actions were taken as a result of the teacher using material containing offensive language, specifically, the word "mother ******" (incestuous son).

Facts: On October 8, 1969, Robert Keefe was suspended for a period of seven days for "unbecoming conduct and other good causes." Causes for proposed dismissal were:

1. Conduct unbecoming a teacher and department coordinator.
2. Undermining public confidence by allowing students to build an outhouse as a symbol of their irrelevance of the school's course work, schedules, and regulations.
3. Use of offensive materials as mentioned above.
4. Refusal to obey direct order not to teach class, but to remain in his office.

Findings: In the opinion, written by District Judge Caffrey, the court denied the petition for temporary injunction.

Rationale: Before obtaining an injunction, a plaintiff must satisfy two requirements. First, plaintiff must demonstrate that if the injunction is denied he will suffer "certain and irreparable" damages. The court found that no irreparable harm could be done because, if the plaintiff prevails, monetary damages would be an adequate remedy.

The second requirement that the plaintiff must show to secure an injunction is a reasonable probability that he will ultimately prevail. Judge Caffrey sited *Parker v. Board of Education* as a very similar case. In this case, a teacher challenged his dismissal for using *Brave New World* as an infringement of his First Amendment right to free speech. The court ruled that the First Amendment guarantee is not absolute. "Where abridgement to the right to free speech results from government action to protect other substantive public rights, no constitutional deprivation will be found to exist."

Robert J. Keefe, Plaintiff, v. George J. Geanakos et al., Defendants, Appellees
No. 7463
U.S. Court of Appeals for the First Circuit

Topic: Plaintiff is appealing the decision of the district court that denied his request for an injunction.

Facts: Plaintiff's position is that his conduct did not warrant discipline and there are no grounds for a hearing to determine if he should be dismissed. His position has two parts. First, his conduct was "within his competence as a teacher, as a matter of academic freedom, whether the defendants approved or not." Secondly, he was not given adequate prior warning that his actions would be considered improper.

Defendants argue that academic freedom is limited to proper classroom materials as determined by the school committee "in light of pertinent conditions." They cite the age of the students in this case.

Findings: The order of the district court denying an injunction is reversed and the case is remanded for further proceedings.

Rationale: In the opinion given by Chief Judge Aldrich, the court stated that the article in which the offensive language was used was in no way pornographic. The article is scholarly and thought provoking. The use of the word is important to the development of the thesis and the conclusions of the author. The court doesn't think the word is unknown or offensive to the senior students and believe that its use is disturbing only to their parents. If students need to be protected from such language then they fear for their futures.

To the charge that the use of such material would undermine public confidence, the court sites *Ginsberg v. New York*, which establishes that what is read or said to students is not to be determined by adult obscenity standards. However, it does not find high school seniors devoid of all discrimination or resistance and the offensiveness must be dependent on the circumstances of its use.

The justices disagreed with the findings of the district court when they site *Parker v. Board of Education*. The teacher in this case was not dismissed; his complaint was that he was not renewed. They also quote Justice Frankfurter in *Wieman v. Updegraff*, "Such unwarranted inhibition upon the free spirit of teachers affects not only those like appellants before the Court. It has an unmistakable tendency to chill that free play of the spirit which all teachers ought especially cultivate and practice."

The justices stated that it was probable that the plaintiff would prevail on the charge of lack of notice, as the school library contained no fewer than five books containing the offensive word.

Finally, they disagree with the district finding that no irreparable injury is involved because the plaintiff may recover money damages. They state, "Academic freedom is not preserved by compulsory retirement, even at full pay."

Simonetti v. School District of Philadelphia
Richard Simonetti, a minor, by his parent and natural guardian, Alberta Simonetti, and Alberta Simonetti, in her own right v. School District of Philadelphia, Appellant
Superior Court of Pennsylvania, 1982
308 Pa. Super. 555, 454 A. 2d 1038

Topic: The question before the Superior Court of Pennsylvania is whether a teacher's momentary absence from the classroom constitutes negligence.

Facts: Richard Simonetti, a fifth-grade student, returned to the classroom from recess and was struck in the left eye by a pencil that had been propelled out of the hand of a classmate when he tripped. The teacher, an employee of the School District of Philadelphia, was outside the classroom, standing at the door, when Simonetti was injured. There she was engaged in monitoring the return of her students from recess and talking with another teacher. The student who dropped or threw the pencil and two other students had been required to remain in the classroom during recess as punishment for misbehavior at breakfast. They had been talking with the teacher during the recess period and were instructed to take their seats when the teacher stepped outside the classroom to supervise the return of the students from recess.

Simonetti filed action against the school district with the Court of Common Pleas of Philadelphia by contending that the teacher had been negligent in failing to provide adequate classroom supervision. The case was tried without a jury, and damages to $15,000 were awarded to the minor plaintiff and his mother. An appeal followed this verdict.

Findings of the Superior Court of Pennsylvania: The Superior Court of Pennsylvania reversed the decision of the Court of Common Pleas of Philadelphia. Citing facts from several precedent cases, the court stated that to require the teacher to anticipate the events, which occurred while the teacher was outside the classroom door, would be to hold that a teacher is required to anticipate the myriad of unexpected acts that occur daily in classrooms in every school in the land. They agreed that this is not the law and perceived no good reason for imposing such an absolute standard on teachers and school districts.

Rationale: Majority Opinion, Judge Wieand

> The following are dominant facts that mark and control the confines of the Court's decision: (1) "It is common knowledge that children may indulge in horseplay. They may throw a pencil, shoot a paper clip or snap a rubber band when a teacher is absent or turns his or her back." (2) The teacher attempted to guard against any horseplay by instructing the three students who were in the classroom to return to their seats and to remain there. (3) Even though the three students who remained in the classroom during recess were being punished for unrelated misconduct at breakfast, there is no evidence that they were hellions who required constant custodial care.
>
> The Court applied the following cases as a proper standard of review:
> (1) In *Bottorf v. Waltz*, 245 Pa. Super. 139, 369 A.2d 332 (1976), a case

in which a student had been burned when melted wax was spilled on his back, this Court defined the standard of care required of a teacher as follows: "What constitutes proper supervision depends largely upon the circumstances attending the event. Thus, the fact that supervisory personnel present when an accident occurs could conceivably have prevented its occurrence does not necessarily render the school agency liable if the supervisory personnel was competent and acted reasonably under all the circumstances."

The Court went on to say,

There is no liability predicated on lack or insufficiency of supervision where the event in connection with which the injury occurred was not reasonably foreseeable. . . . The courts frequently state that a teacher is not required to anticipate the myriad of unexpected acts which occur daily in and about school, to guard against all dangers inherent in the rashness of children, or to watch all movements of children."

(2) *Ohman v. Board of Education of City of New York*, 300 N.Y. 306, 90 N.E.2d 474 (1949). Here a thirteen-year-old student sustained injury when struck in the eye by a pencil. The pencil had been thrown by one student to another, and when the boy for whom it was intended ducked, the pencil hit the minor plaintiff. The accident occurred while the teacher in charge of the classroom was temporarily absent for the purpose of sorting and storing supplies in a corridor closet. The court held that the teacher's absence from the room was insufficient to impose liability upon the Board of Education, saying:

"A teacher may be charged only with reasonable care such as a parent of ordinary prudence would exercise under comparable circumstances. Proper supervision depends largely on the circumstances attending the event but so far as the cases indicate there has been no departure from the usual rules of negligence."

(3) In *Swaitkowski v. Board of Education of the City of Buffalo*, 36 A.D.2d 783 (1971), the Court held that the Board of Education was not liable for injuries sustained by a student who, upon returning to his seat, sat on the point of a pencil placed on the seat by another student while the teacher was absent from the classroom for as short period to assist another teacher locate books in a bookroom 10½ feet away with the doors open.

(4) In *Morris v. Ortiz*, 103 Ariz. 199, 437 P.2d 652, 35 A.L.R.3d 747 (1968), a student in an auto mechanics class was injured when another

student jumped on a car top which the former student was holding. The trial court directed a verdict in favor of the teacher and school district. In affirming, the Arizona Supreme Court said:

"To hold that the teacher had to anticipate the student's act and somehow circumvent it is to say that it is the responsibility of a school teacher to anticipate the myriad of unexpected acts which occur daily in and about schools and school premises, the penalty for failure of which would be financial responsibility in negligence. We do not think that either the teacher or the district should be subject to such harassment nor is there an evocable legal doctrine or principle which can lead to such an absurd result."

(5) In *Butler v. District of Columbia*, 417 F.2d 1150 (D.C.Cir. 1969), a seventh grade student was struck in the left eye by a sharp piece of metal when he entered a printing classroom. The teacher was then absent because he had been assigned as a hall or cafeteria supervisor. The Plaintiff's case was based on alleged negligent supervision of the classroom after the teacher and principal had prior knowledge that the "horseplay" and throwing had occurred in the classroom. In holding that there could be no recovery, the Court took note of the district's dilemma of balancing "the need for a teacher to supervise several hundred students milling about the corridors and the cafeteria against the need to supervise fourteen students in a certain classroom for a period of time."

From these decisions it can safely be concluded that momentary absence from a classroom is not negligence. This is particularly true where the absence was for the authorized and compelling reason of monitoring the return of about thirty students from recess. The teacher could not have been at two places at the same time. It can also be said that it was not negligence for the teacher to give priority to an entire class of approximately thirty students returning from recess rather than to remain in the classroom to supervise three students who had been required to stay in the classroom during the recess period.

Dissenting Opinion: Judge Cirillo

More emphasis is to be placed on three components of the proper standard of review: (1) the fact that the teacher know the behavior-problem children were in the room while she monitored the students returning from recess, (2) that the teacher was distracted by holding a conversation with fellow teachers in the hallway, and (3) the teacher failed to take a position at the doorway where she would have been in view of both the students in the room as well as those returning from recess.

The teacher may have been authorized to stand outside the classroom to monitor those coming in from recess, but this did not relieve her of the duty to supervise the children as they entered the classroom, especially when she knew the behavior-problem children were in the room; nor did it free her to strike up conversations with fellow teachers in the hallway. Unlike the cases cited by the majority, the teacher could have done both tasks, i.e., monitor those in the hallway and watch those in the classroom at the same time by positioning herself in the doorway so she had a view of the inside of the classroom and that of the hallway. Moreover, the distraction of talking to other teachers when she was supposed to be supervising her thirty students is another factor, which should be considered in determining whether there was sufficient evidence for the trial court to find negligence. These additional facts, which are absent in the cases relied upon by the majority, are sufficient to qualify the "momentary absence" of the teacher and support a finding of negligence. Therefore, I would affirm the finding of negligence by the lower court because it was supported by competent evidence.

Note: The dissenting opinion contends that the teacher was negligent because she positioned herself so that she could neither see nor hear what was transpiring in the classroom. This is not in accord with the facts found by the trial judge and recited in his opinion. Even the minor plaintiff testified that the teacher was but a few feet from the classroom door. The trial judge did find that the boy with the pencil had been running in the classroom. Specifically, he was running up the aisle at the time the minor plaintiff was struck in the eye with the pencil.

9

Teacher Negligence

TORTS

Definition of Torts

Torts are defined as a civil wrong independent of contract. There are so many ways that one person may harm another that there are not enough statutes to describe them. Also, many times the person causing the harm did so unintentionally. Therefore, no criminal act was involved, but someone was harmed. Torts are a way to compensate the injured party without charging the perpetrator with a criminal offense.

Types of Torts

There are three kinds of torts; intentional interference, strict liability, and negligence. The courts impose strict liability when blame cannot be established; therefore, they assign the cost to the party that is deemed most capable of paying. Intentional interference occurs when one person deliberately causes harm to another. These two types of torts do not have tremendous relevance to teachers and schools. Therefore, they will not be discussed within the context of this chapter. Instead, emphasis will be given to negligence, which is a common litigation with regard to teachers and schools.

NEGLIGENCE

Elements of Negligence

Duty

For a teacher to be charged with negligence, the person injured must have been under her supervision or care. Duty extends beyond the classroom to other responsibilities that the school has assigned to the teacher, such as hallway supervision, field trips, etc.

Injury or Actual Loss

For negligence to have occurred, there must be an actual injury or loss. A teacher could act in a very negligent way, but if no one was injured, there is no negligence from a legal point of view. Injury is defined as psychological or emotional as well as physical.

Proximate or Legal Cause

The fact that a student was injured does not necessarily mean the teacher was negligent. It must be shown that the teacher was the proximate or legal cause of the injury.

Standard of Care

In determining if the teacher was the proximate or legal cause of a student's injury, the court uses two yardsticks—reasonableness and foreseeability.

1. Reasonable Standard of Care: The word *reasonable* is a subjective term, which needs descriptors to be understood. The courts have defined reasonable as a hypothetical term that means a community ideal of human behavior, a way that any prudent person would act under the same circumstances.
2. Foreseeability: This is the criterion of negligence that has the most impact in most teacher negligent cases. Even though negligent acts

are neither expected nor intended, they are acts that a reasonable person could have foreseen or anticipated as potentially harmful. Therefore, the teacher should have taken action to prevent the harm. (See the *Simonetti* case described in chapter 8.)

Therefore, it can be concluded that if a teacher is charged with negligence, all the following responses must be present for them to be guilty of the charge:

1. Was the student(s) in question under the teacher's duty? Answer: Yes.
2. Was there an actual injury or loss? Answer: Yes
3. Was the teacher the proximate or actual cause of the injury? Answer: Yes.
4. Did the teacher give a reasonable standard of care? Answer: No
5. Did the teacher exercise foreseeability? Answer: No

Defenses for Negligence

Needless to say, a teacher can claim no responsibility for the injury. In addition, there are three other defenses:

Contributory

This defense claims that the injured student was partly responsible for the actions that resulted in injury. The older and more mature the student, the more responsibility he has for his own actions and consequences.

Comparative

If contributory negligence is found to be present by the courts, they will assign comparative blame to each party. For example, if they determine that the student was 50 percent responsible for the injury, and the monetary award was $100,000, the student would be awarded 50 percent of that amount, which is $50,000. The teacher would then be responsible for the other $50,000.

Assumption of Risk

This type of defense claims that the student knew the activity was dangerous, and therefore assumed the risk when she participated. The courts have declared that assumption of risk only applies to interscholastic athletics and cannot be used when the injury occurs within the curriculum offerings, even if participation was voluntary.

For assumption of risk to be a viable defense in interscholastic cases, the burden of proof is on the school to show that the injured athlete had received proper training and was using proper equipment.

Waivers

Many schools ask parents to sign waivers excusing them from liability in interscholastic athletics, field trips, and so forth. Such waivers do not legally lessen the supervisory responsibilities of the school. The same standard of care is required whether the parents have signed a waiver or not.

Unremitting Scrutiny

The courts have held that to hold a teacher to "unremitting scrutiny" is beyond reasonable care. The term means that a teacher should be responsible for 100 percent of the students 100 percent of the time. That, say the courts, is beyond reasonable care.

Educational Malpractice

In the current political climate, this is bound to become a topic of legal contention. The law is emerging on this topic. It is reasonably safe to say that if a school misdiagnoses a child and that child is harmed by such diagnosis, an educational malpractice charge might be upheld. A second instance could be if a parent could show that the school did not follow the curriculum prescribed by the state or local board of education.

In the past, the courts have left educational decisions to the educators. However, the current accountability climate and the attack on the competency of the public school systems lead one to believe that the courts may become more active in educational malpractice suits. (See *Donohue v. Copiague Union Free School District.*)

TEACHER NEGLIGENCE CASE SUMMARIES

Donohue v. Copiague Union Free School District
Court of Appeals of New York
47 N. Y. 2nd 440, 418 N. Y. S. 2nd 375, 391 N. E. 2nd 1352
June 14, 1979 Filed

Prior History: This case was heard in 1977, 1978, and 1979 as it rose through the New York court system.

Topic: Educational Malpractice.

Issues:

1. Should a student be able to receive monetary damages from a school system for educational malpractice?
2. If a student doesn't learn, is there a negligent breach by a state of a constitutional imposed duty to educate?

Facts: Edward Donohue entered Copiague Senior High School in 1972 and graduated in 1976. He claims that although he received a graduation certificate, he lacks the ability to complete a job application. His complaint is that the school system did not perform its duty and obligation to educate him. Donohue alleges that while attending the school system:

- He received some passing as well as minimal or failing grades in various subjects.
- The system failed to evaluate his mental ability and capacity to comprehend.
- The system failed to take reasonable measures and precautions they should have.
- The system failed to provide adequate schools, teachers, psychologists, and so forth to do the evaluation.

This was the first court case to use the term "educational malpractice," and is usually the case that new cases of educational malpractice refer to when making decisions.

Findings: The case was brought before the courts three times and each time the original ruling was affirmed by the court.

Regarding Issue 1 concerning educational malpractice, the court had to use the four basic and necessary elements of any negligence lawsuit:

- Recognition of a duty using accepted standards,
- Showing that the duty was breached by the defendant,
- There must be a reasonable close causal connection between the defendant's conduct and the injury,
- Actual loss or damage to the plaintiff must be demonstrated.

When using the four elements of malpractice, the court had to answer several questions.

- Should teachers be considered professionals?
- Is there some way to create a standard with which to judge a teacher's and the school system's performance?
- Did something the school system did, or didn't do, directly relate to the student's lack of learning?
- Was the student injured?

Regarding Issue 2: The court decided that the state provision, which read "The legislature shall provide for and maintenance and support of a system of free and common schools wherein all the children of this state may be educated" did not intend to impose a duty from the school district to individualize students. Therefore, this issue was quickly dismissed.

Summary of All Three Courts: Although the complaint of educational malpractice might be able to answer to tort law, it doesn't mean the court should acknowledge it. The courts simply decide that as a matter of public policy they should not entertain such claims. The courts felt that they were not qualified to make judgments on broad educational policies and/or the day-to-day implementation of those policies. The courts felt that the control of schools belonged in the hands of the executive branch of the government, not the judicial.

From the first appellate court:

- It is a practical impossibility to demonstrate that a breach of the alleged common law and statutory duties was the proximate cause of the appellant's failure to learn.
- The failure to learn does not bespeak a failure to teach. Other students who were exposed to the same material and teaching style did learn.
- In addition to innate intelligence, the extent to which a child learns is influenced by a host of social, emotional, economic, and other factors that are not subject to control by a system of public education.

From the second appellate court (Judge Jansen):

- The appellate could probably show that all four criteria for educational malpractice could be met. However, they still ruled against the appellate on the grounds that the court should not entertain such claims for "public policy" reasons.
- In the past the courts refused to make decisions on validity of testing due to the fact that the professional educators were better able to handle that decision. The same principle was applied in this case.
- The student/parents could have used the administrative processes provided by state statute to get help from the commissioner of education to ensure that a student gets a proper education.
- Often national and state governments will use the immunity defense when it comes to torts. When it comes to education, it is used to protect the school districts from liability. The reasoning is, "the welfare of a few must be sacrificed for public interest: school districts." And "that public funds and property shouldn't be used to pay damages since that might impair public education."

Concurring Opinion: Judge Wachtler, concurring with the majority, also made these points:

- The law does not provide a remedy for every injury.
- There is a practical impossibility of proving that the alleged malpractice of the teacher proximately caused the learning deficiency.

Many other factors including attitude, motivation, temperament, past experiences, and home environment may all play essential roles in learning.

Dissenting Opinion: Judge Suozzi wrote a dissenting opinion. He felt the other judges ignored the school transcripts, which showed an obvious lack of understanding on the student's part, and could no way be considered "satisfactory completion" of a course of study. He also felt that the school system made no attempt, as they are required to do, to use standard practices to diagnose the nature and extent of the appellant's learning problem, or to make remedial recommendations. Instead the plaintiff was simply moved through the system. Suozzi felt the case should have gone to trial.

Another case involving educational malpractice, though not termed as such, is *Peter W. v. San Francisco School District.* Some of the main points of the case were:

- Classroom methodology affords no readily acceptable standard of care or cause, or injury. Educational pedagogy has many conflicting views about how a child should be taught.
- Literacy is influenced by many factors that affect the student subjectively, from outside the formal teaching process and beyond the control of the teacher, such as physical, neurological, cultural, and environmental problems; the problems may be present but not perceived, recognized but not identified.

10

School Law and Children with Disabilities

A BRIEF HISTORY

In the 1960s and 1970s, concern for the education of handicapped children began to take hold in the American culture and conscience. The watershed event was the passage by Congress of the 1975 landmark legislation entitled the Education for All Handicapped Children Act (EAHCA). This act has been periodically amended and has evolved into today's law, the Individuals with Disabilities Improvement Education Act of 2004 (hereafter referred to as IDEIA). When combined with the other congressional acts dealing with disabilities, such as the Rehabilitation Act of 1973, Section 504, and the American Disabilities Act, they collectively form the legal framework for the protection of students with disabilities.

Needless to say, the complexity of handicapping conditions, and the interrelationship of handicapped and nonhandicapped education, has produced a voluminous set of case law that has given definition to the intent of IDEA-R and its companion legislation.

SOURCES OF DISABLED INDIVIDUALS' PROTECTION

If the disabled person is of school age (ages 3 through 21), specialized instructional services are provided under IDEIA.

504 vs. IDEIA

Public schools provide services to handicapped students under either Section 504 of the Civil Rights Act or IDEA-R. The differences are explained below.

504	**IDEIA**
antidiscrimination	mandates services
managed by regular education	disability must adversely affect
no money source	performance to such a degree that
no mandate for services	specialized instruction is needed
is meant to provide "level the	money is provided
playing field"	

Rehabilitation Act, Section 504

Section 504 of the Rehabilitation Act is monitored by the Office of Civil Rights. Schools must provide special accommodations to persons who have mental or physical impairments that substantially limit one or more of the person's major life activities (caring for one's self, performing manual tasks, walking, seeing, hearing, breathing, speaking, learning, and working). For a more thorough discussion of the disorders covered by 504, please refer to the *Diagnostic and Statistical Manual for Mental Disorders*.

IDEIA

The Individuals with Disabilities Education Act was initially written into effect in 1978 as Public Law 94-142. It was written in part as a response to Section 504 so that schools could respond to the challenge of educating children with disabilities. The act is reauthorized on a regular cycle. The current regulations went into effect in July 1998, and will be reviewed on a regular basis by Congress. This historic act

- defines FAPE (free and appropriate public education) as special education and related services (*see Tatro case*) that are provided at public expense, under public supervision and direction, and without charge;

- meets state rules for special education adopted by the State Board of Education;
- includes preschool, elementary, and secondary education;
- is provided in conformity with an IEP;
- and provides a free and appropriate education to all children with disabilities, three through twenty-one years of age, unless the child has completed the twelfth grade and has been issued a diploma.

The act also defines Related Services as:

- Speech/language therapy
- Occupational and physical therapy
- Interpreter services
- School health services/medical services
- Counseling services
- Aide services
- Transportation

Through the reauthorization process, the act has redefined the thirteen disability conditions that qualify a child for services under IDEA-R. Currently, these disability conditions are defined as:

- Autism
- Cognitive disability/mental retardation (previously known as developmentally handicapped)
- Deaf-blindness
- Deafness
- Emotional disturbance (previously known as severe behavioral handicapped)
- Hearing impairment
- Multiple disabilities (previously known as multiple handicapped)
- Orthopedic impairment
- Other health impairment, such as having limited strength, limited alertness, and so on
- Specific learning disability
- Speech or language impairment

- Traumatic brain injury
- Visual impairment

The provisions of IDEIA provide that all disabled students who qualify for services must be placed in what is defined as the *least restrictive environment*. The least restrictive environment could be any of the following:

- the regular classroom
- a learning center located in a public school building, separate school within the school district or separate facility, such as a county board of mental retardation or developmentally disabled (applicable to Ohio and Missouri only), a school for the blind, or deaf, or an institution operated by a state department of mental health or department of youth services
- hospital/institution
- home
- other appropriate environments

In most states, the following philosophical position with regard to least restrictive environment is being pursued:

It should be emphasized that, once a child has been identified as being eligible for special education, the connection between special education and related services, and the child's opportunity to experience and benefit from the general education curriculum should be strengthened. The majority of the children identified as eligible for special education and related services are capable of participating in the general education curriculum to varying degrees with some adaptations and modifications. This provision is intended to ensure that children's special education and related services are in addition to and are affected by the general education curriculum, not separate from it.

Since the parents of disabled students must agree to the placement of the child in the least restrictive environment, disagreements between the school and the parents sometimes occur. When this happens, procedural safeguards to resolve the conflict occur and take the following form (varies slightly from state-to-state).

1. Case conference
2. Administrative review
3. Prehearing conference (mediation)
4. Impartial due process hearing
5. State level review
6. Appeal to the courts

Individual Education Plan (IEP) Development

The IEP is designed to meet the unique educational needs of the child. The IEP must include related services necessary for the child to benefit from the special education program. The IEP must be reviewed and revised at least yearly.

IDEIA

In recent years some major changes have been reflected in IDEA-R. The most significant include:

1. Disciplinary procedures and manifestation determination,
2. Reevaluation process improved,
3. Strengthens role of the parent,
4. Strengthens the language about least restrictive environment,
5. Clearer language about children in private schools,
6. Adds components to the IEP,
7. Insists regular education teachers participate in the IEP development,
8. Transfer of rights, age of majority,
9. Focus on improving results through the regular classroom.

The Major Components of IDEIA

1. Child identification
2. Procedural safeguards
3. Multifactored evaluation

4. Individualized education program (IEP)
5. Least restrictive environment
6. Confidentiality of data
7. Due process
8. Testing program

Manifestation

The issue of suspension and/or expulsion of disabled students has been the subject of controversy since the inception of special education. As a result, the process of manifestation was passed by Congress as a part of the reauthorization of IDEA. The formal determination of suspension or expulsion must follow these steps:

1. For disciplinary action beyond ten days, parents must be notified of action and procedural safeguards must be in place no later than the day of the infraction.
2. Immediately, but no later than ten days after the action, a manifest determination review must be held and a formal determination established through the following process:
   • Conduct a review. The ARC must first consider, in terms of behavior subject to disciplinary action, all relevant information (i.e., evaluation results, observations, IEP/placement) and then determine (by asking):
   • "If in relationship to the behavior subject to disciplinary action the child's IEP and placement, were appropriate and the special education services, supplementary aids and services, and behavior intervention strategies were provided consistent with IEP and placement?" If the answer is no, then provide FAPE consistent with IEP/placement and suspension/expulsion is not allowed.
   • If the answer is yes, then ask, "Did the child's disability impair the ability of the child to (1) Understand the impact and consequences of the behavior and/or (2) control the behavior subject to disciplinary action?"
   • If yes to either, suspension or expulsion is not allowed.
   • If no to both, suspension or expulsion is permitted.

HANDICAPPED STUDENT (SPECIAL EDUCATION)
CASE SUMMARIES

Timothy W. v. Rochester, New Hampshire, School District
U.S. Court of Appeals, First Circuit 1989
875 P.2d 954

Topic: Education of severely handicapped children.

Issue: Can a school district deny education to a handicapped child based on that child's ability to benefit from educational services?

Facts: Timothy W. was born two months premature on December 8, 1975. He suffered numerous complications at birth and, as a result, Timothy is multiple-handicapped and profoundly mentally retarded. Timothy suffers from complex developmental disabilities, spastic quadriplegia, cerebral palsy, seizure disorders, and cortical blindness. He did not receive any educational services when he became school age.

March 7, 1980: Rochester Schools decided Timothy was not educationally handicapped. Since his handicap was so severe, he was not capable of benefiting from an education and therefore was not entitled to one.

January 17, 1984: In response to a letter from Timothy's lawyer, the district placement team recommended that he be placed at the Child Development Center so that he could be provided with special education services The school board refused to authorize this, stating it needed more information. They requested a CAT scan and his mother refused.

November 17, 1984: Timothy filed a complaint is U.S. District Court alleging his rights were violated under Education for All Handicapped Children Act (EAHCA), New Hampshire state law, Sections 504, and equal protection/due process clauses of the Constitution. The complaint sought preliminary and permanent injunctions directing the school district to provide Timothy with special education and $175.00 in damages.

July 1988: Opinion of the First District court: Timothy is not capable of benefiting from special education; as a result, the school district is not obligated to provide special education under the EAHCA or New Hampshire law.

May 24, 1989: U.S. Court of Appeals, First District heard the case.

Findings: Circuit Judges Bowies, Aldrich, and Bryer reversed the ruling of the district court. They found for the plaintiff Timothy W., and ordered the case to return to district court until an IEP could be put into place. They ordered immediate interim services and damages to be assessed against the school district.

Rationale: Language of the Act (EAHCA)

- The statute is permeated with the words "all handicapped children."
- The act gives priority to the most severely handicapped.
- There is no language requiring a prerequisite that the child demonstrate that he or she will "benefit" from an educational program.
- It is the state's responsibility to design special education to meet the unique needs of handicapped children.
- Language makes clear "zero-reject" policy.

Legislative History:

- Congress intended the act to provide a public education for all handicapped children.
- The act was a response to testimony and evidence that handicapped children were being systemically excluded from public school and receiving inadequate education.
- The Office of Education provided a report documenting eight million handicapped children, four million of whom were not receiving appropriate services.
- Subsequent amendments to the act: In fourteen years, it has been amended seven times, repeatedly affirming the original intent and in fact expanding provisions. The act never required proof of benefit for eligibility.
- Remarks from Senate hearings: "What we are after in this legislation is to rewrite one of the saddest chapters in American education, a chapter in which we were alert while young children were shut away and condemned to a life without hope. This legislation offers them hope, hope that whatever their handicap, they will be given the chance to develop their abilities as individuals and to reach out with their peers for their own personal goals and dreams" (Senator Mondale).

Case Law: Two landmark cases, *Pennsylvania Association for Retarded Citizens v. Commonwealth of Pennsylvania* (1972) and *Mills v. Board of Education of District of Columbia* (1972), established that exclusion from public school of any handicapped child was unconstitutional.

Board of Education of the Hendrick Hudson Central School District
v.
Amy Rowley, by her parents, Clifford and Nancy Rowley
102 S.Ct.3034; 458 U.S. 176; 73 L. Ed.2d 690; No. 801002
Argued March 23, 1982   **Decided June 28, 1982**

Topic: Parents of a deaf child requested to have their daughter receive services from a qualified sign-language interpreter for all of her academic classes. The parents argued that their daughter was being denied the right to a "free appropriate public education" or FAPE.

Issue: Was Amy Rowley's "free appropriate public education" being denied?

Facts:

1. The Education for All Handicapped Children Act requires that students must receive a "free appropriate public education" whether the student is "mentally retarded, hard of hearing, deaf, speech impaired, visually handicapped, seriously emotionally disturbed, orthopedically impaired, and/or other health impaired children with specific learning disabilities."

2. The school district prepared for Amy's success by providing her with an FM hearing aid that amplified the teacher's words, several teachers and administrators took sign language classes, and the principal had a teletype machine in his office to be able to communicate with Amy's parents who were deaf as well. There was a sign language interpreter placed for a trial period in the classroom; however, the findings were that Amy was an excellent lip reader and was able to be successful with her academics and socially without this service. This service was not written in the IEP for Amy's kindergarten or first-grade year. Mr. and Mrs. Rowley, on behalf of their daughter, demanded a hearing.

3. The district court found for the parents and said that though Amy "is performing better than the average student . . . she understands much

less of what goes on in class than if she were not deaf thus she is not learning as much, or performing as well." The court found that Amy was not receiving her required FAPE.

4. The court and all involved had many questions to what the Education of the Handicapped Act and its FAPE requirements really meant for a handicapped student and the school he or she attended. The Supreme Court granted a writ of certiorari to review the lower courts' analysis of the act and identified two questions to consider:

   • What is meant by the act's requirement of a "free appropriate public education?" and

   • What is the role of the state and federal courts in exercising the review granted by the act?

Findings of the Supreme Court: The Supreme Court found for the school district and that Amy's educational setting and services were being met by the requirements of FAPE. The Supreme Court expressed that the act does define the term "free appropriate public education" as "special education and related services which have been provided at public expense, under public supervision and direction, and without charge, meet state standards, include appropriate grade levels from preschool to secondary education, and provide in conformity with the individualized education program required."

The Court also noted that FAPE should "consist of providing the student with instruction to meet his or her unique needs that are necessary for the student to 'benefit' from the instruction." FAPE provides the student with a reasonable opportunity to learn and does not mean that the student must reach maximum potential. The act opens the door for the handicapped student but does not predict a level of performance.

The Court held that the state, according to the act, is required to provide educational services to those children who are not receiving education at all and secondly to those children receiving "inadequate education."

The Court found that there was not a need for a sign language interpreter in Amy's classroom.

Rationale: Justice Rehnquist delivered the majority opinion by first looking at the history of special education.

At the time of the act's ratification, there were approximately eight million handicapped children in the United States. Of those eight million, one million were "excluded entirely from the public school system" and more than half were receiving an inappropriate education. The act was designed to require states to have procedures to meet the "unique needs" of the handicapped students. Rehnquist continued the opinion by quoting definitions from above and that the intent of the act itself was to give handicapped students the opportunity to learn in a public school setting.

There has been an increased awareness of the educational needs of handicapped children because of this act; however, the Rowley family did not think the act was specific enough. This came about because the act (FNIO) contains that special education needs need to be supported by related services. Rehnquist defined related services from the act itself as "transportation, and such development, corrective, and other supportive services as may be required to assist a handicapped child to benefit from special education." Although the definitions are vague and conveyed, the intent of the act was to provide "free appropriate public education" and does not contain specific requirements. The history and interpretation of the act was at the focal point of this case.

Concurring: Written and delivered opinion by Justice Blackmun, along with Powell, Stevens, O'Connor, and Burger discussing history of Congress' intent of the act. Congress intended to take a "more active role under its responsibility for equal protection" and "it seems plain to me that Congress in enacting this statute, intended to do more that merely set out politically self-serving but essentially meaningless language about what the handicapped children deserve at the hands of the state." Blackmun questioned Amy's program and whether it offered her the opportunity to understand and participate in the classroom. Blackmun suggested "the courts focused too narrowly on the presence or absence of a particular service, the sign language interpreter, rather than on the total package of services Amy was receiving by the School Board."

Dissenting: Justice White wrote this opinion, with Justice Brennan and Justice Marshall joining. White stated that the language of the act contradicts the history. The dissent emphasized that "the Act does guarantee that handicapped children are provided equal educational opportunity." However, at times the purpose of the act was described as tailoring each handicapped child's educational plan to enable the child "to achieve his or her maximum potential."

The dissent also noted that it was unsuitable that the Court found that because Amy was "receiving specialized instruction and she was benefiting, that she was receiving meaningful and therefore appropriate education" without the sign-language interpreter.

Justice White also established that "without a sign-language interpreter, Amy comprehended less than half of what is said in the classroom; therefore she was not given the 'equal opportunity to learn.'"

Honig v. Doe
U.S. Supreme Court
484 U.S. 305 (1988)
484 U.S. 305
Honig, California Superintendent of Public Instruction
v. Doe et al.
Certiorari to the United States Court of Appeals
for the Ninth Circuit
No. 86-728.

Argued November 9, 1987   **Decided January 20, 1988**

The Problem: The Education of the Handicapped Act requires states to ensure a "free appropriate public education" for all disabled children within their jurisdictions. This act provides for parental participation in decisions regarding the education of their disabled child as well as a process for administrative and judicial review. Among these safeguards is the so-called stay-put provision, which directs that a disabled child "shall remain in [his or her] then current educational placement" pending completion of any review proceedings, unless the parents and state or local educational agencies otherwise agree (20 U.S.C. 1415[e][3]). This asks whether state or local school authorities may nevertheless unilaterally exclude disabled children from the classroom for dangerous or disruptive conduct growing out of their disabilities. In addition, the Court was called upon to decide whether a district court may, in the exercise of its equitable powers, order a state to provide educational services directly to a disabled child when the local agency fails to do so (484 U.S. 305, 309).

The Background: This case concerns two emotionally disturbed students in the San Francisco School District in 1980. Student "Doe" was an emotionally disturbed student in a special school. He was emotionally abused as a child and he had become a target for other students due to physical, speech, and grooming abnormalities. He was seventeen and attending a developmental center for disabled students when he assaulted and choked another student, and kicked out a window in response to a verbal taunt. Even though this type of explosive behavior was clearly targeted in his IEP, the principal suspended him for five days and recommended expulsion.

Respondent Jack Smith was identified as an emotionally disturbed child by the time he entered the second grade in 1976. School records prepared that year indicated that he was unable "to control verbal or physical outburst[s]" and exhibited a "[s]evere disturbance in relationships with peers and adults." Further evaluations subsequently revealed that he had been physically and emotionally abused as an infant and young child and that, despite above average intelligence, he experienced academic and social difficulties as a result of extreme hyperactivity and low self-esteem. Of particular concern was Smith's propensity for verbal hostility; one evaluator noted that the child reacted to stress by "attempt[ing] to cover his feelings of low self-worth through aggressive behavior[,] . . . primarily verbal provocations."

Based on these evaluations, SFUSD placed Smith in a learning center for emotionally disturbed children. His grandparents, however, believed that his needs would be better served in the public school setting and, in September 1979, the school district acceded to their requests and enrolled him at A. P. Giannini Middle School. His February 1980 IEP recommended placement in a learning disability group, stressing the need for close supervision and a highly structured environment. Like earlier evaluations, the February 1980 IEP noted that Smith was easily distracted, impulsive, and anxious; it therefore proposed a half-day schedule and suggested that the placement be undertaken on a trial basis.

At the beginning of the next school year, Smith was assigned to a full-day program; almost immediately thereafter he began misbehaving. School officials met twice with his grandparents in October 1980 to discuss returning him to a half-day program; although the grandparents agreed to the reduction, they apparently were never apprised of their right to challenge the decision through EHA procedures. The school officials also warned them that if the child continued his disruptive behavior— which included stealing, extorting money from fellow students, and making sexual comments to female classmates—they would seek to expel him. On November 14, they made good on this threat, suspending Smith for five days after he made further lewd comments. His principal referred the matter to the SPC, which recommended exclusion from SFUSD. As it did in John Doe's case, the committee scheduled a hearing and extended the suspension indefinitely pending a final disposition in the matter. On November 28, Smith's counsel protested these actions on grounds essentially identical to those raised by Doe, and the SPC agreed to cancel the hearing and to return Smith to a half-day program at A. P. Giannini or to provide home tutoring. Smith's grandparents chose the latter option and the school began home instruction on December 10; on January 6, 1981, an IEP team convened to discuss alternative placements.

Next Step: On the day the suspension was to end, the SPC notified Doe's mother that it was proposing to exclude her child permanently from SFUSD and was therefore extending his suspension until such time as the expulsion proceedings were completed. The committee further advised her that she was entitled to attend the November 25 hearing at which it planned to discuss the proposed expulsion.

After unsuccessfully protesting these actions by letter, Doe brought this suit against a host of local school officials and the state superintendent of public instruction. Alleging that the suspension and proposed expulsion violated the EHA, he sought a temporary restraining order canceling the SPC hearing and requiring school officials to convene an IEP meeting. The district judge granted the requested injunctive relief and further ordered defendants to provide home tutoring for Doe on an interim basis; shortly thereafter, she issued a preliminary injunction directing defendants to return Doe to his then-current educational placement at Louise Lombard School pending completion of the IEP review process. Doe reentered school on December 15, five and one-half weeks, or twenty-four school days, after his initial suspension. In Jack Smith's case, it was recommended that he attend a half-day program at a school or receive home tutoring. The grandparents decided that they would prefer home tutoring, but when they heard about John Doe's case, they joined the suit.

The district court said that removing the students resulted in a change of placement since the children weren't receiving the services identified in their IEPs. In the original Education of Handicapped Children Act, there was a section called the "stay put" provision. This basically states that while parents and districts are trying to work out problems with a placement, the child stays in the placement that has been identified in the existing IEP. In a series of decisions, the district judge found that the proposed expulsions and indefinite suspensions of respondents for conduct attributable to their disabilities deprived them of their congressionally mandated right to a free appropriate public education, as well as their right to have that education provided in accordance with the procedures set out in the EHA. The district judge therefore permanently enjoined the school district from taking any disciplinary action other than a two- or five-day suspension against any disabled child for disability-related misconduct, or from effecting any other change in the educational placement of any such child without parental consent pending completion of any EHA proceedings. In addition, the judge barred the state from authorizing unilateral placement changes and directed it to establish an ERA compliance-monitoring system or, alternatively, to enact guidelines governing local school responses to disability-related misconduct. Finally, the judge ordered the state to provide services directly to disabled children when, in any individual case, the state determined that the local educational agency was unable or unwilling to do so.

The Supreme Court: Justice Brennan delivered the opinion of the Court as to holdings number 1 and 2, in which Chief Justice Rehnquist and Justices White, Marshall, Blackmun, and Stevens joined. Chief Justice Rehnquist filed a concurring opinion, post. Justice Scalia filed a dissenting opinion, in which Justice O'Connor joined, post.

As a condition of federal financial assistance, the Education of the Handicapped Act requires states to ensure a "free appropriate public education" for all disabled children within their jurisdictions. In aid of this goal, the act establishes a comprehensive system of procedural safeguards designed to ensure parental participation in decisions concerning the education of their disabled children and to provide administrative and judicial review of any decisions with which those parents disagree. Among these safeguards is the so-called stat-put provision, which directs that a disabled child "shall remain in [his or her] then current educational placement" pending completion of any review proceedings, unless the parents and state or local educational agencies otherwise agree (20 U.S.C. 1415[e][30]). Today we must decide whether, in the face of this statutory proscription, state or local school authorities may nevertheless unilaterally exclude disabled children from the classroom for dangerous or disruptive conduct growing out of their disabilities. In addition, we are called upon to decide whether a district court may, in the exercise of its equitable powers, order a State to provide educational services directly to a disabled child when the local agency fails to do so.

The Court was sensitive to the fact that the original EHA law was designed specifically to make sure that disabled students were not excluded from educational services. Doe's portion was thrown out because there was no likelihood that the situation would happen again. In the present case (Smith), the court has jurisdiction because there is a reasonable likelihood that the respondent will again suffer the deprivation of EHA-mandated rights that gave rise to this suit. We believe that, at least with respect to respondent Smith, such a possibility does in fact exist and that the case therefore remains justifiable.

The Supreme Court rejected the school's argument that they couldn't educate him because he was dangerous to other children, determining that schools could not unilaterally exclude students with disabilities from school. "It is respondent Smith's very inability to conform his conduct to socially accepted behavior that renders him handicapped." The schools could temporarily suspend the child for up to ten days. Within that time, if things had not cooled down or changes been agreed on by the parents, the school could seek court assistance. That court review has become known as a Honig injunction—a process in which the school must prove that maintaining the child in his/her current placement would be substantially likely to result in injury to the child or others. From these holdings the ten-day cut off for suspensions and the availability of emergency injunctive review, emerged the current regulatory scheme. The Court agreed with the District Court and the Court of Appeals. One comment about the Court of Appeals was that they allowed more than 10 days to work things out without calling it a change in placement. The Supreme Court said that it disagreed on this issue.

Oberti v. Board of Education
of the Borough of Clementon School District
995 F.2d 1204 (3rd Cir. 1993)
Rafael Oberti, by His Parents and Friends v.
Board of Education of the Borough of Clementon School District
Argued March 9, 1993   **Decided May 28, 1993**

Topic: Mainstreaming requirement of school districts for children with special education needs.

Issue: Whether schools should fully explore ways to teach students with disabilities in regular classrooms before segregating them in special education settings

Facts:

- Raphael was an eight-year-old child with Down syndrome, a genetic defect that impairs intellectual functioning and ability to communicate.
- [a] The IEP (individualized education plan) for Raphael during the 1989–1990 school year, assigned all eighteen academic goals to the afternoon special education class. The morning kindergarten class goals were to only observe, model, and socialize with nondisabled children.
- While some academic and social progress was made, several behavioral problems arose in the morning kindergarten classroom, including toileting accidents, temper tantrums, crawling and hiding under furniture, touching, hitting and spitting on other children. Raphael also struck the teacher and the teacher's aide.
- The IEP made no plans to address behavior issues, nor did it provide special education consultation or communication between the classroom teacher and the special education teacher. A second aide was provided, but little success was obtained. Raphael did not experience similar behavior problems in the afternoon special education class.
- At the end of the year, the child study team decided to place Raphael in a segregated special education classroom for "educable mentally retarded." Since this was not available in the Clementon School District, Raphael would have to travel to another district.
- The Obertis objected to the segregated placement and requested that Raphael be placed in a regular kindergarten class in Clementon Elementary School. The school district refused and the Obertis asked for a due process hearing. Through mediation, the parents agreed to place Raphael for 1990–1991 in a special education class for "multiple handicaps" at Winslow Township School District (a forty-five minute bus ride). As part of the agreement, Winslow promised to explore mainstreaming possibilities and consider a future placement in a regular classroom at Clementon.

- By January, however, there was no evidence of any plans to consider mainstreaming and Raphael had no contact with nondisabled students at Winslow.
- In January 1991, the Obertis brought another due process complaint under IDEA that Raphael be placed in a regular classroom in his home school, Clementon. The New Jersey Office of Administrative Law decided that the segregated special education class at Winslow was the "least restrictive environment" for Raphael, based on testimony of the kindergarten teacher and other witnesses of the disruptive behavior. Alternate expert witnesses about the education of children with disabilities brought by the Oberti side were discounted.
- As a result of the findings, the Obertis filed civil action in the U.S. District Court for the District of New Jersey under IDEA and unlawful discrimination under 504 of the Rehabilitation Act of 1973, 29 U.S.C 794.

Findings of the Third U.S. District Court: The district court decided that the school district had failed to establish by a preponderance of evidence that Raphael could not at this time be educated in a regular classroom with supplementary aids and services. The court decided that the school district had violated IDEA. The court also found that the school district was discriminating against Raphael in violation of Section 504 of the Rehabilitation Act. The court ordered the school district "to develop an inclusive plan for Raphael Oberti for the 1992–1993 school year consistent with the requirements of IDEA and Section 504 of the Rehabilitation Act.

Rationale:

1. It found many of the techniques the expert said were needed could be implemented in a regular classroom.
2. The school district did not make reasonable efforts to include Raphael in a regular classroom.
3. The behavior problems in 1989–1990 were largely a result of the school district's failure to provide supplementary aides and services.
4. The court discounted the New Jersey Office of Administrative law because "they were largely and improperly based upon Raphael's behavior problems in the developmental kindergarten as well as

upon his intellectual limitations, without proper considerations of the inadequate level of supplementary aids and services provided by the school district."

5. The court used the Roncker test to determine the case: "In a case where the segregated facility is considered superior (academically) the court should determine whether the services which make that placement superior could be feasibly provided in a non-segregated setting. If they can, the placement in the segregated school would be inappropriate under the Act."

6. The Daniel RR test would be better because it gives specific direction to the court in determining whether the school district has met the requirements of IDEA: "whether the school district has made reasonable efforts to accommodate the child in regular classroom; the educational benefits available to the child in a regular class, with appropriate supplementary aids and services, as compared to benefits provided in special education class; and the possible negative effects of the inclusion of the child on the education of the other students in the class." (*see Sacramento v. Holland*)

7. Mainstreaming Test:

   First part of mainstreaming test:

   a) Whether the school district has made efforts to accommodate the child in regular classroom.

   b) The educational benefits available to the child in a regular class, with appropriate supplementary aids and services, as compared to the benefits provided in a special education class.

   c) The possible negative effects of the inclusion of the child on the education of the other students in the class.

   Second part of mainstreaming test:

   Whether the school has included the child in school programs with nondisabled children to the maximum extent appropriate.

The school must take intermediate steps wherever appropriate, such as placing the child in regular education for some academic classes and in special education for others, mainstreaming the child for nonacademic classes only, or providing interaction with nonhandicapped children during lunch and recess. The appropriate mix will vary from child to child, and, from school year to school year as the child develops.

Martinez v. School Board of Hillsborough County, Florida
No. 883667
U.S. Court of Appeals for the 11th Circuit
Argued July 13 and 14, 1988
Reargued December 1, 1988
Decided April 26, 1989

Prior History: Appeal from U.S. District Court for the Middle District of Florida.

Topic: Appropriate placement of a special education student.

Issue: The case involves a mentally retarded child infected with human immunodeficiency virus (HIV), which causes Acquired immunodeficiency syndrome (AIDS), wanting to enroll in the Hillsborough County, Florida School System.

Facts: The child involved deals with the following health-related issues:

- Seven-year-old female student with IQ of 41
- HIV positive
- Student is not toilet trained
- Suffers from thrush, a disease that can produce blood in saliva
- Thumb and finger sucking, which gets saliva on her fingers
- Some skin lesions; which parent would keep child at home if they appeared

In the summer of 1986 Mrs. Martinez attempted to enroll her child in the special education program for the Trainable Mentally Handicapped (THM) in the Hillsborough County School System. The Hillsborough County School System found that home instruction was the appropriate educational placement for the student.

Mrs. Martinez requested an administrative hearing, based on the Education of the Handicapped Act, 84 Stat. 175 (1970) which was codified as amended by the Education for All Handicapped Children Act, 89 Stet. 775 (1975) (EHA). On August 25, 1987, a hearing officer of the Florida Division of Administrative Hearings upheld the school board's decision.

Mrs. Martinez appealed, saying that the hearing officer and board's decision violated her daughter's rights under the EHA, Section 504 of the

Rehabilitation Act of 1973, and the equal protection clause of the Fourteenth Amendment.

The case went to trial without a jury in 1988. Mrs. Martinez gave her suggestion as to what reasonable accommodations could be made that would reduce the risk of transmission by keeping her daughter a safe distance from the other students. The following is a list of suggestions made by Mrs. Martinez:

- assigning a full-time aide
- placing Eliana with nonambulatory TMH students
- using disposable diapers
- using a separate potty chair for toilet training
- limiting the number of students in the room
- using gloves, disinfectants, and other precautions in handling and disposing of waste

The school board still contended that home instruction was the least restrictive environment because some mentally handicapped children did not have control over their bodily functions, and there was a risk of transmission of the AIDS virus to other children. There was also a chance that the other children could spread communicable diseases to Eliana.

The court listened to expert testimony on the risk of transmission. There was a "remote theoretical possibility" of transmission of the AIDS virus through tears, saliva, and urine. The experts believed the most appropriate educational placement for Eliana was as follows:

- Eliana could be taught in a special room with a large glass window and sound system so Eliana could see and hear other students.
- There would be a full-time aide who would remain with Eliana and attempt to toilet train her and teach her not to put her fingers in her mouth.
- Other children could enter the special room only if a waiver was obtained from the child's parents absolving the school board of any liability.
- Eliana could be taught in the main classroom when she became toilet trained, and didn't suck her fingers.
- Once Eliana was potty trained and did not suck her fingers, she could enter the classroom. The full-time aide would ensure appropriate dis-

tance was maintained once Eliana entered the classroom full time, and the school nurse would be available for consultations throughout the day.

Mrs. Martinez appealed the trial court's decision.

Opinion of the Court, Judge Vance:

There are two federal statutes that overlap in this case. The Education of the Handicapped Act "EHA" and section 504 of the Rehabilitation Act of 1973. With these statutes in mind the trial judge must first determine the most appropriate educational placement for the handicapped child under ERA. Next the court must determine whether the child is otherwise qualified within the meaning of section 504 to be educated in the classroom despite the communicable disease. If not, the court must consider what would make the child "otherwise qualified" to be educated in the least restrictive environment. Also, the court must consider the financial burden the accommodations would impose on the institution in making the least restrictive environment for the student.

If Eliana was not infected with AIDS, under the EHA, she would be entitled to attend the regular TMH Classroom. Now you must look at the 504 section to see if it is unlawful to exclude Eliana because of AIDS. The trial court found that there was a "remote theoretical possibility" of transmission with respect to tears, saliva, and urine. This does not rise to the "significant" risk level that is required for Eliana to be excluded from the regular TMH classroom. The Middle District Court of Florida made no decisions with respect to the overall risk of transmission from all bodily substances, including blood in the saliva, to which other children might be exposed in the TMH classroom.

With a decision of 3-0, the Eleventh Circuit Court vacated and remanded the case back to the district court to determine the overall risk of transmission and whether Eliana was otherwise qualified to attend classes in the TMH classroom.

Memorandum Opinion: Elizabeth A. Kovachevich

Based on expert medical judgment and the state of medical knowledge there is a "remote theoretical possibility" of transmission of HIV through bodily secretions such as urine and saliva. Because of this the court does not feel

Children with AIDS are qualified handicapped persons as defined by Section 504; therefore, if a child is handicapped by AIDS, and is of school age, he or she is considered a qualified handicapped person.

The surgeon general, Centers for Disease Control, and other health authorities have reinforced their position stating that "there is no significant risk of contracting AIDS in the classroom."

The Family Educational Rights and Privacy Act protects against unwarranted disclosure of school records. If school districts report any cases of AIDS to public health authorities, school districts should convey such information in a manner that respects the privacy of the individual and the confidential nature of the information, in the same way that information about other diseases is treated.

11

Desegregation

HISTORICAL DEVELOPMENT

In 1868, after the U.S. Civil War, Congress passed—and all the states (including the former Confederate States of America) ratified—the Fourteenth Amendment to the Constitution guaranteeing due process and equal protection to all citizens. Soon thereafter, southern states passed Jim Crow laws, which, in essence, separated the races in relation to travel, facilities, and education. Educational segregation was also practiced in many northern states. Such was the state of affairs in the year 1896, when the U.S. Supreme Court established the separate but equal doctrine, which remained the law of the land until 1954.

The evolution from school segregation to desegregation can best be studied through a case-by-case analysis beginning with the separate but equal doctrine as established by *Plessy v. Ferguson* in 1896 and practiced by public schools in many states during the first half of the twentieth century. *Plessy* was reversed by *Brown I* in 1954, and since then the courts have ruled on various issues and strategies that collectively form the current law on school desegregation.

However, social and cultural events that contributed to the eventual overthrow of the separate but equal doctrine should not be overlooked. For example, World War II was a watershed event for African American aspirations for a better life. Black men who fought and survived the war

236

expected that they would come home to a more inviting society. When they didn't find it, they were more inclined to seek it through legal means. In 1947, Jackie Robinson broke the color barrier in major league baseball, the country's national pastime. In Texas, a black man was admitted to law school because the state did not provide a separate and equal black law college. These and other natural and human initiatives brought the country closer and closer to the reexamination of the separate but equal doctrine. The NAACP became active in fighting the inequalities of separate but equal; however, they were not calling for its elimination—to proceed too quickly, it was felt, would only lead to further and deeper entrenchment of segregation in society. Therefore, the NAACP, under the leadership of Thurgood Marshall, would go to communities who requested their assistance to legally gain separate but equal status for their schools. Four simultaneous conflicts arose in the late 1940s—one in each of the states of Kansas, Delaware, Virginia, and South Carolina. Marshall went to Clarenden County, South Carolina, to assist in an equality challenge. In his brief before a federal district judge, Marshall, although asking for equal treatment for the black children of Clarenden County, stated that he felt that the South Carolina statute separating the races for education was unconstitutional. The judge, John Warring, asked if he was challenging the South Carolina law that segregated schools on a separate but equal basis. When Marshall replied in the affirmative, the judge, citing South Carolina law, convened a three-judge panel to decide the constitutional question.

In the presentation of the case by the plaintiffs, the NAACP on behalf of citizens included testimony and an experiment by a black psychologist, Tom Clark, on the negative effects of school segregation on black children. The famous "black doll" experiment clearly showed that black children, through segregation, had been harmed emotionally and psychologically. In spite of overwhelming testimony that the schools of South Carolina were separate but *not* equal, the panel voted 2-1 to uphold segregation.

Separate but Equal Doctrine

The separate but equal doctrine was quickly applied to public schools. This doctrine, which was upheld seven times in the twentieth century by the U.S. Supreme Court, took the position that so long as facilities were equal for both blacks and whites, the practice did not violate the equal protection clause of the Fourteenth Amendment. It is interesting to note that there was one dissenting vote in *Plessy v. Ferguson*. This famous dissent of Justice John Harlan accurately predicted the current interpretation of the Constitution and the moral standard that the nation would follow by stating, "In view of the Constitution, in the eyes of the law, there is in this country no superior, dominant, ruling class of citizens." He also stated, "Our constitution is color-blind, and neither knows nor tolerates classes among its citizens." The majority of the Court, however, felt otherwise.

In succeeding decisions that upheld the separate but equal doctrine, the rationale of the Court seemed to be based on the notions that (a) the solving of local problems should be left to the states, and (b) to rule otherwise would create social and political chaos in the states practicing desegregation.

Erosion of Separate but Equal

After World War II there was movement in the elimination of separate but equal policies, but it was not occurring in K–12 education. In 1950, the U.S. Supreme Court, in *Sweatt v. Painter* (339 I. S. 629, 70 S. Ct.848), the Court ordered the University of Texas to admit a black student to their law school because a separate but equal law school for blacks did not exist. This and subsequent similar decisions shook the foundation of the separate but equal doctrine.

In the realm of K–12 public education the NAACP's strategy seemed to concentrate on making the southern states live up to their separate but equal policy while simultaneously nudging the country toward its elimination. There was a feeling among some African Americans that to push too far too fast could lead to a setback in what was perceived to be progress in race relations. Therefore, the NAACP, under the leadership of Thurgood Marshall, had to constantly tread a "tightrope" in its quest for equality in public education. Eventually, in *Brown v. Board of Education*, the constitutionality of state statutes requiring the segregation of public schools by race was challenged "head on," and the Supreme Court was faced with the resolution of the issue.

Reversal of Separate but Equal

In *Brown v. Board of Education*, the Supreme Court, in a unanimous decision, declared that separate but equal had no place in public education. The opinion, written by Chief Justice Earl Warren, stated,

> We come to the question presented: Does segregation of children in public schools solely on the basis of race, even though the physical facilities and other "tangible" factors may be equal, deprive the children of the minority group of equal educational opportunities? We believe that it does. . . . We conclude that in the field of public education the doctrine of "separate but equal" has no place. Separate educational facilities are inherently unequal.

This historic decision declared segregation unconstitutional but did not prescribe remedies for its elimination. However, in *Brown II* the court ordered states to proceed with desegregation with all deliberate speed. The Court also remanded the monitoring and enforcement of desegregation plans to the lower federal courts. Fifteen years later, in 1969, the U.S. Supreme Court replaced its "all deliberate speed" standard with the "immediate" standard and ordered all states that had legal segregation prior to 1954 to become unitary immediately.

Attempts to Circumvent *Brown v. Board of Education*

In the decade following Brown, school districts pursued various devices to avoid desegregating. Central to these attempts is the way in which the courts differentiated between desegregation and integration. In the *Briggs v. Elliot* case, which was a companion to *Brown v. Board of Education*, the lower court judge stated that a state may not deny to any person on account of race the right to attend any school that it maintains. This means that the Constitution does not require integration, but does prohibit segregation. Later, northern courts defined the difference between desegregation and integration by stating "There is no constitutional duty on the part of the board to bus Negro children or white children out of their neighborhoods or to transfer classes for the sole purpose of alleviating racial imbalance" (*Deal v. Cincinnati Board of Education*).

In Virginia, in the case of *Griffin v. Prince Edward County*, the court disallowed a county's attempt to avoid desegregation by refusing to

operate a public system and providing money for private schools that refused Negro children. The court ruled that such governmental action was
a violation of the equal protection clause of the Fourteenth Amendment.
Also in Virginia, in the case of *Green County v.*

*County School Board of
New Kent County*, the court struck down a desegregation plan based on
freedom of choice because not one white child chose to attend a black
school and 85 percent of the black students were still in segregated
schools. The court said it did not meet the "with all deliberate speed" standard nor did it comply with court order to achieve a unitary system on a
factor other than race.

De Jure verses de Facto Segregation

As the courts attempted to deal with the controversies surrounding the desegregation plans following *Brown*, the complexity of the issues predicted
in the *Brown I* decision surfaced. The courts defined de jure segregation
as one imposed through the governance structure. It was viewed a deliberate attempt by state and local school authorities to create a dual school
system. In ordering the dismantling of these systems, the courts maintained control over the desegregation plans until they met court approval
through the creation of unitary systems. De facto segregation was a condition resulting from housing patterns and was not automatically a violation of desegregation court orders.

The dilemma of the courts was that sometimes, after a school system
had corrected their de jure segregated condition, housing patterns and
other demographic factors would create a de facto segregated situation.
The legal question then became, once a school has remedied it de jure segregation and had been released from court order to desegregate, did the
reappearance of segregation as a result of housing patterns (de facto)
mean that the school officials would be subject to a new court order to desegregate? This question is ancillary to a second concern. Are school systems under court order to desegregate bound to that order permanently or,
once released, not under further obligations with regard to desegregation?

The Supreme Court has tended to be lenient on school districts that meet
their de jure obligations and then find themselves in a de facto environment.
The Court has been reluctant to force schools to guarantee that building enrollment will be identical to the racial makeup of the school district. They

have tended to look at factors that describe a unitary system, such as decision making that is obviously not motivated by racial bias or prejudice.

STRATEGIES AND REMEDIES TO SEGREGATION

The early efforts of desegregation usually centered on the movement of students, teachers, and staff, both black and white, in an effort to make the racial makeup of the schools as close to the general population of the school district as feasible. The movement of students was primarily achieved through busing plans, such as those mandated in *Swann v. Mechlenburg*. In more recent years the courts have allowed other approaches to desegregation. Among them are:

1. The creation of magnet programs or schools to attract students of all races.
2. Voluntary transfer of students to create racial balance.
3. The creation of early childhood intervention programs.
4. The reduction of the teacher-pupil ratio.
5. Open enrollment policies to encourage the mixing of the races.

The purpose of all these programs is to extend relief to those individuals who had been harmed by past segregation policies, and as a means of overcoming the vestiges of past discrimination.

DESEGREGATION CASE SUMMARIES

Homer Adolph Plessy, Plaintiff in Error v.
Judge J. H. Ferguson, The State of Louisiana
U.S. Supreme Court
163 US 537 No. 210,
Argued October Term 1895   **Decided May 28, 1896**

Topic: Thirteenth Amendment: abolition of slavery a part of the fundamental law. Fourteenth Amendment: newly freed African Americans enjoy full rights as U.S. citizens.

Issue: Should Homer Plessy be tried under a law that robbed him of the full rights of a U.S. citizen? Did the law leave him with a "badge of slavery" by confining him to a segregated "colored car"?

Facts: On June 7, 1892, Homer Plessy, seven-eighths Caucasian, entered the first-class railroad car of the East Louisiana Railway in New Orleans. Shortly after he was seated, Plessy told the conductor that he was a "colored man" according to Louisiana law. The conductor asked him to move to the "colored" car but Plessy refused. Plessy was taken to jail where he was arraigned for "remaining in a compartment of a coach by race he did not belong."

State District Court: On October 28, 1892, Homer Plessy appeared in the state criminal district court before Judge John H. Ferguson. Lionel Adams, the assistant district attorney, had filed an "information" and James Walker, Plessy's attorney, filed his brief claiming innocence. James Walker filed a fourteen-point brief pleading that the law in question clashed with the U.S. Constitution. Adams said the state simply wanted to avoid friction between white and black passengers by seating them in separate cars and said the state had the power to make the law under the Tenth Amendment (powers not delegated to the federal government go to the state). On November 18, 1892, Judge Ferguson accepted Adams' arguments finding precedents supporting his case. He decided that the state could choose to regulate railroad companies that operated within Louisiana. Plessy's lawyers immediately appealed Judge Ferguson's decision to the Louisiana Supreme Court.

Louisiana Supreme Court: Justice Charles E. Fenner had to decide whether the statute in question established a discriminatory distinction "between citizens of the United States" based on race. Fenner concluded the law was not discriminatory because it would apply equally to a white person who tried to sit in a car reserved for blacks. The Louisiana Supreme Court agreed with Adams. "The Supreme Court of the United States has clearly decided the Thirteenth Amendment does not refer to rights of the character here involved." It also stated that the fact that the railroad law required "equal but separate" accommodations by race prevented it from clashing with the Fourteenth Amendment. The state supreme court stated that separate railroad cars may have come from a "deep-rooted prejudice in public opinion" that "is not created by law and cannot be changed by law."

U.S. Supreme Court: Albion Tourgee immediately appealed to the U.S. Supreme Court and with the help of Samuel Phillips restated his case. Phillips stated the Fourteenth Amendment was violated because Plessy sustained injury by being treated in an insulting fashion. Tourgee stated the newly freed slaves were granted national citizenship and were guaranteed "equality of right" and the "free enjoyment of all public privileges."

Alexander P. Morse assisted Adams and took over the defense when the case reached the Supreme Court. Morse concluded the federal courts did not set limits to a state's power. Morse also stated that since most of the states blacks lived on farms, there was a "danger of friction from too intimate contact" with the whites. Finally, Morse used the term "equal" in a broad sense and said, "equal accommodations do not mean identity of accommodations."

The nine Supreme Court justices that heard the case turned into eight when Justice David Brewer excused himself for undisclosed reasons. With a vote of 7-1 the Louisiana Supreme Court decision was upheld. The majority, written by Justice Henry Brown, has been called by many one of the worst decisions in Supreme Court history.

Justice Henry Brown (Majority): Why did the Thirteenth Amendment not apply to the case? The Louisiana law made racial "distinctions" but they did not amount to "discrimination." The law merely stated the obvious: that whites and blacks were different.

How did the Fourteenth Amendment not apply to the states? The amendment implied legal equality in such things as voting and jury service, but not necessarily what might be considered fair social treatment. Justice Brown also stated discrimination was not in the law but in the minds of African Americans forced to sit in the Jim Crow cars.

Could laws bring about racial integration? If the African Americans wanted social equality, Brown said "it must be the result of natural affinities, a mutual appreciation of each other's merits and a voluntary consent of individuals." Brown also stated, "Legislation is powerless to eradicate racial instincts or to abolish distinctions based on physical differences."

Justice John Harlan (Lone Dissenter): Focusing on the fact that the case made whites the superior race, Harlan stated "there cannot be a superior, dominant, ruling class of citizens. There is no caste here. Our constitution is colorblind, and neither knows nor tolerates classes among citizens."

Agreeing to the reasoning of the jurors, Harlan said a state could require "white and black jurors to be separate in the jury box partition. They could be forbidden to stand or sit with each other in a political assembly or even walk in common the streets of a city."

Justice Harlan expected the amendments to give "universal civil freedom and citizenship to all born or naturalized in the United States." The amendments should "obliterate the race line from our system of government."

Supreme Court Justices: Chief Justice Melville Fuller, Edward White, Horace Gray, Rufus Peckham, George Shiras, Stephen Field, Henry Brown, David Brewer, John Harlan.

Precedents: Roberts v. City of Boston (1849); *West Chester and Philadelphia Railroad v. Miles* (1867); *Louisville, New Orleans, and Texas Railway Company v. Mississippi*; *Strauder v. West Virginia*; *Barbier v. Connolly.*

Brown v. Board of Education
Argued December 9, 1952
Reargued December 8, 1953
Decided May 17, 1954

Topic: School segregation.

Issue: Is the segregation of children (in school) based on race a violation of the Fourteenth Amendment? Is "separate but equal," as established in *Plessy v. Ferguson*, constitutional?

Related History: In 1896, the Supreme Court ruled that "separate but equal" was acceptable. This became the precedent that courts did not seem to want to challenge.

Facts: Linda Brown was an African American child. She had to go to another part of Topeka to attend a school for black children, while white children could attend the neighborhood school only blocks away. The Topeka School system was segregated on the basis of race, and under the separate but equal doctrine, this arrangement was acceptable and legal. Linda's parents sued in federal district court on the basis that separate facilities for blacks were inherently unequal. The lower courts agreed with the school system that if the facilities were equal, the child was being treated equally with whites as prescribed by the Fourteenth Amendment.

> Fourteenth Amendment, Section 1. All persons born or naturalized in the United States, and subject to the jurisdiction thereof, are citizens of the United States and of the state wherein they reside. No state shall make or enforce any law which shall abridge the privileges or immunities of citizens of the United States; nor shall any state deprive any person of life, liberty, or property, without due process of law; nor deny to any person within its jurisdiction the equal protection of the laws.

The Browns and other families in other school systems appealed to the Supreme Court that even facilities that were physically equal did not take into account "intangible" factors, and that segregation itself has a deleterious effect on the education of black children. Their case was encouraged by the National Association for the Advancement of Colored People (NAACP) and was argued before the Supreme Court by Thurgood Marshall, who would later become the first black justice on the Supreme Court.

Defense: The board of education's defense was that, because segregation in Topeka and elsewhere pervaded many other aspects of life, segregated schools simply prepared black children for the segregation they would face during adulthood. The board also argued that segregated schools were not necessarily harmful to black children; great African Americans such as Frederick Douglass, Booker T. Washington, and George Washington Carver had overcome more than just segregated schools to accomplish what they achieved.

Supreme Court Ruling: The Supreme Court ruled unanimously to end racial segregation in public schools.

Rationale: The high court ruled unanimously to overturn the *Plessy v. Ferguson* decision. Chief Justice Earl Warren delivered the decision of the Court. After outlining the facts of the case and history of the Court's thinking on the separate but equal doctrine, Warren stressed the importance of education in the consciousness of American life:

> Today, education is perhaps the most important function of state and local governments. Compulsory school attendance laws and the great expenditures

for education both demonstrate our recognition of the importance of education to our democratic society. It is required in the performance of our most basic public responsibilities, even service in the armed forces. It is the very foundation of good citizenship. Today it is a principal instrument in awakening the child to cultural values, in preparing him for later professional training, and in helping him to adjust normally to his environment. In these days, it is doubtful that any child may reasonably be expected to succeed in life if he is denied the opportunity of an education. Such an opportunity, where the state has undertaken to provide it, is a right which must be made available to all on equal terms.

We come then to the question presented: Does segregation of children in public schools solely on the basis of race, even though the physical facilities and other "tangible" factors may be equal, deprive the children of the minority group of equal educational opportunities? We believe that it does.

The rational of the Court's decision was based on the dehumanizing effects of segregation:

Segregation of white and colored children in public schools has a detrimental effect upon the colored children. The impact is greater when it has the sanction of the law, for the policy of separating the races is usually interpreted as denoting the inferiority of the Negro group. A sense of inferiority affects the motivation of a child to learn. Segregation with the sanction of law, therefore, has a tendency to [retard] the educational and mental development of Negro children and to deprive them of some of the benefits they would receive in a racial[ly] integrated school system.

The basis of the decision rested on the equal protection clause of the Fourteenth Amendment, which applied the standard of equality to the actions of the states as well as the federal government in a concept known in legal circles as "incorporation." Warren wrote:

We conclude that, in the field of public education, the doctrine of "separate but equal" has no place. Separate educational facilities are inherently unequal. Therefore, we hold that the plaintiffs and others similarly situated for whom the actions have been brought are, by reason of the segregation complained of, deprived of the equal protection of the laws guaranteed by the Fourteenth Amendment.

Facts for Features
US Census Bureau
CB04-FFSE.02   **February 4, 2004**
Special Edition*
Brown v. Board of Education:
50th Anniversary

On May 17, 1954, the U.S. Supreme Court ruled unanimously that segregation of public schools "solely on the basis of race" denied black children equal educational opportunity, even though "physical facilities and other 'tangible' factors may have been equal." The plaintiff's case was argued by Thurgood Marshall, later to become the first black Supreme Court justice. To commemorate that landmark decision, the Census Bureau has assembled data on the educational attainment and school enrollment of blacks—then and now.

Enrollment: 1954 to 2002

69%
Percentage of black children ages 5 and 6 who were enrolled in school in 1954. By 2002, enrollment for black children of those ages was 96 percent.

<http://www.census.gov/population/www/socdemo/school.html>

24%
Percentage of young, black adults ages 18 and 19 who were enrolled in school in 1954. In 2002, the comparable enrollment was 58 percent.

<http://www.census.gov/population/www/socdemo/school.html>

High School Graduates: 1952 to 2002

15%
Percentage of blacks age 25 and over in 1952 who were at least high school graduates. By 2002, this rate had risen to 79 percent.

<http://www.census.gov/population/www/socdemo/educ-attn.html>

1.6 million
Number of blacks 25 years old and over with at least a high school diploma in 1957. This number had risen to 16.0 million by 2002.

<http://www.census.gov/population/socdemo/education/ppl-169/tab01.pdf>

College Graduates: 1952 to 2002

2%

Percentage of blacks age 25 and over in 1952 who were college graduates. By 2002, the rate had risen to 17 percent.

<http://www.census.gov/population/socdemo/education/tabA-2.pdf>

252,000

Number of blacks who had at least a bachelor's degree in 1957. In 2002, 3.5 million blacks had at least a bachelor's degree.

<http://www.census.gov/population/socdemo/education/ppl-169/tab01 .pdf>

Students: 1955 to 2002

4.5 million

Number of blacks enrolled in schools (nursery through college) in 1955. This number had risen to 11.7 million by 2002.

<http://www.census.gov/population/socdemo/school/tabA-1.pdf>

155,000

Number of black college students in 1955. By 2002, this number had risen to 2.3 million.

<http://www.census.gov/population/socdemo/school/tabA-1.pdf>

926,000

Number of black high school students in 1955. In 2002, this number was 2.6 million.

<http://www.census.gov/population/socdemo/school/tabA-1.pdf>

On an occasional basis, the U.S. Census Bureau issues special editions of Facts for Features to commemorate anniversaries or observances, or to provide background information for topics in the news. Below is a listing of previous such editions:

U.S. Armed Forces and Veterans (April 10, 2003)

Tax Time (April 11, 2003)

Louisiana Purchase Bicentennial (May 12, 2003)

Dialing for Dollars (Sept. 24, 2003)

First Flight Centennial (Dec. 3, 2003)

Social Security COLA (Dec. 11, 2003)

The 2004 Presidential Election (Jan. 6, 2004)

Editor's note: Some of the preceding data were collected in surveys and, therefore, are subject to sampling error. Questions or comments should be directed to the Census Bureau's Public Information Office: telephone: (301) 763-3030; fax: (301) 457-3670; or e-mail: <pio@census.gov>.

Brown v. Board of Education
Myths v. Truths

Today's public understanding of the landmark U.S. Supreme Court decision in *Brown v. Board of Education* has been shaped by misconception and inaccurate information.

While *Brown v. Board of Education* is one of the most important milestones in U.S. history, it is often misunderstood. Below are commonly held myths about the case, and the realities of what actually transpired.

Table 11.1.

Myth	Truth
Brown v. Board of Education was the first legal challenge to racially segregated schools in the United States.	African American parents began to challenge racial segregation in public education as early as 1849 in the case of *Roberts v. City of Boston, Massachusetts.* Kansas was the site of eleven such cases spanning from 1881 to 1949.
The *Brown* case in Kansas came about because Linda Brown was denied access to her neighborhood school and had to walk dozens of blocks to attend an African American school.	The *Brown* case was initiated and organized by the National Association for the Advancement of Colored People (NAACP) leadership who recruited African American parents in Topeka for a class action suit against the local school board. Although school buses were provided for African American children, they were only allowed to attend designated public schools based on race.
The only plaintiff in the *Brown* case was Oliver Brown on behalf of his daughter.	In 1952, *Brown v. Board* was brought before the U.S. Supreme Court as a combination of five cases from various parts of the country, representing nearly 200 hundred plaintiffs.
Oliver Brown's name led the roster in the Topeka case because it was the first alphabetically of the thirteen NAACP plaintiffs.	The Kansas case was named after Oliver Brown as a legal strategy to have a man at the head of the roster. There actually were two plaintiffs with the surname of Brown: Darlene Brown and Oliver Brown. The only male plaintiff was Oliver Brown, for whom the Topeka case was named.

(continued)

Table 11.1. *(continued)*

Myth	Truth
Oliver Brown initiated the suit against the Topeka Board of Education.	Oliver Brown was asked to join the class action suit by Charles Scott, one of three serving as legal counsel for the Topeka NAACP.
The U.S. Supreme Court decision in *Brown v. Board of Education* was based on the Topeka case.	The Supreme Court combined five cases under the heading of *Brown v. Board of Education* from Delaware, Kansas, South Carolina, Virginia, and the District of Columbia. Those individual cases were: • *Belton v. Gebhardt* (*Bulah v. Gebhardt*) (Delaware) • *Brown v. Board of Education* (Kansas) • *Briggs v. Elliot* (South Carolina) • *Davis v. Prince Edwards County School Board* (Virginia) • *Bolling v. Sharpe* (District of Columbia)
Thurgood Marshall was the NAACP attorney for the case of *Brown v. Board of Education.*	The strategy to use the courts to challenge segregation in public education began with the NAACP under the leadership of attorney Charles Hamilton Houston during the 1930s. Houston was the former dean of Howard University Law School. Thurgood Marshall was hired into the NAACP by Houston, and worked on *Brown* with a team of attorneys.
The objective of the NAACP's legal challenge in the *Brown v. Board of Education* was to eliminate segregation in public education.	Ultimately, the NAACP sought to end the practice of "separate but equal" throughout every segment of society, including public transportation, dining facilities, public schools, and all forms of public accommodation.

The initial Court ruling rendered in 1954 that determined racial segregation in public education was unconstitutional is known as *Brown I*. The Court implementation mandate of "with all deliberate speed" in 1955 is known as *Brown II*. In 1979, three young African American attorneys in Topeka petitioned the court to reopen the original *Brown* case to examine whether or not the local school board had in fact ended all vestiges of segregation in public schools. That case is known as *Brown III*, which resulted in Topeka public schools building three magnet schools to comply with the Court's findings.

Freeman v. Pitts
503 U.S. 467 (1992)

Topic: A federal district court partially withdrew its supervision and control of DeKalb County School System's (DCSS) desegregation plan.

Issue: Does a court have the authority to relinquish remedial control in those areas where unitary status has been achieved as defined by the Green factors? (The Green factors, a result of *Green v. County School Board of New Kent County*, are framework providing six areas where a school district can demonstrate it is a unitarian and not a de jure district. These six determinants are student assignment, faculty, staff, transportation, extracurricular activities, and facilities. The court looks in these areas to determine whether or not sufficient movement has been made in the desegregation effort.)

Facts: In 1969 the U.S. District Court for the Northern District of Georgia entered a consent order to dismantle the de jure segregation in the DeKalb County School System (DCSS) as a result of a suit filed by black schoolchildren and their parents. The district court held jurisdiction through 1986 when DCSS filed a petition for dismissal, stating they have achieved unitary status. The court found DCSS had achieved unitary status in four of the six Green factors, and ordered no further relief in those areas. Additionally, the court retained supervision only in those two areas not meeting the unitary definition.

The case went to the Court of Appeals for the Eleventh Circuit (1989) and they reversed the district court's decision. The appellate court stated the district court could not relinquish full remedial authority until all six of the Green factors were met for a period of several years. The case was argued before the Supreme Court in October 1991.

Findings of the Supreme Court: The decision of the appeals court was reversed on two points. First, the Supreme Court held that a district court does have the authority to relinquish supervision and control in incremental stages before full compliance of the court-ordered consent. Second, the court of appeals erred in holding that, as a matter of law, the district court had no discretion to permit DCSS to regain supervision and control over the four Green factors for which the school district provided a remedy.

Rationale: In the opinion of the Court delivered by Justice Kennedy, the Supreme Court determined the term *unitary* did not have a fixed meaning. The duty impressed upon the district court by the consent order was to supervise the transition into desegregation, eventually restoring control back to the district now in compliance. Additionally, the four complying areas were scrutinized individually to ensure whether full and satisfactory compliance had been achieved, whether retention of control was still necessary to achieve compliance in other areas, and whether the district had acted in good faith to remedy the situation, before court supervision could be relinquished. DCSS demonstrated through their policies and subsequent court directives adequacy in four areas of measurement.

The error of the application of law found by the Supreme Court rests on the premise that the above question, could the district court relinquish partial control, was answered in the affirmative. The district court used equitable discretion in that they decided to concentrate on the areas where de jure discrimination had not been sufficiently eliminated. An important distinction is made between de jure and de facto discrimination. A district that provides a remedy for de jure discrimination will not be liable for any de facto discrimination that may occur in the same time period. A "racial balance is not to be achieved for its own sake." As in the DCSS case, population demographics changed such that they would have failed the student assignment test under a de jure eye.

Regents of the University of California v. Bakke
No. 7811
438 U.S. 265

Argued: October 12, 1977   **Decided: June 28, 1978**

Topic: Did the University of California (Davis campus) violate the Fourteenth Amendment's equal protection clause and the Civil Rights Act of 1964, by practicing an affirmative action policy that resulted in the repeated rejection of Bakke's application for admission to its medical school?

Issue: Alan Bakke, a thirty-five-year-old white man, had twice applied for admission to the University Medical School at Davis. He was rejected both times. The school reserved sixteen places in each entering class of one hundred for "qualified" minorities, as part of the university's affirmative action program, in an effort to redress longstanding, unfair minority exclusions from the medical profession.

Bakke's qualifications (college GPA and test scores) exceeded those of any of the minority students admitted in the two years Bakke's application was rejected. Bakke contended, first in California courts, then in the Supreme Court, that he was excluded from admission solely on the basis of race.

Facts: The medical school of the University of California at Davis had two admissions programs and the special admissions program for the entering class of 100 students—the regular admissions program and the special admissions program; under the regular procedure, candidates whose overall undergraduate grade point averages fell below 2.5 on a scale of 4.0 were rejected. About one out of six applicants was given an interview, following which he or she was rated on a scale of 1 to 100, based on the interviewers' summaries, his overall grade point average, his science course GPA, his Medical College Admissions Test (MCAT), letters of recommendations, extracurricular activities, and other biographical data, all which resulted in a total "benchmark score." The full admissions committee then made offers of admission on the basis of their review of the applicant's file and score. The committee chairperson was responsible for placing names on the waiting list and had discretion to include persons with "special skills."

A separate committee, a majority of who were members of minority groups, operated the special admissions program. The application forms asked the candidates whether they wished to be considered members of "economically and/or educationally disadvantaged " applicants and members of a "minority" (blacks, Chicanos, Asians, American Indians). Special candidates did not have to meet the 2.5 grade cutoff and were not ranked against candidates in the general admission process. About one-fifth of the special applicants were invited for interviews in 1973/1974, following which they were given benchmark scores, and the top choices were then given to the general admissions committee, which could reject special candidates for failure to meet course requirements or specific deficiencies. The special committee continued to recommend candidates until sixteen special admission selections had been made.

Allan Bakke, a white male, applied to the medical school in 1973 and 1974 under the general admissions program. He had scored 468 out of 500 in 1973; he was rejected, since no general applicant scored less than 470 was being accepted. At that time, four special admission slots were still unfilled. In 1974, Bakke applied again and received a scored of 549 out of 600, but was rejected again. In neither year was his name placed on the discretionary list. In both years, special applicants were admitted with significantly lower scores than Bakke.

Action: Bakke (respondent) filed action in state trial court for mandatory, injunctive, and declaratory relief to compel his admission to the medical school. He alleged the special admission program operated to exclude on the basis of race in violation of the equal protection clause of the Fourteenth Amendment, a provision of the California Constitution and section 601 of Title VI of the Civil Rights Act of 1964, which provides inter alia that no person shall, on the ground of race or color, be excluded from participating in any program receiving federal financial assistance.

The university (petitioner) claimed that the special admissions program was lawful. The trial court found that the special program operated a racial quota, because minority applicants in that program were rated against one another, and sixteen places in the class of 100 were reserved for them. The trial declared that the university could not take race into account in making decisions for the program. The program was held to violate the federal and state constitutions and Title VI. Bakke's admission was not ordered by the court; also he did not have proof that he would have been admitted if the special program did not exist.

Bakke appealed from the portion of the trial court denying his admission and the university appealed from the decision that its special admissions program was unlawful and the order enjoining it from considering race in the process of applications. The California Supreme Court concluded that the special admissions program was not the least intrusive means of achieving the goals of integrating the medical profession and increasing the number of doctors willing to serve minority patients, even though both were compelling state interests. The California court held that the equal protection clause of the Fourteenth Amendment required that no applicant be rejected because of his race, in favor of another who is less qualified, as measure applied without regard to race. Since the university could not satisfy the burden of demonstrating that Bakke, absent the special program, would not have been admitted, the court ordered his admission to Davis.

The order was stayed pending review in the U.S. Supreme Court, which granted certiorari to consider the important constitutional issue.

Conclusion: There was no single majority opinion. Four of the justices contended that any racial quota system supported by the government violated the Civil Right Act of 1964. Justice Lewis Powell Jr. agreed, casting the deciding vote and ordering the medical school to admit Bakke.

More Facts: Justice Powell concluded:

> Title VI proscribes those racial classifications that would violate the Equal Protection Clause if employed by a State or its agencies. Racial and ethnic classifications of any sort are inherently suspect and call for the most exacting scrutiny. While the goal of achieving a diverse student body is sufficiently consideration of race in admissions under some circumstances, University (petitioners) special admissions program, which forecloses consideration to persons like Bakke (respondent) is unnecessary to the achievement of this compelling goal, and therefore invalid under the Equal Protection Clause. Since petitioner could not satisfy its burden of proving the respondent would not have been admitted if there had been no special admission program, he must be admitted.

Justice Brennan, Justice White, Justice Marshall, and Justice Blackmun concluded:

> Title VI proscribes those racial classifications that would violate the Equal Protection Clause if employed by a State or its agencies. Racial classification calls for strict judicial scrutiny. Nonetheless, the purpose of overcoming chronic minority under presentation in the medical profession is sufficiently important to justify petitioner's remedial use of race. Thus, the judgment below must be reversed in that it prohibits race from being used as a factor in university admissions.

Justice Stevens, Chief Justice, Justice Stewart, and Justice Rehnquist held the view that whether race can ever be a factor in an admissions policy is not the issue here, that Title VI applies, and that the respondent (Bakke) was excluded from Davis Medical School in violation of Title VI concurs in the Court's judgment insofar as it affirms the judgment of the court below ordering Bakke admitted to Davis.

The Civil Rights Act intended that "No person in the United States shall, on the ground, color, or national origin, Be excluded from participation in, be denied of, or be subjected to discrimination under any program or activity receiving Federal financial assistance."

Title VI of the Civil Rights Act of 1964 was "intended to halt federal funding of entities that violate a prohibition of racial discrimination as in the constitution, and to assure the existing right to equal treatment in the enjoyment of Federal Funds."

There is constitutional restriction against discrimination in the use of federal funds; and Title VI spells out the procedure to be used in enforcing the restriction.

Milliken v. Bradley
Supreme Court of the United States, 1974
418 U.S. 717, 94 S.Ct.3112

Issue: Whether a federal court may impose a multidistrict, area-wide remedy to a single-district segregation problem without any finding that the other included school districts have failed to operate unitary school systems within their district.

Facts: School districts around Detroit, Michigan, were found by a lower federal district court to be so constituted as to create school segregation in the central city. The federal district court and the federal court of appeals concluded that desegregation of the Detroit schools was impossible, unless the racial composition of the entire metropolitan area was taken into account.

According to these federal courts, the dismantling of segregation required interdistrict busing between inner-city school districts and school districts in the surrounding suburbs. Fifty-four independent school districts would be involved.

The case was appealed to the Supreme Court.

Ruling of the U.S. Supreme Court: Chief Justice Burger delivered the opinion. The Supreme Court held that there was no evidence in the record to show that the original boundaries of the school districts were established for the purpose of segregation of race. There was also no evidence that the included districts had committed acts that affected segregation within the other districts, and the included districts had not been given a chance to present evidence or to be heard.

The Supreme Court also pointed out all the operational problems that would be presented.

Finally, the Court held that from the scope of the interdistrict remedy that absent a complete restructuring of the laws of Michigan relating to the school districts, the district court would become the "de facto legislative authority" to resolve complex questions, and then the "superintendent" for the entire area. According to this ruling, this was not a task for a judge.

The judgment of the court of appeals was reversed and the case was remanded for further proceedings.

Swann v. CharlotteMecklenberg Board of Education
402 U.S. 1.91 Supreme Court 1267, 1971

Topic: Desegregation of Schools

Issue: Does state-imposed segregation by race in the public schools deny equal protection of the law?

Facts:

1. The Charlotte-Mecklenburg school system, which includes the city Charlotte, N.C., had more than 84,000 students in 107 schools in 1968–1969. The Charlotte-Mecklenburg system had been operating separate systems of education, one for black children and one for white children.
2. Approximately 24,000 of the students were African American; around 14,000 of these students were in twenty-one schools that were at least 99 percent African American. This was due to the desegregation plan approved by the district court in 1985 by way of zoning and transfer free provisions.
3. In 1968 petitioner Swann moved to further relieve these schools of segregation based on *Green v. County Board*, 391 U.S. 430, which requires school boards to come forward with a "plan that promises to realistically work . . . now . . . until it is clear that state imposed segregation has been completely removed."
4. The district court ordered the school board in April of 1969 to provide a plan for faculty and student desegregation. The board submitted an unsatisfactory plan, so the court appointed an educational expert to devise an alternative desegregation plan.

5. The district court was presented in February of 1969 with two plans: the school board's final plan and Dr. Finger's plan. The board's plan restructured school attendance zones to gain racial balance but rejected as strategies such as pairing and clustering to achieve desegregation. The proposed attendance zones for the high schools would allow students in the inner city access to the outlying schools.

6. The Finger plan was similar to the upper-level schools but differed greatly for the seventy-six elementary schools. He proposed the pairing and clustering strategy for those schools.

7. On February 5, 1970, the district court approved the board plan but with the modifications as stated by Dr. Finger for the junior and senior high schools. The court also adopted the Finger plan for the elementary schools.

8. The school board appealed. The court of appeals affirmed the district court's order as to the junior and senior high schools, but rejected the order in regards to the elementary schools. The court feared that the pairing and clustering of elementary schools would place an undue burden on the board and the students.

9. The U.S. Supreme Court granted certiorari.

10. The focal point in this case was that of student placement. The Court recognized four problem areas.

   a. To what extent can racial balance or racial quotas be used to implement a remedial order to correct segregated school system?

   b. Whether an all African American and an all-white school must be eliminated as part of the process of desegregation?

   c. What are the limits on the rearrangement of school districts and attendance zones as a measure of desegregation?

   d. What are the limits on the use of transportation facilities to correct state-imposed racial segregation?

Findings: On April 20, 1971, by a unanimous vote (9-0) the U.S. Supreme Court affirmed the judgment of the court of appeals as to those parts that were affirmed by the district court. Based on the facts of this case, the Court was unable to conclude that the order of the district court is not reasonable, economical, and workable. The Court stated that busing to overcome racial segregation is a judicially appropriate alternative where de jure segregation has existed.

Rationale: Chief Justice Berger wrote the opinion of the Court.

- Racial balance and racial quotas using mathematical ratios were just a starting point in the process of reshaping the schools. The school authority's remedial plan or district court decree is to be judged by its effectiveness. The limited use of mathematical ratios was within the remedial discretion of the district court.
- One-race schools, a familiar phenomenon in the metropolitan areas, are often found concentrated in one location in the city. Schools of all or predominately one race in a district of mixed population will need close scrutiny to determine that the school assignments are genuinely nondiscriminatory. The burden is now upon the school to satisfy the Court that the racial composition is not the result of present or past discriminatory practice on their part.
- The Court held that the pairing and grouping of noncontiguous school zones as a tool to alter attendance zones is permissible and such action is to be considered in light of the objectives sought.
- As for the transportation of students, no strict guidelines can be given due to the variety of problems presented in thousands of cases. The strategy used in the district court's order was within that court's power to provide equitable relief. The implementation of the decree is within the capacity of the school authority. Desegregation plans cannot be limited to the "walk-in" schools. An objection to the transportation of students could have validity when the time and/or distance is so great that it is either a risk to the health of students or can significantly impinge on the educational process.

A

The Constitution of the United States: Selected Provisions

We the People of the United States, in Order to form a more perfect Union, establish Justice, insure domestic Tranquility, provide for the common defense, promote the general Welfare, and secure the Blessings of Liberty to ourselves and our Posterity, do ordain and establish this Constitution for the United States of America.

ARTICLE I.

Section 1.

All legislative Powers herein granted shall be vested in a Congress of the United States, which shall consist of a Senate and House of Representatives.

Section 2.

The House of Representatives shall be composed of Members chosen every second Year by the People of the several States, and the Electors in each State shall have the Qualifications requisite for Electors of the most numerous Branch of the State Legislature.

Section 7.

All Bills for raising Revenue shall originate in the House of Representatives; but the Senate may propose or concur with Amendments as on other Bills.

Every Bill which shall have passed the House of Representatives and the Senate, shall, before it become a Law, be presented to the President of the United States: If he approves he shall sign it, but if not he shall return it, with his Objections to that House in which it shall have originated, who shall enter the Objections at large on their Journal, and proceed to reconsider it. If after such Reconsideration two thirds of that House shall agree to pass the Bill, it shall be sent, together with the Objections, to the other House, by which it shall likewise be reconsidered, and if approved by two thirds of that House, it shall become a Law. But in all such Cases the Votes of both Houses shall be determined by yeas and Nays, and the Names of the Persons voting for and against the Bill shall be entered on the Journal of each House respectively. If any Bill shall not be returned by the President within ten Days (Sundays excepted) after it shall have been presented to him, the Same shall be a Law, in like Manner as if he had signed it, unless the Congress by their Adjournment prevent its Return, in which Case it shall not be a Law.

Every Order, Resolution, or Vote to which the Concurrence of the Senate and House of Representatives may be necessary (except on a question of Adjournment) shall be presented to the President of the United States; and before the Same shall take Effect, shall be approved by him, or being disapproved by him, shall be re-passed by two thirds of the Senate and House of Representatives, according to the Rules and Limitations prescribed in the Case of a Bill.

Section 8.

The Congress shall have Power To lay and collect Taxes, Duties, Imposts and Excises, to pay the Debts and provide for the common Defense and general Welfare of the United States; but all Duties, Imposts and Excises shall be uniform throughout the United States;

To borrow Money on the credit of the United States;

To regulate Commerce with foreign Nations, and among the several States, and with the Indian Tribes;

To establish an uniform Rule of Naturalization, and uniform Laws on the subject of Bankruptcies throughout the United States;

To coin Money, regulate the Value thereof, and of foreign Coin, and fix the Standard of Weights and Measures;

To provide for the Punishment of counterfeiting the Securities and current Coin of the United States;

To establish Post Offices and post Roads;

To promote the Progress of Science and useful Arts, by securing for limited Times to Authors and Inventors the exclusive Right to their respective Writings and Discoveries;

To constitute Tribunals inferior to the Supreme Court;

To define and punish Piracies and Felonies committed on the high Seas, and Offences against the Law of Nations;

To declare War, grant Letters of Marque and Reprisal, and make Rules concerning Captures on Land and Water;

To raise and support Armies, but no Appropriation of Money to that Use shall be for a longer Term than two Years;

To provide and maintain a Navy;

To make Rules for the Government and Regulation of the land and naval Forces;

To provide for calling forth the Militia to execute the Laws of the Union, suppress Insurrections and repel Invasions;

To provide for organizing, arming, and disciplining, the Militia, and for governing such Part of them as may be employed in the Service of the United States, reserving to the States respectively, the Appointment of the Officers, and the Authority of training the Militia according to the discipline prescribed by Congress;

To exercise exclusive Legislation in all Cases whatsoever, over such District (not exceeding ten Miles square) as may, by Cession of particular States, and the Acceptance of Congress, become the Seat of the Government of the United States, and to exercise like Authority over all Places purchased by the Consent of the Legislature of the State in which the Same shall be, for the Erection of Forts, Magazines, Arsenals, dock-Yards, and other needful Buildings;—And

To make all Laws which shall be necessary and proper for carrying into Execution the foregoing Powers, and all other Powers vested by this Constitution in the Government of the United States, or in any Department or Officer thereof.

Section 9.

The Privilege of the Writ of Habeas Corpus shall not be suspended, unless when in Cases of Rebellion or Invasion the public Safety may require it.
No Bill of Attainder or ex post facto Law shall be passed.

Section 10.

No State shall enter into any Treaty, Alliance, or Confederation; grant Letters of Marque and Reprisal; coin Money; emit Bills of Credit; make any Thing but gold and silver Coin a Tender in Payment of Debts; pass any Bill of Attainder, ex post facto Law, or Law impairing the Obligation of Contracts, or grant any Title of Nobility.

ARTICLE II.

Section 1.

The executive Power shall be vested in a President of the United States of America. He shall hold his Office during the Term of four Years, and, together with the Vice President, chosen for the same Term, be elected, as follows:
No Person except a natural born Citizen, or a Citizen of the United States, at the time of the Adoption of this Constitution, shall be eligible to the Office of President; neither shall any Person be eligible to that Office who shall not have attained to the Age of thirty five Years, and been fourteen Years a Resident within the United States.
Before he enter on the Execution of his Office, he shall take the following Oath or Affirmation: — "I do solemnly swear (or affirm) that I will faithfully execute the Office of President of the United States, and will to the best of my Ability, preserve, protect and defend the Constitution of the United States."

Section 2.

The President shall be Commander in Chief of the Army and Navy of the United States, and of the Militia of the several States, when called into the actual Service of the United States; he may require the Opinion, in writing, of the principal Officer in each of the executive Departments, upon any Subject relating to the Duties of their respective Offices, and he shall have Power to grant Reprieves and Pardons for Offences against the United States, except in Cases of Impeachment.

He shall have Power, by and with the Advice and Consent of the Senate, to make Treaties, provided two thirds of the Senators present concur; and he shall nominate, and by and with the Advice and Consent of the Senate, shall appoint Ambassadors, other public Ministers and Consuls, Judges of the supreme Court, and all other Officers of the United States, whose Appointments are not herein otherwise provided for, and which shall be established by Law: but the Congress may by Law vest the Appointment of such inferior Officers, as they think proper, in the President alone, in the Courts of Law, or in the Heads of Departments.

The President shall have Power to fill up all Vacancies that may happen during the Recess of the Senate, by granting Commissions which shall expire at the End of their next Session.

Section 3.

He shall from time to time give to the Congress Information of the State of the Union, and recommend to their Consideration such Measures as he shall judge necessary and expedient; he may, on extraordinary Occasions, convene both Houses, or either of them, and in Case of Disagreement between them, with Respect to the Time of Adjournment, he may adjourn them to such Time as he shall think proper; he shall receive Ambassadors and other public Ministers; he shall take Care that the Laws be faithfully executed, and shall Commission all the Officers of the United States.

ARTICLE III.

Section 1.

The judicial Power of the United States shall be vested in one Supreme Court, and in such inferior Courts as the Congress may from time to time ordain and establish. The Judges, both of the supreme and inferior Courts, shall hold their Offices during good Behaviour, and shall, at stated Times, receive for their Services a Compensation, which shall not be diminished during their Continuance in Office.

Section 2.

The judicial Power shall extend to all Cases, in Law and Equity, arising under this Constitution, the Laws of the United States, and Treaties made, or which shall be made, under their Authority;—to all Cases affecting Ambassadors, other public Ministers and Consuls;—to all Cases of admiralty and maritime Jurisdiction;—to Controversies to which the United States shall be a Party;—to Controversies between two or more States;—between a State and Citizens of another State;—between Citizens of different States;—between Citizens of the same State claiming Lands under Grants of different States, and between a State, or the Citizens thereof, and foreign States, Citizens or Subjects.

In all Cases affecting Ambassadors, other public Ministers and Consuls, and those in which a State shall be Party, the Supreme Court shall have original Jurisdiction. In all the other Cases before mentioned, the Supreme Court shall have appellate Jurisdiction, both as to Law and Fact, with such Exceptions, and under such Regulations as the Congress shall make.

The Trial of all Crimes, except in Cases of Impeachment, shall be by Jury; and such Trial shall be held in the State where the said Crimes shall have been committed; but when not committed within any State, the Trial shall be at such Place or Places as the Congress may by Law have directed.

ARTICLE IV.

Section 1.

Full Faith and Credit shall be given in each State to the public Acts, Records, and judicial Proceedings of every other State. And the Congress may by general Laws prescribe the Manner in which such Acts, Records and Proceedings shall be proved, and the Effect thereof.

Section 2.

The Citizens of each State shall be entitled to all Privileges and Immunities of Citizens in the several States.

A Person charged in any State with Treason, Felony, or other Crime, who shall flee from Justice, and be found in another State, shall on Demand of the executive Authority of the State from which he fled, be delivered up, to be removed to the State having Jurisdiction of the Crime.

Section 3.

New States may be admitted by the Congress into this Union; but no new State shall be formed or erected within the Jurisdiction of any other State; nor any State be formed by the Junction of two or more States, or Parts of States, without the Consent of the Legislatures of the States concerned as well as of the Congress.

The Congress shall have Power to dispose of and make all needful Rules and Regulations respecting the Territory or other Property belonging to the United States; and nothing in this Constitution shall be so construed as to Prejudice any Claims of the United States, or of any particular State.

Section 4.

The United States shall guarantee to every State in this Union a Republican Form of Government, and shall protect each of them against Invasion; and on Application of the Legislature, or of the Executive (when the Legislature cannot be convened), against domestic Violence.

ARTICLE V.

The Congress, whenever two thirds of both Houses shall deem it necessary, shall propose Amendments to this Constitution, or, on the Application of the Legislatures of two thirds of the several States, shall call a Convention for proposing Amendments, which, in either Case, shall be valid to all Intents and Purposes, as Part of this Constitution, when ratified by the Legislatures of three fourths of the several States, or by Conventions in three fourths thereof, as the one or the other Mode of Ratification may be proposed by the Congress; Provided that no Amendment which may be made prior to the Year One thousand eight hundred and eight shall in any Manner affect the first and fourth Clauses in the Ninth Section of the first Article; and that no State, without its Consent, shall be deprived of its equal Suffrage in the Senate.

ARTICLE VI.

All Debts contracted and Engagements entered into, before the Adoption of this Constitution, shall be as valid against the United States under this Constitution, as under the Confederation.

This Constitution, and the Laws of the United States which shall be made in Pursuance thereof; and all Treaties made, or which shall be made, under the Authority of the United States, shall be the supreme Law of the Land; and the Judges in every State shall be bound thereby, any Thing in the Constitution or Laws of any State to the Contrary notwithstanding.

The Senators and Representatives before mentioned, and the Members of the several State Legislatures, and all executive and judicial Officers, both of the United States and of the several States, shall be bound by Oath or Affirmation, to support this Constitution; but no religious Test shall ever be required as a Qualification to any Office or public Trust under the United States.

ARTICLE VII.

The Ratification of the Conventions of nine States, shall be sufficient for the Establishment of this Constitution between the States so ratifying the Same.

George Washington
President and deputy from Virginia

Delaware
Geo: Read
Gunning Bedford jun

John Dickinson
Richard Bassett
Jaco: Broom

Maryland
James McHenry
Dan of St Thos. Jenifer
Danl. Carroll

Virginia
John Blair
James Madison Jr.

North Carolina
Wm. Blount
Richd. Dobbs Spaight
Hu Williamson

South Carolina
J. Rutledge
Charles Cotesworth Pinckney
Charles Pinckney
Pierce Butler

Georgia
William Few
Abr Baldwin

New Hampshire
John Langdon
Nicholas Gilman

Massachusetts
Nathaniel Gorham
Rufus King

Connecticut
Wm. Saml. Johnson
Roger Sherman

New York
Alexander Hamilton

New Jersey
Wil. Livingston
David Brearley
Wm. Paterson
Jona. Dayton

Pennsylvania
B Franklin
Thomas Mifflin
Robt. Morris
Geo. Clymer
Thos. FitzSimons
Jared Ingersoll
James Wilson
Gouv Morris
The Bill of Rights

These amendments were ratified December 15, 1791, and form what is known as the "Bill of Rights."

AMENDMENT I

Congress shall make no law respecting an establishment of religion, or prohibiting the free exercise thereof; or abridging the freedom of speech, or of the press; or the right of the people peaceably to assemble, and to petition the Government for a redress of grievances.

AMENDMENT II

A well regulated Militia, being necessary to the security of a free State, the right of the people to keep and bear Arms, shall not be infringed.

AMENDMENT III

No Soldier shall, in time of peace be quartered in any house, without the consent of the Owner, nor in time of war, but in a manner to be prescribed by law.

AMENDMENT IV

The right of the people to be secure in their persons, houses, papers, and effects, against unreasonable searches and seizures, shall not be violated, and no Warrants shall issue, but upon probable cause, supported by Oath or affirmation, and particularly describing the place to be searched, and the persons or things to be seized.

AMENDMENT V

No person shall be held to answer for a capital, or otherwise infamous crime, unless on a presentment or indictment of a Grand Jury, except in cases arising in the land or naval forces, or in the Militia, when in actual service in time of War or public danger; nor shall any person be subject for the same offence to be twice put in jeopardy of life or limb; nor shall be compelled in any criminal case to be a witness against himself, nor be deprived of life, liberty, or property, without due process of law; nor shall private property be taken for public use, without just compensation.

AMENDMENT VI

In all criminal prosecutions, the accused shall enjoy the right to a speedy and public trial, by an impartial jury of the State and district wherein the crime shall have been committed, which district shall have been previously ascertained by law, and to be informed of the nature and cause of the accusation; to be confronted with the witnesses against him; to have compulsory process for obtaining witnesses in his favor, and to have the Assistance of Counsel for his defence.

AMENDMENT VII

In Suits at common law, where the value in controversy shall exceed twenty dollars, the right of trial by jury shall be preserved, and no fact tried by a jury, shall be otherwise re-examined in any Court of the United States, than according to the rules of the common law.

AMENDMENT VIII

Excessive bail shall not be required, nor excessive fines imposed, nor cruel and unusual punishments inflicted.

AMENDMENT IX

The enumeration in the Constitution, of certain rights, shall not be construed to deny or disparage others retained by the people.

AMENDMENT X

The powers not delegated to the United States by the Constitution, nor prohibited by it to the States, are reserved to the States respectively, or to the people.

AMENDMENT XI

Passed by Congress March 4, 1794. Ratified February 7, 1795.
Note: Article III, section 2, of the Constitution was modified by amendment 11.

The Judicial power of the United States shall not be construed to extend to any suit in law or equity, commenced or prosecuted against one of the

United States by Citizens of another State, or by Citizens or Subjects of any Foreign State.

AMENDMENT XII

Passed by Congress December 9, 1803. Ratified June 15, 1804.
Note: A portion of Article II, section 1 of the Constitution was superseded by the Twelfth Amendment.

The Electors shall meet in their respective states and vote by ballot for President and Vice-President, one of whom, at least, shall not be an inhabitant of the same state with themselves; they shall name in their ballots the person voted for as President, and in distinct ballots the person voted for as Vice-President, and they shall make distinct lists of all persons voted for as President, and of all persons voted for as Vice-President, and of the number of votes for each, which lists they shall sign and certify, and transmit sealed to the seat of the government of the United States, directed to the President of the Senate;—the President of the Senate shall, in the presence of the Senate and House of Representatives, open all the certificates and the votes shall then be counted;—The person having the greatest number of votes for President, shall be the President, if such number be a majority of the whole number of Electors appointed; and if no person have such majority, then from the persons having the highest numbers not exceeding three on the list of those voted for as President, the House of Representatives shall choose immediately, by ballot, the President. But in choosing the President, the votes shall be taken by states, the representation from each state having one vote; a quorum for this purpose shall consist of a member or members from two-thirds of the states, and a majority of all the states shall be necessary to a choice. [And if the House of Representatives shall not choose a President whenever the right of choice shall devolve upon them, before the fourth day of March next following, then the Vice-President shall act as President, as in case of the death or other constitutional disability of the President.—]* The person having the greatest number of votes as Vice-President, shall be the Vice-President, if such number be a majority of the whole number of Electors appointed, and if no person have a majority, then from the two highest numbers on the list, the Senate shall choose the Vice-President; a quorum for the purpose shall consist of two-thirds of the whole number of Senators, and a majority of the whole number shall be necessary to a choice. But no person constitutionally ineligible to the office of President shall be eligible to that of Vice-President of the United States.

*Superseded by section 3 of the Twentieth Amendment.

AMENDMENT XIII

Passed by Congress January 31, 1865. Ratified December 6, 1865.
Note: A portion of Article IV, section 2, of the Constitution was superseded by the Thirteenth Amendment.

Section 1.

Neither slavery nor involuntary servitude, except as a punishment for crime whereof the party shall have been duly convicted, shall exist within the United States, or any place subject to their jurisdiction.

Section 2.

Congress shall have power to enforce this article by appropriate legislation.

AMENDMENT XIV

Passed by Congress June 13, 1866. Ratified July 9, 1868.
Note: Article I, section 2, of the Constitution was modified by section 2 of the Fourteenth Amendment.

Section 1.

All persons born or naturalized in the United States, and subject to the jurisdiction thereof, are citizens of the United States and of the State wherein they reside. No State shall make or enforce any law which shall abridge the privileges or immunities of citizens of the United States; nor shall any State deprive any person of life, liberty, or property, without due process of law; nor deny to any person within its jurisdiction the equal protection of the laws.

Section 2.

Representatives shall be apportioned among the several States according to their respective numbers, counting the whole number of persons in each State, excluding Indians not taxed. But when the right to vote at any election for the choice of electors for President and Vice-President of the United States, Representatives in Congress, the Executive and Judicial officers of a State, or the members of the Legislature thereof, is denied to any of the male inhabitants of such State, being twenty-one years of age,* and citizens of the United States, or in any way abridged, except for participation in rebellion, or other crime, the basis of representation therein shall be reduced in the proportion which the number of such male citizens shall bear to the whole number of male citizens twenty-one years of age in such State.

Section 3.

No person shall be a Senator or Representative in Congress, or elector of President and Vice-President, or hold any office, civil or military, under the United States, or under any State, who, having previously taken an oath, as a member of Congress, or as an officer of the United States, or as a member of any State legislature, or as an executive or judicial officer of any State, to support the Constitution of the United States, shall have engaged in insurrection or rebellion against the same, or given aid or comfort to the enemies thereof. But Congress may by a vote of two-thirds of each House, remove such disability.

Section 4.

The validity of the public debt of the United States, authorized by law, including debts incurred for payment of pensions and bounties for services in suppressing insurrection or rebellion, shall not be questioned. But

neither the United States nor any State shall assume or pay any debt or obligation incurred in aid of insurrection or rebellion against the United
States, or any claim for the loss or emancipation of any slave; but all such
debts, obligations and claims shall be held illegal and void.

Section 5.

The Congress shall have the power to enforce, by appropriate legislation,
the provisions of this article.

Changed by section 1 of the Twenty-Sixth Amendment.

AMENDMENT XV

Passed by Congress February 26, 1869. Ratified February 3, 1870.

Section 1.

The right of citizens of the United States to vote shall not be denied or
abridged by the United States or by any State on account of race, color, or
previous condition of servitude—

Section 2.

The Congress shall have the power to enforce this article by appropriate
legislation.

AMENDMENT XVI

Passed by Congress July 2, 1909. Ratified February 3, 1913.
Note: Article I, section 9, of the Constitution was modified by the Six-
teenth Amendment.

The Congress shall have power to lay and collect taxes on incomes,
from whatever source derived, without apportionment among the several
States, and without regard to any census or enumeration.

AMENDMENT XVII

Passed by Congress May 13, 1912. Ratified April 8, 1913.
Note: Article I, section 3, of the Constitution was modified by the Seventeenth Amendment.

The Senate of the United States shall be composed of two Senators from each State, elected by the people thereof, for six years; and each Senator shall have one vote. The electors in each State shall have the qualifications requisite for electors of the most numerous branch of the State legislatures.

When vacancies happen in the representation of any State in the Senate, the executive authority of such State shall issue writs of election to fill such vacancies: *Provided,* That the legislature of any State may empower the executive thereof to make temporary appointments until the people fill the vacancies by election as the legislature may direct.

This amendment shall not be so construed as to affect the election or term of any Senator chosen before it becomes valid as part of the Constitution.

AMENDMENT XVIII

Passed by Congress December 18, 1917. Ratified January 16, 1919. Repealed by the Twenty-First Amendment.

Section 1.

After one year from the ratification of this article the manufacture, sale, or transportation of intoxicating liquors within, the importation thereof into, or the exportation thereof from the United States and all territory subject to the jurisdiction thereof for beverage purposes is hereby prohibited.

Section 2.

The Congress and the several States shall have concurrent power to enforce this article by appropriate legislation.

Section 3.

This article shall be inoperative unless it shall have been ratified as an amendment to the Constitution by the legislatures of the several States, as provided in the Constitution, within seven years from the date of the submission hereof to the States by the Congress.

AMENDMENT XIX

Passed by Congress June 4, 1919. Ratified August 18, 1920.
The right of citizens of the United States to vote shall not be denied or abridged by the United States or by any State on account of sex.

Congress shall have power to enforce this article by appropriate legislation.

AMENDMENT XX

Passed by Congress March 2, 1932. Ratified January 23, 1933.
Note: Article I, section 4, of the Constitution was modified by section 2 of this amendment. In addition, a portion of the Twelfth Amendment was superseded by section 3.

Section 1.

The terms of the President and the Vice President shall end at noon on the 20th day of January, and the terms of Senators and Representatives at noon on the 3d day of January, of the years in which such terms would have ended if this article had not been ratified; and the terms of their successors shall then begin.

Section 2.

The Congress shall assemble at least once in every year, and such meeting shall begin at noon on the 3d day of January, unless they shall by law appoint a different day.

Section 3.

If, at the time fixed for the beginning of the term of the President, the President elect shall have died, the Vice President elect shall become President. If a President shall not have been chosen before the time fixed for the beginning of his term, or if the President elect shall have failed to qualify, then the Vice President elect shall act as President until a President shall have qualified; and the Congress may by law provide for the case wherein neither a President elect nor a Vice President shall have qualified, declaring who shall then act as President, or the manner in which one who is to act shall be selected, and such person shall act accordingly until a President or Vice President shall have qualified.

Section 4.

The Congress may by law provide for the case of the death of any of the persons from whom the House of Representatives may choose a President whenever the right of choice shall have devolved upon them, and for the case of the death of any of the persons from whom the Senate may choose a Vice President whenever the right of choice shall have devolved upon them.

Section 5.

Sections 1 and 2 shall take effect on the 15th day of October following the ratification of this article.

Section 6.

This article shall be inoperative unless it shall have been ratified as an amendment to the Constitution by the legislatures of three-fourths of the several States within seven years from the date of its submission.

AMENDMENT XXI

Passed by Congress February 20, 1933. Ratified December 5, 1933.

Section 1.

The eighteenth article of amendment to the Constitution of the United States is hereby repealed.

Section 2.

The transportation or importation into any State, Territory, or Possession of the United States for delivery or use therein of intoxicating liquors, in violation of the laws thereof, is hereby prohibited.

Section 3.

This article shall be inoperative unless it shall have been ratified as an amendment to the Constitution by conventions in the several States, as provided in the Constitution, within seven years from the date of the submission hereof to the States by the Congress.

AMENDMENT XXII

Passed by Congress March 21, 1947. Ratified February 27, 1951.

Section 1.

No person shall be elected to the office of the President more than twice, and no person who has held the office of President, or acted as President, for more than two years of a term to which some other person was elected President shall be elected to the office of President more than once. But this Article shall not apply to any person holding the office of President when this Article was proposed by Congress, and shall not prevent any person who may be holding the office of President, or acting as President, during the term within which this Article becomes operative from holding the office of President or acting as President during the remainder of such term.

Section 2.

This article shall be inoperative unless it shall have been ratified as an amendment to the Constitution by the legislatures of three-fourths of the several States within seven years from the date of its submission to the States by the Congress.

AMENDMENT XXIII

Passed by Congress June 16, 1960. Ratified March 29, 1961.

Section 1.

The District constituting the seat of Government of the United States shall appoint in such manner as Congress may direct:

A number of electors of President and Vice President equal to the whole number of Senators and Representatives in Congress to which the District would be entitled if it were a State, but in no event more than the least populous State; they shall be in addition to those appointed by the States, but they shall be considered, for the purposes of the election of President and Vice President, to be electors appointed by a State; and they shall meet in the District and perform such duties as provided by the twelfth article of amendment.

Section 2.

The Congress shall have power to enforce this article by appropriate legislation.

AMENDMENT XXIV

Passed by Congress August 27, 1962. Ratified January 23, 1964.

Section 1.

The right of citizens of the United States to vote in any primary or other election for President or Vice President, for electors for President or Vice President, or for Senator or Representative in Congress, shall not be denied or abridged by the United States or any State by reason of failure to pay poll tax or other tax.

Section 2.

The Congress shall have power to enforce this article by appropriate legislation.

AMENDMENT XXV

Passed by Congress July 6, 1965. Ratified February 10, 1967.
Note: Article II, section 1, of the Constitution was affected by the Twenty-Fifth Amendment.

Section 1.

In case of the removal of the President from office or of his death or resignation, the Vice President shall become President.

Section 2.

Whenever there is a vacancy in the office of the Vice President, the President shall nominate a Vice President who shall take office upon confirmation by a majority vote of both Houses of Congress.

Section 3.

Whenever the President transmits to the President pro tempore of the Senate and the Speaker of the House of Representatives his written declaration that he is unable to discharge the powers and duties of his office, and until he transmits to them a written declaration to the contrary, such powers and duties shall be discharged by the Vice President as Acting President.

Section 4.

Whenever the Vice President and a majority of either the principal officers of the executive departments or of such other body as Congress may by law provide, transmit to the President pro tempore of the Senate and the Speaker of the House of Representatives their written declaration that the President is unable to discharge the powers and duties of his office, the Vice President shall immediately assume the powers and duties of the office as Acting President.

Thereafter, when the President transmits to the President pro tempore of the Senate and the Speaker of the House of Representatives his written declaration that no inability exists, he shall resume the powers and duties of his office unless the Vice President and a majority of either the principal officers of the executive department or of such other body as Congress may by law provide, transmit within four days to the President pro tempore of the Senate and the Speaker of the House of Representatives their written declaration that the President is unable to discharge the powers and duties of his office. Thereupon Congress shall decide the issue, assembling within forty-eight hours for that purpose if not in session. If the Congress, within twenty-one days after receipt of the latter written declaration, or, if Congress is not in session, within twenty-one days after Congress is required to assemble, determines by two-thirds vote of both Houses that the President is unable to discharge the powers and duties of his office, the Vice President shall continue to discharge the same as Acting President; otherwise, the President shall resume the powers and duties of his office.

AMENDMENT XXVI

Passed by Congress March 23, 1971. Ratified July 1, 1971.
Note: Amendment 14, section 2, of the Constitution was modified by section 1 of the Twenty-Sixth amendment.

Section 1.

The right of citizens of the United States, who are eighteen years of age or older, to vote shall not be denied or abridged by the United States or by any State on account of age.

Section 2.

The Congress shall have power to enforce this article by appropriate legislation.

AMENDMENT XXVII

Originally proposed Sept. 25, 1789. Ratified May 7, 1992.

No law, varying the compensation for the services of the Senators and Representatives, shall take effect, until an election of representatives shall have intervened.

B

Equal Access Act, 20 U.S.C. Sections 4071 and 4072

Section 4071. Denial of Equal Access Prohibited

a. Restriction of limited open forum on basis of religion, political, philosophical, or other speech content prohibited.

It shall be unlawful for any public secondary school which receives Federal assistance and which has a limited open forum to deny equal access or a fair opportunity to, or discriminate against, any students who wish to conduct a meeting within that limited open forum on the basis of the religious, political, philosophical, or other content of the speech at such meetings.

b. "Limited open forum" defined:

A public secondary school has a limited open forum whenever such school grants an offering to or opportunity for one or more noncurriculum related student groups to meet on school premises during noninstructional time.

c. Fair opportunity criteria:

Schools shall be deemed to offer a fair opportunity to students who wish to conduct a meeting within its limited open forum if such a school uniformly provides that;

1. the meeting is voluntary and student initiated;
2. there is no sponsorship of the meeting by the school or government, or its agents or employees;

285

3. employees or agents of the school or government are present at religious meetings only in a nonparticipatory capacity;
4. the meeting does not materially and substantially interfere with the orderly conduct of educational activities within the school; and
5. nonschool persons may not direct, conduct, control, or regularly attend activities of student groups.

d. Construction of subchapter with respect to certain rights.

Nothing in this subchapter shall be construed to authorize the United States or political subdivisions thereof;

1. to influence the form or content of any prayer or other religious activity;
2. to require any person to participate in prayer or other religious activity;
3. to expend public funds beyond the incidental cost of providing the space for student initiated activities;
4. to compel any school agent or employee to attend a school meeting if the content of the speech at the meeting is contrary to the beliefs of the agent or employee;
5. to sanction meetings that are otherwise unlawful;
6. to limit the rights of groups of students which are not of a specified numerical size; or
7. the abridge the constitutional rights of any person

e. Federal financial assistance to schools unaffected.

Notwithstanding the availability of any other remedy under the Constitution or the laws of the United States, nothing in this subchapter shall be construed to authorize the United States to deny or withhold any Federal assistance to any school

f. Authority of schools with respect to order, discipline, well-being, and attendance concerns.

Nothing in this subchapter shall be construed to limit the authority of the school, its agents or employees, to maintain order and discipline on school premises, to protect the well-being of students and faculty, and to assure that attendance of students at meetings is voluntary.

Section 4072. Definitions

As used in this subchapter:

1. The term "secondary school" means a public school which provides secondary education as determined by State law.
2. The term "sponsorship" includes the act of promoting, leading, or participating in a meeting. The assignment of a teacher, administrator, or other school employees to a meeting for custodial purposes does not constitute sponsorship of the meeting.
3. The term "meeting" includes those activities of student groups which are permitted under a school's limited open forum and are not directly related to the school curriculum.
4. The term "noninstructional time" means time set aside by the school before actual classroom instruction begins or after actual classroom instruction ends.

C

Family Educational Rights and Privacy Act (Buckley Amendment)

The federal Family Educational Rights and Privacy Act of 1974 established standards for schools to follow when handling student records. Before FERPA was enacted, students sometimes had difficulty obtaining access to their school records even though some courts had held that parents and students had the right of access unless it was detrimental to the public interest. However, parents and students had little leverage over schools in the control of students' records, and had to resort to litigation to obtain redress. The FERPA created uniformity in the handling of student records. The main features of the act are:

1. Requires school districts to establish a written policy concerning student records and inform parents of their rights under the act each year.
2. Guarantees parents the right to inspect and review the educational records of their children.
3. Establishes procedures through which parents can challenge the accuracy of school records.
4. Protects the confidentiality of student records by preventing disclosure of personally identifiable information to outsiders without prior parental consent.
5. Entitles parents to file complaints with the FERPA Office concerning alleged failures to comply with the act.

Records accessible

Any information directly related the education of the student.

Records not accessible

Personal notes of educators if in "sole possession."

Records of physicians, psychologists, or other professionals used only in connection with their treatment.

Law enforcement records used solely for police purposes.

Job-related records of students employed by the school.

A school can disclose directory information but does not have to under FERPA.

School districts that do not follow the procedures outlined in FERPA are subject to losing federal funds administered by the U.S. Department of Education.

Index

About the Author

Leo Bradley holds a bachelor's degree in history, a master's degree in educational administration, and a doctorate in educational administration with minors in curriculum and twentieth-century American history.

Dr. Bradley's scholarly works include sole authorship for four books, *Curriculum Leadership and Development*, *Competency-Based Education*, *Total Quality Management for Schools* (both book and accompanying educational video), and *Curriculum Leadership: Beyond Boiler-Plate Standards*. In addition, he coauthored *Profits and Productivity: A Workplace Productivity Skills Development Program for CEOs*. Among his journal article topics are entry-year programs, mentorships, ethics, school law, curriculum design, factors in student achievement, and leadership theory. Dr. Bradley is a nationally recognized consultant for schools and businesses in the areas of curriculum, school law, total quality management, and leadership.

In his professional life, he has held the positions of teacher, high school principal, assistant superintendent, and superintendent of schools. For the past fourteen years he has been a professor and program director in educational administration for Xavier University in Cincinnati, Ohio.

Dr. Bradley is also a baseball historian, songwriter, musician, and singer. He has written and recorded over forty songs for Fraternity Records, including the 1999 album *One Bounce and You're Out: The History of Baseball in Song*, and the 2003 album, *Remembering the Reds: The History of the Cincinnati Reds in Song*.

Breinigsville, PA USA
24 January 2010
231280BV00005B/85/P